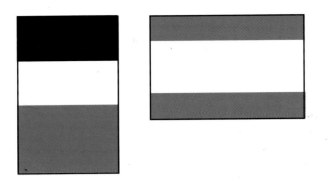

Canatlantic Ltd.

John T. Rennie and Sons

Cardiff Hall Line
Managers: Edward Nicholl and Co.

The first funnel was used on Nicholl's first ship, *Whateley Hall*, but was discontinued in favour of the version with green and white bands. The third funnel was used on the *Grindon Hall* (1) of 1905.

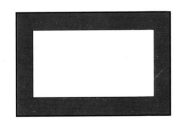

The Carron Company
Original flag on the left.

BRITISH SHIPPING FLEETS

Editors: Roy Fenton and John Clarkson

Contributors: David Burrell, Roy Fenton, Peter Newall, Seán Patterson, Graeme Somner, with additional material from Captain Eric Askew and Alan Phipps.

Ships in Focus Publications

Published in the UK in 2000 by Ships in Focus Publications,
18 Franklands, Longton
Preston PR4 5PD

Printed by Amadeus Press Ltd., Cleckheaton, West Yorkshire
ISBN 1 901703 21 5

Cover: *Manchester Regiment* (2). *[World Ship Photo Library]*
Above: *Manchester Faith* (1) outward bound on her maiden voyage, 28th March 1959. *[John Slavin]*

Manchester Merchant (4), see page 49. *[Fotoflite incorporating Skyfotos]*

2

CONTENTS

Fisher's *Walnut* (1) sailing from Preston (see page 93).

FOREWORD

British Shipping Fleets is a new venture for Ships in Focus, a collection of company histories and fleet lists which cover the spectrum of British shipping, from sailing ships, through steam coasters and coastal liners, to deep-sea tramps, specialist freighters, cargo liners and container ships. Too large for an article in our journal *Record*, these fleets are yet rather small for books of their own, hence this compendium.

Inspiration for *British Shipping Fleets* comes from two sources: Gert Uwe Detlefsen's *Deutsche Reederein*, each volume of which covers a number of German shipping companies, and *Mersey Rovers* by one of the editors, a compendium of histories and fleet lists of Liverpool coaster owners. Both share our aims of accurate, readable texts and as comprehensive as possible a range of illustrations, with the best reproduction available.

We will be asked whether *British Shipping Fleets* is the start of a series. Clearly, there is enormous potential for further volumes, and the publishers have a long wish-list of companies for possible inclusion. But *British Shipping Fleets* must prove itself in the marketplace before we commit ourselves to further volumes. This is one reason why we have mixed the companies in this book, in order to include operators of liner and tramp, deep-sea and coastal ships. We hope that those whose interest is focussed on one type of ship will find that, despite its wide coverage, *British Shipping Fleets* is well worth having, and will appreciate that we have also kept the price to a reasonable level. We expect that even those with a narrow interest will find much to appeal to them in every chapter, including the boxes we have used to elaborate on topics referred to in the text, and to add colour with memories of those who sailed on the ships.

Great efforts have been made to ensure accuracy and completeness. Ships' histories have been checked in the Closed Registers held at the Public Record Office and elsewhere. Although not faultless, and by no means complete, these can be regarded as the definitive source for the history of a ship under British ownership. To ensure maximum photographic coverage, we have had the wholehearted support of many individual photographers and collectors, and administrators of large collections. However, we acknowledge that it is impossible to say the last word on a company, or turn up every photograph. The editors therefore welcome additions and amendments to *British Shipping Fleets,* and any substantial further information or photographs of vessels unrepresented here will be published in our journal *Record*.

It is our belief that there is no such thing as an uninteresting shipping company, and we trust our various authors have succeeded in bringing out the aspects of each fleet's history which made it an individual.

Roy Fenton   John Clarkson
Wimbledon   Longton
            October 2000

NOTES, SOURCES AND ACKNOWLEDGEMENTS

Notes on the fleet lists

Fleet lists are presented in the format used in our journal *Record*, and which is adapted from that developed and refined by the World Ship Society. This format has the merits of being concise, familiar, and flexible.

On the first line, the number in brackets following the ship's name indicates how many times that name has been used in the fleet. The dates are those of entering and leaving the company's ownership or management. Next is indicated the hull material and, for sailing vessels, the rig. Ships not otherwise described are steel steamers or motor vessels.

On the second line is given the ship's official number (O.N.) in the British Register; then her tonnages, gross (g), net (n), and in some cases deadweight (d) or burden (b); followed by overall length x breadth x depth in feet or metres. All tonnages and dimensions are those at the time of acquisition. Substantial alterations following a rebuild, for instance, are noted on the next line.

On the following line is a description of the engine(s) fitted and the name of their builder. Steam engines may be single cylinder (1-cyl.), two cylinder compounds (C. 2-cyl.), three or four cylinder triple expansion (T. 3-cyl. or T. 4-cyl.), or quadruple expansion four cylinder (Q. 4-cyl.). For oil engines are given the type (e.g. Sulzer, Burmeister & Wain), the number of cylinders, whether two stroke (2SC) or four stroke (4SC) cycle, single acting (SA) or double acting (DA). Various figures for horsepower are given: nominal (NHP), brake (BHP), indicated (IHP), or shaft (SHP) for turbines. Nominal horsepower bears least relationship to the engine's actual power, but is often the only figure available. The speed is taken from registration documents or *Lloyd's Register,* and is usually an estimate not a trial's figure. Any changes of engine are listed, with dates, on subsequent lines.

Ships' careers and technical details have been derived from or checked against the Closed Registers in Class BT110 in the Public Records Office, Kew whenever these are accessible, to find the exact dates of registration, sales, and renamings, and dimensions whilst under British ownership. This applies mainly to ships whose British registry was open beyond 1895 and closed before the end of 1955, as - tragically - most registers closed later than 1955 seem not to have survived to be transferred to the Public Record Office. Some details before 1895 have been taken from registration documents in Class BT108 at the Public Record Office or held locally.

Photographic sources

Photographs are from the collection of John Clarkson unless otherwise credited. We thank all who gave permission for their photographs to be used, and are particularly grateful to Martin Dobson, Edward Gray, Peter Newall, Ivor Rooke, William Schell, George Scott, John Slavin, Phil Thomas; to David Whiteside and Tony Smith of the World Ship Photo Library; to David Hodge and Bob Todd of the National Maritime Museum; Dr. David Jenkins of the Welsh Industrial and Maritime Museum; Bill Lind of the Ballast Trust, and other individuals, museums and institutions credited.

Flags and funnels

Artwork was very kindly provided by J.L.Loughran, custodian of the Ships' Liveries section of the World Ship Society's Central Record.

General sources and acknowledgements

Sources for fleet lists include *Lloyd's Register, Lloyd's Confidential Index, Mercantile Navy Lists, Lloyd's War Losses, Marine News* and the *Registers* of William Schell and Tony Starke. Use of the facilities of the World Ship Society's Central Record, the Guildhall Library and Lloyd's Register of Shipping are gratefully acknowledged. Particular thanks also to John Bartlett, Fred Hawks and William Schell for information, to Heather Fenton for editorial and indexing work, and to Marion Clarkson for accountancy services.

Manchester Liners Ltd.

Reference has been made to minute books, annual reports, fleet records and miscellaneous papers of Manchester Liners Ltd. Thanks also to David Attenborough and Peter Wynne. Published sources comprise:
Sea Breezes 1948, V: 268; 1958, XXVI: 34; 1984, LVIII: 799, 853; 1985, LIX: 41
Robert B. Stoker, *Fifty Years on the Western Ocean*
Robert B. Stoker, *The Saga of Manchester Liners*
James E. Cowden and John O.C. Duffy, *The Elder Dempster Fleet History 1852-1985*
David Farnie, *The Manchester Ship Canal and the Rise of the Port of Manchester*
David Burrell, *Furness Withy* 1891-1991
Edward Gray, *Manchester Liners: a Pictorial History.*

Joseph Fisher and Sons.

The narrative is based largely on research by Seán Patterson, presented in 1994 as *Newry Shipping 1900-1981.* One of Seán's major informants was John D.F. Fisher, who very generously supplied additional information on the Fisher family, business and ships, and read various drafts of the text. Other informants were D. Brennan, David Donnan, Eddie Bell Gallagher, Thomas Johannesson, P. McKeown, C.J. McCarthy, J. Murphy, and Brian O'Keefe. Thanks are also due to Terry O'Conallain and Ian Wilson for reading and commenting on drafts of the text. Published sources comprise:
T. O'Driscoll *et al,* in *Irish Shipping* Summer 1965
J.A. Macrae and C.V. Waine, *The Steam Collier Fleets*
There's the Last of Her broadcast by BBC Radio Ulster on 26th September 1978
Frontier Sentinel, Irish Times, Newry Reporter and *Lloyd's Lists.*
Manuscripts sources include:
Log book of *Poplar* loaned by J. Boylan
Crew agreements for *Ulidia* and *Upas* in the PRO (NI) Trans. 46/3248.

Runciman (London) Ltd. and Canatlantic Ltd.

Paul Boot must take credit for pointing out that this company would make an interesting article, and for compiling an initial fleet list, although with typical modesty he declined to appear as co-author. Information on the foundation of the owning companies and valuable background came from contemporary issues of *The World's Paper Trade Review*, and for bringing these to his attention the author is most grateful to the librarians at St. Brides Printing Library, Fleet Street, London. Reports of some vessels' construction appeared in *Shipbuilding and Shipping Record* and *Merchant Ships World Built*.

J. T. Rennie and Sons

Generous help came from Dag Bakka, Ambrose Greenway, Fred Hawks, Rick Hogben, John Landels, Bill Laxon, Jenny Meilhon, Dr John Naylon, Mrs Anne Rennie, Bill Schell, Graeme Somner, The Ship Society of Southern Africa, Catherine Walker and Brian Ingpen, author of *Horizons - The Story of Rennies 1849-1999*.

Cardiff Hall Line

Three individuals made large contributions to this chapter. Ivor Rooke originally suggested that the company was worthy of coverage, and supplied many photographs. Richard Pryde contributed his own fleet list and brief history, but magnanimously declined to be listed as a co-author. Dr. David Jenkins read and gave comments on the text based on his own research into Nicholl, and

alerted us to photographs held by the National Museums and Galleries of Wales. Information also came from Tyne and Wear Archives. Published sources comprise:

Leonard Gray and John Lingwood, *The Doxford Turret Ships*
H.E. Hancock, *Wireless at Sea*
P. Harley, *My Life in Shipping 1881-1938*
J. Geraint and David Jenkins, *Cardiff Shipowners*
David Jenkins, *Shipowners of Cardiff: a Class by Themselves*
D. Masters, *Crimes of the High Seas*
J.R. Scobie, *Revolution on the Pampas*
A.J. Tennent, *British Merchant Ships sunk by U-Boats in the 1914-1918 War*
P.N. Thomas, *British Ocean Tramps*
T.C. Wignall, *The Life of Commander Sir Edward Nichol*
C. Wright and C.E. Fayle, *A History of Lloyd's*
W.R. Wright, *British-Owned Railways in Argentina*.

The Carron Company

Thanks to Mrs Elspeth Reid, Archivist, Falkirk Museums, for supplying copies of material in the Museum; to the Scottish Record Office in Edinburgh for access to the vast collection of material passed to them by the Carron Company; to the Public Record Office, Kew; and the Guildhall Library, London. For further reading on the Carron Company see Brian Watters, *When Iron Runs Like Water* 1998.

Representatives of three of the fleets whose histories appear in this book:
Manchester Liners' *Manchester Progress* (2): see page 60 (opposite).
Joseph Fisher's motorship Oak (2) at Preston: see page 104 (top). *[World Ship Photo Library]*.
Rennie's *Ingoma* in Harrison's colours: see page 139 (left).

MANCHESTER LINERS LTD.
David Burrell

The dirty ditch

Victorian Manchester, a growing city flourishing on cotton, faced a problem: the cost of landing raw materials at Liverpool and delivering them 36 miles to Manchester. The answer, a ship canal, had been propounded as early as 1721, but it was not until June 1882 that, at the instigation of Daniel Adamson (1820-1890), a start was made to realise this ambition. Despite opposition in Liverpool and elsewhere an Act of Parliament was obtained and £8 million capital raised to commence work in 1887. Construction problems and cost escalations followed, the Corporation of Manchester arranging extra loans of £5 million. Finally, on 1st January 1894 Manchester was declared a customs port, the first ship arrived and on 21st May Queen Victoria officially opened the 'dirty ditch'. By 1911, Manchester had become Britain's second city and its fourth port.

A challenge remained: attracting trade to the port. Liverpool owners saw no need to call there. Support came from elsewhere: Herbert Watson from Glasgow, George Renwick from Newcastle-on-Tyne, and the Bacon, Sivewright and Furness families from Hartlepool. Some attempts failed, such as the Manchester, Bombay and General Navigation Company. Furness, Withy and Co. made thirteen sailings to Canada. Strong local support and start-up subsidy was needed. A deputation to Canada in 1897 returned with the promise of a three-year Government subsidy of £8,000 for a fortnightly service, plus the support of the Canadian Pacific Railway and others.

The founding fathers

Christopher Furness promised to support local interests in the proposed Manchester Steamship Liners Ltd., intended to carry produce and live cattle across the Atlantic. On 3rd May 1898 the company was registered with the simpler title, Manchester Liners Ltd. £350,000 of the authorised £1 million capital was issued, Furness taking £150,000. The prospectus named the directors as Christopher Furness (chairman), Charles Schiff, Alderman James Southern, Sir Edward Jenkinson KCB, and Sir Richard Mottram. Furness seconded his principal trusted aide and a Furness, Withy director, R.B. Stoker, to Manchester as managing director of the venture.

Robert Burdon Stoker (1859-1919) had been recruited by Furness in 1882. He helped build the business, opening offices in Newcastle and London, and was a founding director of Furness, Withy and Co. Ltd. in 1891. He was to become the first of three generations of the Stoker family to lead Manchester Liners.

The early fleet

Two ships were purchased for £60,000, the ten-year-old *Queensmore* and *Parkmore*, renamed *Manchester Enterprise* and *Manchester Trader* (1). Initially they traded under their old names alongside *Cynthiana* (2,923/1891) and *Straits of Menai* (2,870/1894), chartered from the Furness-controlled British Maritime Trust. More ships were required for a fortnightly Canadian service and several speculative orders placed by Furness with his own and other yards were acquired. The first was nearing completion by Sir Raylton Dixon and Co., and went into the water on 6th June 1898 as *Manchester City* (1). Two more were part of a series of four ordered by Furness from Palmers, four-masted cargo liners over 450 feet long with cargo capacities well in excess of 8,000 tons. Furness gave the new Manchester Liners an option on two of these, which were completed as *Manchester Port* (1) and *Manchester Merchant* (1). The other two went to the Hamburg America Line as *Bosnia* (7,436/1899) and *Bengalia* (7,661/1898).

The multiple interests of Christopher Furness placed the directors in a delicate position. They did not always agree with him on the suitability of certain ships for their service. He would announce the availability of ships under construction, then withdraw to permit discussion by his fellow directors. They would express thanks and defer the offer for future discussion. At a later meeting their relief can almost be felt as the chairman expressed regret that the proffered ships had been sold in the meantime.

One of Manchester Liners' first two ships, *Manchester Trader* (1) passing through Barton aqueduct (opposite). *[Captain Eric Askew collection]*

Manchester Corporation (above) and *Manchester Importer* (1) (right). *[Right: World Ship Photo Library]*

At a directors' meeting on 7th June 1898 it was decided to invite tenders for five ships, two each of 5,500/5,600dwt and 6,400/6,500dwt, and one of 6,900/7,000dwt. The final outcome was slightly different: the Furness, Withy yard delivering in 1899 the *Manchester Corporation* and *Manchester Commerce* (1), large 430-feet vessels like the earlier ships. They were followed, from Irvines' yard, by the smaller 370-feet *Manchester Importer* and *Manchester Shipper* (1). It was originally intended that the second of these was to be built by Earle's yard in Hull, but second thoughts redirected it to Irvines. By this time experience had been gained in the trade and the optimum size of ship was found to be smaller than the big cargo carriers then in service. The early ships, in the main, soon disappeared; in 1906 *Manchester City* (1) was converted into the world's largest reefer ship, with a 375,000 cubic feet insulated capacity, at a cost of £30,000 and was in the River Plate meat trade for the rest of her life, whilst in 1901 *Manchester Port* (1) was sold and became the *Hydaspes* in Houston's South American trade. *Manchester Merchant* (1) was lost in 1903, leaving only *Manchester Corporation* and *Manchester Commerce* (1) (which had 10,000 cubic feet of refrigerated cargo capacity).

The *Manchester Exchange* of 1901, a Furness, Withy-built spar decker just over 4,000g and 360 feet long, proved to be the ideal ship, and between then and 1904 eight sisters were delivered, three from Furness, Withy and five from Northumberland, named *Manchester Engineer* (1), *Manchester Inventor* (1), *Manchester Market*, *Manchester Spinner* (1), *Manchester Miller* (1), *Manchester Port* (2), *Manchester Merchant* (2) and *Manchester Mariner* (1). Rather than issue more capital they were partially financed by £300,000 of 4.5% debentures, followed a few years later by a further £100,000 at 5.5%. Both were repaid by the end of 1921.

Marine risks

Manchester Liners had an inauspicious start, losing three ships to maritime risks in their first five years - it was to be 1939 before a similar loss occurred. The service was only months old when *Cynthiana*, bound for Montreal, went ashore in fog at Port Ellen on 22nd August 1898. Refloated, she was repaired at Belfast. More seriously, in October, the new *Manchester City* (1) on passage from her builders to load in Canada had her steering gear wrecked in the Pentland Firth, lost her anchors and managed to reach shelter in Cromarty Firth, only to be driven ashore. Refloated, she returned to the Tyne for repairs. Hardly had *Manchester City* been repaired than came news that Cunard's *Cephalonia* (5,606/1882) had towed *Manchester Enterprise* into Queenstown with hold and stokehold flooded.

The next casualty was the new *Manchester Port* (1), on her maiden voyage, striking an iceberg on 13th July 1899 whilst on passage from Montreal for Manchester. She put back to St. John's, Newfoundland for repairs. The first loss was *Manchester Enterprise* which foundered on 14th November 1899, on her eleventh voyage. Water was found rising in the holds and engine room, the pumps were unable to cope and, when Donaldson's *Lakonia* (4,686/1899) was sighted, she was abandoned. The subsequent enquiry was the first held in Manchester. Liners also aided other ships; September 1899 finding *Manchester Trader* (1) assisting the whaler *Era* with supplies.

Manchester Merchant (1) was chartered as a transport to South Africa, returning to commercial service in October 1902. She was on passage from New Orleans for Manchester when, on 12th January 1903, fire was discovered in the cargo of cotton, pitch pine lumber, turpentine resin, soap and grain. Three days later she reached Dingle Bay on fire from forward to aft of the bridge and, entering Castlemaine Harbour, was scuttled in nine fathoms of water to extinguish the blaze. The Liverpool Salvage Association despatched their *Ranger* (408/1888), but the position was exposed and by the end of the month the *Manchester Merchant* was breaking up. The third total loss in the early years was *Manchester Market*. From Manchester for Philadelphia, on 26th April 1903 she stranded during fog in an exposed position off the Tuskar. Again, *Ranger* attended but three days later *Manchester Market* was abandoned in heavy seas.

The Boer War

Manchester Liners was formed at a time of buoyant freight rates, due partly to a series of wars, between the USA and Spain, with the Boer Republics in South Africa and the Boxer Rising in China. These required the services of many transports and supply ships. The operations during the South African War (1899-1902) were the largest yet undertaken to support British forces overseas.

Four ships were chartered by the Government for varying periods, three to carry cavalry regiments and the *Manchester City* (1) for a trip with mules from New Orleans. A Government offer to purchase *Manchester Port* (1) and *Manchester Merchant* (1) was declined. *Manchester Port* (Transport No. 41) on her three trips started by carrying the 1st Royal Dragoons, and later went to Brisbane for a contingent of bushmen. *Manchester Corporation* (Transport No. 70) took a mixed contingent, two batteries of the Royal Horse Artillery and a detachment from the 2nd battalion Royal Irish Fusiliers. *Manchester Merchant* (1) commenced her service in February 1900 by transporting part of the West Country battalion of the Imperial Yeomanry to the front. As Transport No. 92 she made numerous trips to South Africa until coming off charter in October 1902. The charter paid for *Manchester City* (1) is not known, but the other three earned a useful £229,296.

The freight market slumped in the first decade of the twentieth century. No dividend was paid on ordinary shares from 1903 to 1912, and by 1911 there was a five and a half year backlog on preference shares which was not cleared until 1913. No ships joined the fleet between 1904 and 1912, and although in most years something was transferred to depreciation, the amount was nominal. By careful management the accounts remained in the black, even though the profits were small when compared with the investment involved.

During this period Annual General Meetings were lively as shareholders voiced concern. Gentlemen like F. Sandiford regularly questioned board actions, suggested withdrawing from Manchester, looking for better-paying trades, selling the fleet, cutting depreciation to pay dividends and disposing of investments. At the Annual General Meeting held on 30th September 1911 he was quoted as saying '... in a few years some of them [the shareholders] would be where dividends were not wanted, they would be of no use to them ...' Wiser counsel prevailed, and explanations were accepted. Where opportunities were seen ships were chartered out or placed in better trades and the only investment made was 20,000 £1 shares in the Excess Marine Insurance Co., a Furness company which not only showed a good dividend but also ensured preferential rates on the fleet.

The four-masted *Manchester Merchant* (1) as Boer War Transport No. 92. *[National Maritime Museum G30]*

Manchester Mariner (1) at a North American port.

Trades increase

The original service was to Montreal, and to St. John during the winter. In 1900 ships commenced calling at New Orleans and Galveston to load cotton, and Boston was served by chartered British Maritime Trust ships. Philadelphia appeared on the sailing list in 1901, a joint service with R.W. Leyland and Co. supported by the Reading Railroad, with *Manchester Corporation* and *Planet Neptune* (4,329/1901) taking the first sailings. By 1904 a fleet of fourteen ships was trading and a monthly service was inaugurated to the River Plate, becoming fortnightly in 1906 in partnership with F. Leyland and Co. This service was suspended in 1908 due to lack of support, although *Manchester City* (1) remained on the route, chartered to the Anglo-Argentine Shipping Co. Other charters included *Manchester City* (1) and *Manchester Port* (2) to Gulf Line in 1904, and *Manchester Miller* (1) and *Manchester Port* (2) to Watts, Watts and Co. during 1906. At the AGM in 1908 it was reported that six of the fourteen-strong fleet were chartered out.

On 13th November 1910 *Manchester Commerce* (1), proceeding down the Mersey, collided with the Norwegian *Truma* (1,557/1896) which was crossing the river. The matter ended up in the Admiralty Court where the Norwegian ship was judged to blame. *Manchester Engineer* (1) rendered salvage services to the destroyer USS *Wilkes* in 1911, for which the US courts made an award of £7,000 in 1918. *Manchester Commerce* (1) was again in the news, colliding with an iceberg and limping into St. John's, Newfoundland, to spend two months under repair using 70 tons of steelwork shipped from the UK. On 12th November 1915 *Manchester Merchant* (2) took 15 men off the Brazilian schooner *Storeng* (333/1904) which was sinking in a gale, and in December 1917 *Manchester Mariner* (1) was able to tow the *Labicum* (4,358/1907) 500 miles to Madeira for which an award of £6,750 was received. In 1911 the first member of the fleet, *Manchester City* (1), was fitted with Marconi's radio telegraphy.

The First World War

With no additions to the fleet since 1904, it was desirable to replace the older ships with new tonnage, so in February 1912 two ships were ordered, one each from Northumberland and Irvines. *Manchester Trader* (1), the oldest ship in the fleet, was sold to Norwegian owners and

the two new ships were named *Manchester Citizen* (1) and *Manchester Civilian* on delivery in August 1912 and August 1913. On the outbreak of war early in August 1914 the Manchester Liners' fleet numbered fifteen ships. Most were on the Canadian and Philadelphia services, *Manchester Civilian* was in the River Plate and *Manchester Port* (2) on passage, under charter, from New York for Maceio.

The company was rapidly embroiled in the conflict. *Manchester Citizen* (1) avoided the German commerce raider *Kaiser Wilhelm Der Grosse*, outward bound from Bremerhaven, and *Manchester Commerce* (1) became the first loss on 27th October 1914 when she hit a mine off Tory Island. The same day the battleship HMS *Audacious* was sunk by another mine in the field, laid by the minelayer SMS *Berlin*. Within days of the declaration of war *Manchester Engineer* (1) and *Manchester Importer* were requisitioned to carry the British Expeditionary Force across the Channel to France. *Manchester Engineer* (1) continued as a supply ship for the British forces until June 1915, and *Manchester Importer* continued until torpedoed and damaged in 1918. *Manchester Civilian* was taken up as Collier No. 414, and was coaling Admiral Sturdee's battlecruisers at Port Stanley in the Falkland Islands when Admiral Von Spee's fleet was sighted and annihilated at the Battle of the Falkland Islands on 8th December 1914.

In August 1914 Lloyd Austriaco of Trieste, had a ship under construction in the Northumberland yard. Seized on the declaration of war, she was purchased on the stocks by Manchester Liners in December 1914 as a replacement for the lost *Manchester Commerce* (1), and completed in 1916 as *Manchester Hero*. Ten ships were sunk by enemy action, but fortunately the total loss of life amounted to only 25. *Manchester Engineer* (1) was lost to *U 44* in March 1916, but the real massacre commenced after unrestricted submarine warfare was declared early in 1917. The twelve months from January 1917 saw eight ships of the fleet lost and others damaged. To offset this, four secondhand vessels were purchased for £546,000 (well in excess of twice their new cost) in 1916 and 1917 to partially fill the gaps.

Manchester Liners were not always easy targets for the enemy. On 4th June 1917 *Manchester Trader* (2) had a running fight with *U 65* before being sunk, for which resistance both Captain F.D. Struss and Chief Engineer

W.R. Stobo were awarded the DSC. *Manchester Port* (2), on 4th June 1917, succeeded in beating off a submarine attack in a gunnery action. *Manchester Mariner* (1) was damaged by a mine in December 1917, and after being hit by a torpedo *Manchester Importer* reached port in May 1918 and was repaired.

The war had a massive impact on ship prices and values. In 1914 when *Manchester Commerce* (1) was lost the insurance payment exceeded her book value by only £1,641. In 1916 when *Manchester Engineer* (1) was sunk values had increased so that her war loss payment of £105,600 exceeded her book value by £74,000, which was credited to depreciation. Thereafter, a steamer replacement account was opened and the excess of insurance over book values was credited. For the eight ships lost in 1917-1918, the Government war risk scheme paid £1,121,285 and the replacement account stood at £704,003 in October 1918. Together with full employment from the war, this meant that the accounts were healthier than they had ever been. Having recommenced paying dividends in 1913, the three years 1916 to 1918 saw Manchester Liners paying 25% each year.

The Canadian service had continued to run during hostilities and, in 1915, a joint Furness-Johnston-Manchester Liners service to Baltimore commenced. In 1920 the New Orleans service resumed and the Baltimore route was extended to Norfolk, Virginia. The Gulf service did not last long, closing in the face of competition from a service sponsored by the United States Shipping Board and employing some of the massive fleet of US-built war emergency ships. Manchester was chosen as one of the terminal ports for the new Furness North Pacific service via the Panama Canal, and in 1921 the first ship, *Mongolian Prince* (5,880/1913), was loaded.

Peace restored

The closing months of the war saw delivery of two new ships from Irvine's. They were ordered late in 1914 but had been delayed for years by urgent war work. They were appropriately named *Manchester Brigade* and *Manchester Division*. Following them into the fleet came two vessels transferred in 1921 from within the Furness, Withy group for £480,000 and renamed *Manchester Producer* and *Manchester Spinner* (2). The latter was too slow for the main line service and was employed on whatever was available. With *Manchester Civilian* she made several trips from the USA to Japan with relief supplies following the Yokohama Earthquake in 1923 and subsequently became well known in the Sydney, Cape Breton coal trade.

Early 1920 saw the formation of a subsidiary, Manchester Ocean Services Ltd., to which the three oldest ships were transferred, *Manchester Mariner* (1), *Merchant* (2) and *Port* (2), for £48,228. Ocean Services lasted until 1930 when only *Manchester Merchant* (2) remained, and she was returned to Manchester Liners. It was intended that three of a class of six 7,900g turbine steamers ordered by Furness, Withy from Furness's yard at Haverton Hill-on-Tees be taken by Manchester Liners and placed with Ocean Services. This was reduced to one vessel in view of the price, £458,598, which was so high that she is reputed never to have made a profit. When delivered in 1922 as *Manchester Regiment* (1) she was retained by Manchester Liners, and became the only one of her class to remain with the Furness Group throughout her life - the others passed in 1935 to T. and J. Harrison where one become famous as *Politician,* whose wreck was to be the inspiration for Sir Compton Mackenzie's *Whisky Galore.* In May 1926 Captain Foale of *Manchester Regiment* (1) became the first Manchester Liners' master to received the Gold-Headed Cane from the Port of Montreal for being the first ship to arrive in the navigation season. A total of ten Manchester Liners ships feature in the list of these awards, which dates back to 1840. Since the amalgamation with Orient

Overseas Container Lines, a further three OOCL ships have joined the list.

Casualties

Manchester Brigade towed the tanker *Le Coq* (3,419/1895), which had suffered rudder damage, into St. John's, Newfoundland, in January 1919 and received a salvage award of £15,000. Later that year her assistance was refused by the US-owned *Davidson County* (3,642/1919), which waited on the arrival of her sister *West Lashaway* (6,087/1918). This case ended in the US courts who found that *Manchester Brigade's* services amounted to salvage, and awarded 25% of the sum she would have received had she towed *Davidson County* into port. *Manchester Division*, at anchor 75 miles below Quebec, was run down and damaged by the Allen Liner *Tunisian* (10,743/1900), both being damaged. It was the turn of *Manchester Shipper* (1) in January 1923 when she towed the abandoned and dismasted barquentine *Maid of England* (690/1919) into Halifax.

Manchester Liners suffered a number of casualties themselves in 1926. In January *Manchester Merchant* (2), berthed at Philadelphia, was badly damaged when hit amidships by the *Margaret* (3,352/1916). *Manchester Civilian* was ashore from May to July in the Gulf of St. Lawrence. With coal and coke loaded at Sydney, Cape Breton, she was in an exposed position and reinsurance premiums reached 35 guineas before she was refloated. The coal and coke was jettisoned and pig iron and rails discharged to a coaster before she floated and proceeded under her own power to Quebec, escorted by the salvage vessel *Reindeer 1* (532/1884). The major casualty in this period was *Manchester Producer* (1) which lost her rudder early in February 1926 on passage with cattle from Canada for Manchester. The *Comino* (4,618/1918), *Menominee* (6,919/1897), *Mongolian Prince* and *London Commerce* (7,886/1923) all took her in tow, but the weather was so bad that their lines soon parted. It was seventeen days after the casualty before the Dutch tug *Zwarte Zee* (604/1906) arrived and connected up, by which time cattle feed was running out. Grain from the cargo was fed to the cattle, and those on deck were sacrificed to allow those below decks to survive. On arrival at Fayal it was reported that 253 had survived and 133 had been lost. *Zwarte Zee* then towed *Manchester Producer* to the Mersey. The storms that winter were bad; a few days before *Manchester Producer* lost her rudder the *Antinoe* (3,708/1902) had foundered after being abandoned.

In December 1927 *Manchester Producer* responded to a distress call from *Bellasco* (2,494/1922), whose pumps were unable to stem a leak in number 1 hold. *Bellasco* made for St. John's, Newfoundland, escorted for 550 miles by *Manchester Producer*. A year later *Manchester Citizen* (2) grounded on the Irish coast. Although she came off without delay the bottom damage was so extensive she put into Belfast and was not allowed to sail until repairs had been completed. *Manchester Division* called and transhipped her cargo for St. John, New Brunswick and Philadelphia. The outstanding service of the decade came in December 1929 when *Manchester Regiment* (1) answered the distress calls of the *Volumnia* (5,608/1911), sinking in a North Atlantic hurricane. With the help of oil pumped on to the water by the tanker *Saco* (5,106/1919), *Manchester Regiment* launched a boat which made two trips to the *Volumnia* to rescue all 45 crew. The boat crew received Board of Trade Sea Gallantry Medals, Lloyd's Medals for Saving Life at Sea and other tokens of appreciation.

The cattle trade

The casualty suffered by *Manchester Producer* is a reminder of the importance of the live cattle trade up to the Second World War. The first year of operations had seen 12,956 cattle shipped, of which 35 died on passage to

Manchester Brigade (top).

Manchester Division (middle).

Manchester Commerce (1) discharging cattle into the lairage at Birkenhead (bottom).

Manchester. On her first arrival on 16th January 1899, *Manchester City* (1) landed 450 cattle and 150 sheep at the Foreign Animals Wharf at Mode Wheel (commissioned in August 1896). The trade was under the control of the Board of Agriculture who could ban imports under the Contagious Diseases (Animals) Act 1878. An outbreak of foot-and-mouth disease could completely halt the trade. To protect British agriculture, animals were not permitted to leave the port, hence the lairage into which cattle were landed was alongside the slaughter house from which the meat was distributed. From 1899 to 1938, Manchester Liners carried a total of 2,636,369 cattle, of which 746 died at sea (0.028% of the total). The record was even better if the *Manchester Producer* casualty is excluded.

The price of new ships was such that not only were sisters of *Manchester Regiment* (1) declined, but further orders were deferred. In March 1923 prices tendered for one or two ships were considered prohibitive and no action was taken. But, nevertheless, the fleet was ageing, with half dating from before the war. Finally, in May 1924, a Furness tender for two ships of 8,500dwt was accepted at £134,000 each. These were delivered in 1925 as *Manchester Commerce* (3) and *Manchester Citizen* (2). Three pre-war ships were sold for further trading that year, *Manchester Exchange*, *Manchester Port* (2) and *Manchester Mariner* (1), with *Manchester Importer* (1) following in 1927. The need to replace the ageing *Manchester City* (1) and retain the interest in the Plate trade was met by the purchase, for £206,000, of a half share in the new Fairfield-built *El Argentino* (9,501/28), an investment retained until she was sold to Furness, Withy for £122,500 in 1937. The final addition to the fleet in the 1920s was *Rexmore* in 1929, for which £55,000 was paid. She was renamed *Manchester Exporter* (1).

The depression

The depression of the 1930s, together with competition from subsidised US lines out of Philadelphia, reduced the cargo available and number of ships required. Hence the reduction in fleet size continued with *Manchester Corporation* going for scrap with *Manchester*

City (1) in 1929, followed by *Manchester Shipper* (1) in 1930. In the main, the fleet was kept in operation, although some lay-ups could not be avoided, such as *Manchester Civilian* and *Manchester Spinner* (2) in 1932. *Manchester Merchant* (2) went for scrap in 1933, and *Manchester Civilian* was sold the same year for further trading.

Like most shipowners the First World War had left them with healthy balance sheets which, in the case of the Furness, Withy Group had financed the management buy-out in 1919. For Manchester Liners this also enabled them to double their stake in the Economic Insurance Co. in 1920, followed by acquisition of more shares in 1927. Another investment was £100,000 of preference shares in the Neptune Steam Navigation Co. Ltd., converted to shares in Johnston Warren Lines Ltd. when Neptune was wound up in 1934.

The fleet received attention as the depression lifted. The first of a series from the Blythswood yard was *Manchester Port* (3) in 1935, followed by *Manchester City* (2) (1937), *Manchester Progress* (1) (1938), *Manchester Merchant* (3) (1940), *Manchester Trader* (3) (1941) and *Manchester Shipper* (2) (1943). The first cost £129,000, the last pair £210,000 each. As the new ships entered service older ships left the fleet, *Manchester Hero* being sold in 1937 and *Manchester Producer* (1) in 1939. As part of the Shipping (Assistance) Bill, 1939, the Board of Trade established a Merchant Ship Reserve, in which *Manchester Producer* became *Botwey*. Ten ships were purchased for this reserve before the outbreak of war ended the need for it.

Manchester Regiment (1) was in the news when, on 23rd October 1937, she was in collision with *Clan Mackenzie* (6,554/1917). Sailing from Liverpool for East London, the Clan Liner overtook *Manchester Regiment* which was flying the flags 'JI', the signal that she was adjusting compasses. *Clan Mackenzie* was rammed on the port side and had to be beached. Later refloated she was declared a total loss, sold and broken up at Troon in 1938. The case went to court where the judge considered which rule of the road should apply, and decided fault lay *Manchester Regiment* 80% and *Clan Mackenzie* 20%.

Manchester Exporter (1) entering the Liverpool docks system.

The Second World War

When war was declared in September 1939 Manchester Liners had a fleet of ten, five of which were to be lost during the conflict, three from enemy action, with 109 killed. The first loss came on 4th December 1939, when *Manchester Regiment* was the victim of a convoy collision. The Pacific Steam Navigation Co.'s *Oropesa* (14,118/1920) had been detached to pick up the crew of Harrison's *Chancellor* (4,607/1916), sunk in collision with *Athelchief* (7,707/1925). Returning to the convoy, *Oropesa* ran down and sank *Manchester Regiment* with the loss of nine lives.

The first loss through enemy action came when *U 137* sank *Manchester Brigade* on 26th September 1940, the first sinking in convoy OB 218. Only four of her crew survived. Captain Clough, Vice Admiral Smith (Convoy Commodore) and 56 others were lost. The other two sinkings came in 1943, the first being *Manchester Merchant* (3) by *U 628* on 25th February with the loss of 36 of her crew. She was the last ship sunk in convoy ON

166 which had been subject to a running battle with U-boats for five days. Both these sinkings had been on the company's normal North Atlantic route, the third was in strange territory for Manchester Liners. *Manchester Citizen* (2) met her end on 9th July at the hands of *U 508,* on passage from Freetown to Lagos, with another fifteen names added to Manchester Liners War Memorial. The final loss was *Manchester Spinner* (2), now the oldest ship in the fleet, when purchased and expended on 7th June 1944 as a blockship protecting the temporary harbour off Juno Beach at Courseulles, seven miles east of Arromanches, during the Normandy invasion.

During the war the ships visited many strange places and undertook duties never before envisaged in Manchester. *Manchester City* (2) was taken over and commissioned as a controlled minelayer mother ship, spending much time in the Indian Ocean maintaining minefields protecting British bases. *Manchester Progress* (1) was one of the last ships to leave Rangoon before Japanese forces arrived in March 1942. Manchester Liners

Manchester Liners at war (1): *Manchester Division* with balloon (above), and *Manchester Commerce* (3) at anchor, Bedford Basin, Halifax on 7th May 1943 (below). *[National Maritime Museum P23334 and P23333]*

Manchester Liners at war (2): *Manchester Exporter* (1) on 7th June 1943 (top); *Manchester Port* (3) entering the Manchester Ship Canal (middle); and *Manchester Progress* (1) off Cammell, Laird's yard (bottom). *[National Maritime Museum P23335, P23337, and G3943]*

Manchester Liners at war (3): *Manchester Trader* (3) at anchor in the Mersey (top) and *Manchester Shipper* (2) underway, rigged with anti-torpedo nets (middle). *[National Maritime Museum G3944 and P23339]*

were strongly represented in the fleet assembled for Operation Torch, the Allied invasion of North Africa in November 1942. In the fleet were *Manchester Citizen* (2), *Manchester Port* (3) and *Manchester Commerce* (3), with *Manchester Trader* (3) and *Manchester Merchant* (3) later taking supplies to this theatre.

Normal maritime risks also had to be faced such as *Manchester Exporter* (1) nearly sinking after a December 1942 collision in Belfast Lough. The same year *Manchester Progress* (1) towed the *Forest* (4,998/1937) towards Iceland without the benefit of naval escort. *Manchester Division* found herself a player in the epic of the *Dunedin Star*. Late in November 1942 *Dunedin Star* (11,168/1936) was beached after striking an underwater obstruction on South Africa's notorious Skeleton Coast. With other ships, *Manchester Division* took part in rescuing the 116 passengers and crew, taking 40 off the wreck. Others had landed through the surf and could not be reached. They were rescued by a land expedition across the unexplored desert backing the coast and did not reach safety until 24th December. In addition to caring for their own ships, Manchester Liners Ltd. were also appointed

managers of three of the Canadian-built Park ships.

Eight Manchester Liners were left to carry the company colours as they returned to their normal haunts in the summer of 1945. Those of the pre-war fleet were now six years older. Not only were there many deferred repairs to be undertaken, the ongoing need for new tonnage had to be faced in a time when all owners were eager to replace their losses. The shipyards were full. Unlike many owners Manchester Liners did not purchase war-built Empire, Liberty or Victory ships. As the war progressed the Government introduced the Ships Disposal Scheme under which ships were allocated to owners for management and then purchased after the war. In October 1944 the decision was taken not to take ships under the scheme, and instead Blythswood were asked to quote for a ship similar to *Manchester Shipper* (2), built under licence in 1943. Although intended for 1945 delivery she did not enter service until 1947 as *Manchester Regiment* (2), by which time another order was in hand at Blythswood for delivery as *Manchester Merchant* (4) in 1951. At the same time *Manchester Exporter* (1) was sold.

The Great Lakes service

At their meeting on 7th November 1950, the directors made an important decision, to commence a service into the Great Lakes. The St. Lawrence and the Great Lakes had, since the earliest times, been an artery of communication, but in the twentieth century the locks passing the river rapids limited ships to a size of 255 x 44 x 14 feet. Alfred Shaw in the early 1930s had started sending coasters into the Lakes, followed by Olsen and Ugelstad's Fjell Line. Later, the Dutch Oranje Line (Anthony Veder N.V.) followed, commencing with two ships bought from Fjell.

After the Welland Canal had been enlarged and re-opened in 1932, the next bottleneck, starting at Montreal's Lachine Canal, had to be removed so that Labrador iron ore could be moved upstream to the industrial regions round the Lakes. Already talks were in hand to harness power, to which navigation was added and agreement reached between the USA and Canada in 1954. The first ships used the seven St. Lawrence Seaway locks in April 1959, with the official opening by Queen Elizabeth II and President Eisenhower on 26th June 1959. Thereafter ships up to 768 x 80 x 30 feet could penetrate 2,000 miles inland and rise 600 feet above sea level. A 400-year-old dream had been realised.

Vessels built and bought for the Great Lakes trade before the St. Lawrence Seaway opened: *Manchester Explorer* (opposite upper) and *Manchester Prospector* (opposite lower). *[Upper: John Slavin; lower Peter Kenyon collection]*

Manchester Vanguard (1) in the Manchester Ship Canal on her maiden voyage (above). *[John Slavin]*

Manchester Faith with black hull on the Welland Canal (right). *[Captain Eric Askew collection]*

Two ships could provide a monthly service into the Lakes, and a design based on the Fjell Line 'tween deckers was considered the most suitable. One problem was winter employment when ice closed the Lakes to navigation. The Fjell ships, after completing surveys and repairs in mid January, and before loading again for the Lakes late in March, were in the habit of going to the Mediterranean and the Spanish orange trade '... where they are a nuisance to the Conference Lines!' To open the new service a two-ship order was placed with Cammell, Laird and Co. Ltd., delivered in time to enter service in the 1952 season. Named *Manchester Pioneer* and *Manchester Explorer*, they were said to be the smallest steam turbine-powered ships afloat. Demand for cargo space was such that early in 1953 the Norwegian *Vigør* was purchased to be the third ship in the service as *Manchester Prospector*.

In September 1955 the names *Manchester Vanguard* (1) and *Manchester Venture* (2) were chosen for two further Lakers, the first Manchester Liners' order placed with foreign builders, in this case A.G. Weser of Bremerhaven. The *Manchester Vanguard* was the first

motorship to be owned by the company. Winter employment for these Lakers was a problem, and from 1956 to 1958 the *Manchester Vanguard* and *Manchester Venture* ran for Yeoward Brothers carrying Canary Island tomatoes and bananas to Britain. With work on the Seaway proceeding apace in July 1957 it was decided to order two larger vessels from Austin and Pickersgill Ltd. Delivered in 1959 as the engines-aft motorships *Manchester Faith* (1) and *Manchester Fame* (1), they were designed for both the Great Lakes trade through the Seaway and as fruit carriers on the Canary and Mediterranean trades. The completion of the Seaway in 1959, opening the trade to larger ships, ended the need for the five small ships. *Manchester Pioneer* was lengthened by 40 feet in February 1960, but all five were sold for further trading between 1960 and 1963.

In addition to the Great Lakes service, approval was given in April 1954 to commence a service to Churchill, in Hudson Bay. The route via Churchill from the Prairies was 1,000 miles shorter than by the St. Lawrence, but this was offset by the very short navigation season, from late July to late October. The port had been

Manchester Regiment (2) at Manchester (above). [M.J. Dobson]

Manchester Spinner (3) at Manchester (right). [M.J. Dobson]

Manchester Mariner (2) (below). [Captain Eric Askew collection]

Manchester Miller (2) at Manchester with her twin uptakes painted in Manchester Liners' funnel colours; as delivered these were mast-coloured (opposite). [M.J. Dobson]

opened by Dalgliesh's *Farnworth* (4,944/1924) in September 1931. Manchester Liners only operated to Churchill for two seasons, the first sailing, in July 1954, being taken by *Cairnavon* (6,333/1941), chartered from the associated Cairn Line. An officer in Manchester Liners remembers the first call to collect grain at Head of the Lakes, where his ship towered above a town which reminded him of cowboy movies, complete with hitching rail.

Fleet renewals

Inflation became a problem after the war. In 1938 *Manchester Progress* (1) had cost £190,000, the *Manchester Regiment* (2) of 1947 was ordered at £447,000 and the *Manchester Spinner* (3) of 1952 cost £606,500. Hence, in 1953, the decision was taken to increase the authorised capital of Manchester Liners Ltd. from £1,000,000, at which it had stood since the company was formed, to £1,500,000. The new shares, both preference and ordinary, were offered to shareholders on the basis of one new share for every two shares held previously.

By 1953 all the old pre-depression ships had been sold. For the next decade the main line services were maintained by the five ships built between 1935 and 1943, strengthened by the five deliveries between 1947 and 1959, the steam turbine-powered *Manchester Regiment* (2) (1947), *Manchester Merchant* (4) (1951), *Manchester Spinner* (3) (1952), *Manchester Mariner* (2) (1955) and *Manchester Miller* (2) (1959). The last, *Manchester Miller* (2), had been ordered from Harland and Wolff Ltd. in 1956 at a price of £992,000 and had a distinctive profile with bridge midships and engines aft with two slim funnels abreast. She was destined to bridge the gap between conventional and container operations when converted by Smith's Dock Co. Ltd. into the cellular container ship *Manchester Quest* in the summer of 1970.

Manchester Shipper (3) and *Manchester Pioneer* were involved in an unusual casualty in August 1954, when a Convair RB36 bomber crossing the Atlantic ditched after its engines caught fire. The two Manchester Liners answered the SOS and between them rescued the four survivors from the crew of 23. *Manchester Pioneer* was equipped with a radio telephone and was able to communicate with searching aircraft, hence she co-ordinated the five ships which took part in the rescue. They formed a line abreast at 10 cable distances and swept the area for survivors, reminding many of the crew of wartime convoys. A decade later *Manchester Progress* (1) and *Manchester Fame* (1) responded to the ditching of a Lockheed

Constellation airliner in the North Atlantic. Of the 76 on board 48 were rescued. Several cargo fires took place in the 1960s. One was on board *Manchester Merchant* (4), and amongst the ships that answered her distress call was the nuclear-powered *Savannah* (13,890/1962).

On five occasions in the 1950s, Manchester Liners won the Gold-Headed Cane at Montreal. Captain Raper received it twice; in 1952 with *Manchester Merchant* (4) and in 1957 with *Manchester Mariner* (2).

Times a-changing

In the 1960s, change began to accelerate. A Manchester Liners crew from the 1890s would have had little difficulty in taking the latest ships to sea sixty years later, but technology then started to change rapidly. Owners had suffered labour problems both in port and at sea, and the developing container trade appealed because it substituted a capital-intensive system for the previous labour-intensive one. A few well-paid operators would replace hundreds of low-paid labourers, and - it was hoped - avoid strikes.

Manchester Liners played a key role in the changes as they introduced the first British container service on the North Atlantic in 1968. From 1963 to 1967 a series of five container-friendly ships were delivered from Smith's Dock Co. Ltd., Middlesbrough. *Manchester Commerce* (4) came first in June 1963, followed by *Manchester City* (3). With the Seaway opened to traffic in 1959 these ships were fitted to operate right into the far reaches of the Lakes, replacing the small vessels previously employed which could navigate the earlier smaller canals. Included in this series were the first ice-strengthened ships in Manchester Liners' service. The Canadian icebreakers were operating through the winter and Lauritzen's ice-strengthened ships were reaching Montreal during the winter. *Manchester Port* (4) and *Manchester Progress* (2) of 1966 and 1967 were therefore strengthened enabling the company to continue a round-the-year service, rather than divert to St. John during the winter.

In 1965 two Manchester Liners were chartered to the associated Cairn Line, and in return two Cairn Line ships were purchased and another chartered. Cairn Line operated a service from the north east to Canada which was in decline. The Manchester Liner ships were smaller and more suited to the cargo available and to the needs of Cairn Line. *Manchester Faith* (1) and *Manchester Fame* (1) became *Cairnesk* and *Cairnglen* for two years, whilst *Cairngowan* became *Manchester Engineer* (3) for one

On charter to Manchester Liners: the handsome *Cairngowan*, renamed *Manchester Engineer* (3) (above), and Prince Line's *Tartar Prince* (below). *[Top: M.J. Dobson]*

year's charter. *Cairnforth* was chartered and *Cairndhu* bought, being renamed *Manchester Freighter* and *Manchester Exporter* (2), respectively. With Manchester Liners containerised after 1968, Cairn Line withdrew from the Canadian trade and its interests were assumed by Manchester Liners, including the Clyde berth shared with Donaldson and Head Line. Another service to close was the Furness Warren Line from Liverpool to Halifax and Boston. In addition to the Cairn Line ships, Manchester Liners also chartered two Prince Line ships, *Western Prince* (7,917/1955) and *Southern Prince* (7,917/1956). The first was renamed *Manchester Trader* (4) for her charter, which lasted from 1960 until January 1969.

The cost of new ships was growing with *Manchester Commerce* (4) costing £1,080,000 in 1963. When ordered in 1964 the price quoted by Smith's Dock for *Manchester Port* (4) and *Manchester Progress* (2), delivered in 1966 and 1967, was £1,550,000 each. As a consequence, the company's capital was again increased in 1965. More extensive use was made of chartering. *Manchester Renown* (1), the third of the 1963-64 ships, was taken on a seven-year charter from Beaver Industries Ltd., North Shields, at £109,500 per annum. In the decades that followed finance was to be obtained from a number of sources through demise chartering. Containerisation was extremely expensive: the costs involved were resposible for the decisions taken at Donaldson and Head Lines to withdraw from shipowning and close their Canadian services. In the case of Manchester Liners, who had discussed a possible joint venture with Donaldson, the initial investment in ships, facilities and containers came to £16,000,000.

Prince Line

In 1968 Prince Line, in the face of poor trading results, closed their service from Manchester to the Mediterranean, a service which dated from 1898. The interest was taken over by Manchester Liners, who purchased the Prince Line loading brokers, Gough and Crosthwaite Ltd. The idea of a Mediterranean service was not new: in October 1910 the directors had considered a Levant service, although nothing was done at the time.

Half a century later the service became a reality under the name Manchester Prince Line. The first ships employed were chartered and given the names *Trojan Prince* (1,283/1954), *Spartan Prince* (1,202/1954) and

Tartar Prince (1,187/1959). This new approach - trading chartered tonnage - worked and was subsequently adopted by Prince Line on their service from London. The venture was strengthened by the purchase of the Golden Cross and Constantine Lines which brought welcome homeward cargo to the service.

In 1971 the decision was taken by the British lines running to the Mediterranean to explore containerisation. Manchester Liners, with their North Atlantic experience fresh in mind, were able to promote this and *Manchester Merit* became the first British containership to operate into the Mediterranean.

The Furness, Withy Group underwent the trauma of takeover twice within a decade. Having come under the control of C.Y. Tung in 1980 and lived through the absorption and mergers that resulted, the remaining remnants again changed hands in 1990 when they were sold to Oetker's Hamburg-Sud. Manchester Prince Line were part of the package and in due course were integrated with Hamburg-Sud's Middle East interests, the Deutsche Nah-Ost Linie, with the last ship to bear a Manchester name being the chartered *Manchester Trader* (11) in 1992.

The Mediterranean service and the onward delivery of containers to the Middle East saw, in 1977, the formation of Marine Transport International, owned by the Alireza organisation (64%) and Manchester Liners (36%), to fit out and operate a container terminal at Jeddah for the Saudi Ports Authority. A terminal at Khor Fakkah, Sharjah, followed.

Expansion

In 1968 Manchester Liners Ltd. ceased to be a lone trading company when it assumed a group status with the purchase of ship repairers Morrell Mills and Co. Ltd., provision merchants James Walker and Son (Shipping) Ltd., and boiler scalers and cleaners Condrons (Manchester) Ltd. With the continued growth of containerisation further takeovers followed in the container repair and packing, road transport and storage arena to create the facilities to provide the door-to-door seamless service which containerisation became. The growing staff and administration needs of the company, as it moved through the planning stage of containerisation, could not be contained within the offices in St. Ann's Square. A four-acre site close to the docks and a quarter mile from the container terminal was therefore obtained in 1967 and a new ten-storey office block erected. A second block on the site was leased to HM Customs. The new offices were opened in December 1969.

Containerisation

The company had for long taken a great interest in improving and rationalising cargo handling, exploring the use of pallets and containers. The work of Matson and Sea-Land on their services to Hawaii and Puerto Rico were noted. A study group was formed to examine the subject, and in September 1966 their report was accepted. Containerisation was to be a mammoth undertaking, requiring new ships, their containers, terminals, container cranes and transport equipment, backed by extensive repair and maintenance facilities.

Orders were placed with Smith's Dock in early 1967 for three ships at a price of £2,000,000 each. In view of the weather conditions to be faced they were to stow all their 500 20-feet containers below decks and would be ice strengthened to permit the Montreal service to operate year round, rather than divert in the winter to the east coast. Container cranes for Manchester and Montreal came in at £200,000 each. The initial order for 3,500 containers, with an option for another 1,000, attracted a bill for nearly £3,000,000.

November 1968 saw the new *Manchester Challenge* (1) open the first British container service across the North Atlantic. She was followed into service by her sisters, *Manchester Courage*, *Manchester Concorde* and *Manchester Crusade* - a fourth ship having been ordered in 1968 (there was the possibility this fourth ship would have involved Donaldson). The *Manchester Concorde* and *Manchester Crusade* were financed by the Industrial and Commercial Finance Corporation (now 3I plc), owned by their subsidiary Nile Steamship Co. Ltd., and chartered by Manchester Liners. Meanwhile the older *Manchester Miller* (2) and *Manchester Progress* (2) were taken in hand in 1970 and 1971 respectively, to emerge as container ships under the names *Manchester Quest* and *Manchester Concept*. Smaller vessels were also bought and chartered

The purpose-built container ship *Manchester Challenge* (1) up bound in the Manchester Ship Canal, seen from Warburton High Level Bridge on 26th August 1973. [*John Slavin*]

to enable a feeder container service to operate from Montreal through to Chicago, ships that were equally suited to employment on the Manchester Prince Line Mediterranean service. These included the 260teu *Manchester Vigour* and *Manchester Zeal* built at Appledore in 1973. As the new North Atlantic operation settled down the older vessels were placed on the disposal market. To handle heavy lifts, machinery and other cargo not suited to containers, 1973 saw the Golden Cross Line reborn and chartering tonnage for a Manchester Great Lakes service.

Manchester Courage made her mark very early when, on 16th March 1969, she suffered a wild propeller whilst transiting the Manchester Ship Canal and crashed through the lock gates at Irlam. This closed the Canal for a month before the damage was repaired. Prior to the opening in 1894, experts had predicted such an accident would never happen. Soon, in April 1895, *Harold* (1,735/1891) proved them wrong at Latchford, followed by *Starlight* (1,481/1884) at Barton Lock in November 1899 and *Winkfield* (4,009/1900), also at Barton, in December 1902.

The Manchester Liners board were both active and adventurous in their exploration of opportunities. December 1969 saw them considering a 258,000dwt oil/ore carrier for charter to operators. This came to nothing, but another opportunity was taken in ordering container ships for charter. First into service from Smith's Dock were the 1,000teu sisters *Manchester Renown* (2) and *Manchester Reward* in 1974, followed in 1977 by the larger *Manchester Vanguard* (2) and *Manchester Venture* (2). Massive capital was required to finance such a fleet and various channels were employed to raise it. Typical was that used for *Manchester Vanguard* (2), when 75% of the Golden Cross Line was sold to Pilkington Brothers, the glass manufacturers. The attraction was the 100% depreciation on the new ship which was permitted in the first year. This would enable Pilkingtons to benefit and reclaim tax. The Revenue were unhappy, taking the matter to court and winning when the House of Lords ruled in 1982.

Takeovers

During the 1960s the Furness, Withy Group had been actively rationalising itself. For long it had consisted largely of virtually autonomous companies. This had led to the description of the Group as being 'a loose confederation of warring tribes'. The rationalisation saw cross holdings removed, and the purchase of minority holdings and takeovers turn associate companies into subsidiaries.

The turn of Manchester Liners came in 1970, at which time Furness, Withy held 42% of the shares. It was a delicate operation as four directors were on the boards of both companies. Hence, the negotiations were based on the guidance of the merchant bankers of the two companies. The outcome was that the Furness, Withy holding increased to 56%, giving control and subsidiary status.

In 1974 a more serious threat emerged. Frank Narby, a founder of the Cast operation (Eurocanadian Shipholdings Ltd.), made a bid for the 44% not held by Furness, Withy. Cast were operating non-conference competition on the North Atlantic using bulkers with containers loaded on top of bulk steel and copper matte. Cast were not considered suitable bedfellows and would have caused a breakdown in Manchester Liners' association with their fellow liner conference operators. There was also the problem of a third man, a millionaire who had gained control of 30% of Manchester Liner shares as an investment, and was waiting to sell to the highest bidder. The Cast offer rose from 110p per share to 155p and they claimed to control 37% of the shares.

With Furness, Withy holding control Cast adopted new tactics, buying Furness, Withy shares. By June 1976 nearly 25% were in their hands. They then suggested a mathematical solution, that through Furness, Withy they *de facto* owned 25% of Manchester Liners. Added to their direct holding this would give them control with over 50%. They suggested a handover of Manchester Liners. This was refused, and instead the matter went to the Monopolies and Mergers Commission who, in 1976, deemed the takeover was against the public interest and ruled against Cast.

Manchester Vigour at Malta. *[World Ship Photo Library]*

Not big enough

Being first is not always to be recommended. Manchester Liners took a massive step into containerisation, but it was not to be big enough. Within a decade it was realised that bigger was better and proposals were developed in 1978 to take Manchester Liners into their second generation as container carriers. The five ships on the North Atlantic would be sold, replaced by three larger ships. They would withdraw from the Manchester terminal and avoid the size restrictions of the Manchester Ship Canal by relocating to the Royal Seaforth terminal in Liverpool. At the same time the contraction of trade to Manchester led to a policy of rationalisation in Group interests. This saw Morrell, Mills and Co. Ltd. and Manchester Dry Docks Ltd. liquidated and other assets sold.

The 1970s had been a time of fierce rate cutting by non-conference operators on the North Atlantic, which hit Manchester Liners balance sheet and led to a co-operation agreement with Canadian Pacific. Rather than compete with each other it was agreed that Canadian Pacific would operate from East Coast and Continental ports, and Manchester Liners from the West Coast. In 1979 Liverpool became the principal British terminal, able to handle much larger ships than could transit the Ship Canal and berth at Manchester.

Two of the original container ships, *Manchester Challenge* and *Manchester Courage,* were sold in 1979 to C.Y. Tung interests, replaced on the service by the larger *Manchester Reward* and *Manchester Renown* (2). But the following year came the shock. Furness, Withy had been sold, and with it Manchester Liners, to C.Y. Tung of Hong Kong. C.Y. Tung soon purchased the 37.6% of Manchester Liners still held by Cast, transferred *Manchester Vanguard*

(2) and *Manchester Venture* (2) to other of his companies and sold some of the smaller ships. Nothing would ever be the same again for Furness, Withy and Manchester Liners. The 1980s would be as traumatic as the previous decade.

The big change that followed the C.Y. Tung takeover saw Manchester Liners in 1981 join Dart Line and Canadian Pacific to form St. Lawrence Co-Ordinated Service (SLCS). The new arrangement saw four ships operating the service, instead of the eleven previously employed by the partners. Dart was a consortium dating from 1969 when Charles Hill's Bristol City Line, Compagnie Maritime Belge (CMB) and Clarke Traffic Services followed Manchester Liners into the container era. They had commissioned four 31,000g second-generation, ice-strengthened, 20-knot 1,800teu container ships. In the decade that followed changes took place with the Bristol City Line sold to Bibby Brothers in 1972, followed by C.Y. Tung taking over the Clarke interest. In addition to buying Furness, Withy in 1980, Tung also acquired the Bibby share of Dart. Now a minority partner, CMB eventually sold out to C.Y. Tung in 1985. The SLCS concentrated its service at Felixstowe, thus ending the Manchester Liners association with the West Coast. In 1984 the Dart service to the United States passed to C.Y. Tung, leaving the Canadian service partners as Manchester Liners, Canadian Pacific and Compagnie Maritime Belge.

Requiem

The last of the Manchester Liners fleet was sold in 1982, the sisters *Manchester Concorde* and *Manchester Crusade*, plus the larger *Manchester Reward* and *Manchester Renown* (2). The four Dart Line ships continued the service, with Manchester Liners' flag hoisted on *Dart*

Too big for Manchester: the *Manchester Vanguard* (2) sailed between Felixstowe and Montreal. *[Captain Eric Askew collection]*

America, chartered from Tynedale Shipping and renamed *Manchester Challenge* (2) as Manchester Liners' contribution. *Dart Atlantic* (31,036/1971) was renamed *CP Ambassador* to carry the Canadian Pacific interest in the re-organised service. Elsewhere, in the Mediterranean, the Manchester name continued to be carried by chartered tonnage.

C.Y. Tung was developing the Orient Overseas Container Line into a global undertaking, with the Dart Line and Manchester Liners candidates for merger and consolidation into that line. But this would not be yet. C.Y. Tung died in 1982 and his Group faced bankruptcy in 1985. Furness,Withy were one of the main assets, and was ring-fenced to avoid a mass scramble by creditors whilst a co-ordinated restructuring agreement was agreed. A fire sale of Furness, Withy under such circumstances would have realised only a fraction of their true worth. With this danger past the merging of mutual interests continued and led to the 1988 announcement that Manchester Liners' interests on the North Atlantic would be absorbed by the Orient Overseas Container Line. At the same time, *Manchester Challenge* (2) was renamed to recognise the change, becoming *OOCL Challenge*. Sold to Greek interests in 1995 she went to the breakers the following year.

Bereft of its purpose in life, Manchester Liners Ltd. nevertheless survives. The Furness, Withy Group shrank as compatible interests were absorbed by the C.Y. Tung interests and other interests sold. Finally the remnants again changed hands in October 1990, being sold to the Rudolf A. Oetker Group, whose main shipping interest is the Hamburg Sudamerikanische D.G. Eggert and Amsinck. Again a process of rationalisation saw further areas merged with similar Hamburg Sud interests. But this had little effect on Manchester Liners, apart from the Manchester Prince Line, as the remaining assets were limited to property in Manchester, with the offices their main asset. But they were destined to again appear briefly in the list of shipowners when, in 1996, the gas tanker *Darwin* (43,636/1977) was registered in their name for tax reasons. Furness, Withy have a succesful gas distribution operation based in Ecuador. Gas is shipped in and stored on board the *Darwin* before being distributed along the Pacific coast of South America by smaller tankers. Owned by Furness, Withy (Shipping) Ltd she was transferred to Manchester Liners and, the tax purpose having been fulfilled, was returned to Furness, Withy (Shipping) Ltd. by 1998.

Chartered ships which carried Manchester Liners' names

Period	Name	Tons/built	Previous names
1960-69	*Manchester Trader* (4)	5,758/1955	*Western Prince*
1965-66	*Manchester Engineer* (3)	8,275/1952	*Cairndhu*
1965-66	*Manchester Freighter*	8,105/1958	*Cairnforth*
1968-75	*Manchester Trader* (5)	2,479/1952	*Werratal*
1971-80	*Manchester Mercurio*	1,997/1971	
1971-77	*Manchester Rapido*	1,997/1971	*Esther del Mar*
1973-75	*Manchester Trader* (6)	499/1972	*Jeanette Helleskov*
1974-75	*Manchester Shipper* (3)	500/1973	*Peter Theilgaard*
1975-77	*Manchester Fulmar* (1)	2,524/1974	*Fulmar*
1975-76	*Manchester Falcon*	999/1975	*Lappland*
1976-77/ 1978-83	*Manchester Faith* (2)	1,421/1974	*Francop*
1978	*Manchester Trader* (7)	1,598/1976	*Kathe Johanna*
1980	*Manchester Clipper*	1,595/1980	*Clipper*
1981-82	*Manchester Eagle*	965/1972	*Atlantic Eagle, Black Eagle*
1981-83	*Manchester Fulmar* (2)	1,599/1979	*City of Ipswich*
1983-85	*Manchester Crown*	1,599/1979	*Crown Prince*
1984-85	*Manchester Trader* (8)	1,999/1977	*Lamara, Meteor II*
1985	*Manchester Faith* (3)	1,599/1971	*Nahorst Kurier, Pinguin*
1985-86	*Manchester City* (4)	3,598/1978	*City of Lisbon, Eagle, Polaris II, Eurobridge Beam, Polaris*
1985-89	*Manchester Trader* (9)	3,978/1978	*Kormoran, Eagle, Kormoran, Visurgis, Carald, Ville de Saint Pierre, Carald*
1986-89	*Manchester Prince*	1,599/1981	*Njord, City of Oporto, Njord*
1989-91	*Manchester Trader* (10)	3,348/1980	*Karyatein, Altona*
1991-92	*Manchester Trader* (11)	3,818/1991	*Francop*

Chartered tonnage: *Manchester Engineer* (3) (left), and (opposite clockwise from top) *Manchester Mercurio* in the St. Lawrence Seaway during May 1973 *[Rene Beauchamp]*, *Manchester Faith* (2) 14th June 1977, *Manchester Clipper* 1983, *Manchester Fulmar* (2) January 1983, *Manchester Shipper* (3) August 1975. *[All: John Slavin]*

Golden Cross Line Ltd.

In 1898 Owen and Watkin Williams, Cardiff, commenced a service from Welsh ports to Marseilles, Genoa and Leghorn, returning from Spanish Mediterranean ports. This became known as the Golden Cross Line from their flag, a golden cross on a blue ground. On 9th July 1906 they registered the Golden Cross Line Ltd. During the 1920s Williams failed and the Golden Cross Line Ltd. was wound up on 16th May 1930.

In the autumn of 1925 the service was taken over by Lambert, Barnett and Co., Cardiff, and registered on 29th April 1933 as the Golden Cross Line (Bristol Channel) Ltd. In January 1946 the company was sold to Charles Hill and Sons, Bristol, and Turnbull, Scott and Co. Ltd. London. Renamed Golden Cross Line Ltd., in 1952 it passed to Harris and Dixon Ltd., London, who operated a Mediterranean service in association with Anthony and Bainbridge Ltd., Newcastle-on-Tyne. The service was renamed the Gracechurch Line and passed in 1959 to Constantine Lines Ltd., Middlesbrough, and then to Anthony and Bainbridge Ltd., Newcastle-on-Tyne.

The Golden Cross Line Ltd., but not its service rights, was purchased by Manchester Liners Ltd. on 29th November 1968 to become a break-bulk service, using chartered tonnage, to Canada alongside their container operation. Catering for non-container compatible cargo, from 1977 to 1983 the line also owned the container ship *Manchester Vanguard* (2) which spent much of her time on charter.

War and peace with Manchester Liners
Captain Eric Askew

I joined Manchester Liners on 29th December 1942, after spending two months' survivor's leave at my home in Cumberland. Reporting to the Liverpool Officer's Pool, I was sent to Manchester Liners' office where I was appointed third mate of *Manchester Progress* (1).

During my first voyage to St. John, New Brunswick, the convoy was routed well to the north. One afternoon Captain Barclay called me to the bridge and away on the starboard bow were the snow-clad mountains of Greenland, gleaming brightly in the setting sun. 'There you are, young man, Greenland - you might never see it again.' 'I don't want to see it now, sir', was my reply.

On that first outward voyage, *Manchester Progress* was the Vice Commodore ship, having on board a Royal Navy Commodore who was doing his first trip in this role, having just retired as a captain with Royal Mail Lines. Homeward bound we sailed from Halifax in company with a few ships, and joined a homeward convoy from New York, with our Commodore now in sole charge of the convoy. A few days later we were attacked by U-boats and several ships were sunk, including the Commodore ship. Sadly, our Commodore did not survive.

On my second voyage on *Manchester Progress*, we experienced heavy weather after clearing the Irish coast, and after a few days the motor vessel *Forest* belonging to Morel Ltd. of Cardiff lost her rudder. The Commodore appointed us to assist *Forest* (4,998/1937) and tow her to Reykjavik. During a lull, we connected a tow line, and commenced to tow. However, the weather worsened in the night, and next morning the tow broke. After several attempts to reconnect the tow in increasing wind, it was decided we should proceed to Reykjavik and request a tug be sent out. This was just after noon on Saturday, and we arrived at Reykjavik just after breakfast on Sunday. It was Tuesday before a tug went out. Two days later we left in a small convoy to Loch Ewe, where we waited a few days before joining the next outward convoy. For my part in salvaging the *Forest* (which survived the war), I received the sum of £21.

In December 1943 I was promoted second mate and moved to *Manchester Exporter* (1), which was loading in Manchester with military stores for Naples. On joining the Mediterranean convoy we were made Vice Commodore ship, but had no naval personnel to help us with signals. When south of Sicily, Italian destroyers came out to escort us. We received a long message by Morse giving us orders

from the Commodore, and while he steamed on towards Alexandria with a naval escort and just five ships, Captain Downing of the *Manchester Exporter* found himself in charge of over forty bound for the Syracuse anchorage.

Homeward bound we called in at Gibraltar to join a homeward convoy, but received orders to proceed to Valencia to load a full cargo of oranges. We hugged the Spanish coast, keeping inside the three-mile limit, with occasional RAF aircraft flying past to seaward to keep an eye on us. While berthed at Valencia, the French fruiter *Kilissi* (3,723/1934) berthed astern of us, only now she was crewed by Germans and flew the swastika ensign. The Spanish police did a good job of keeping our crew and the Germans apart for a few days until she sailed. We heard the RAF sank her on her way north up the Spanish coast (she was bombed and sunk off the River Ebro on 12th March 1944, *Ed.*). We brought our oranges safely back to Manchester, where I left to sit for my first mates' certificate.

When the war ended, eight ships were left to carry on Manchester Liners' Canadian and US trades. Canadian ports served were Montreal in summer, and St. John, New Brunswick in the winter. US ports served were Philadelphia, Baltimore and Norfolk. Occasionally, the company used to extend the route to Florida to take scotch whisky from Glasgow for the season in Miami.

During the late 1940s a decision was made to open up a trade to the Great Lakes using existing canals, and two vessels 258 feet long were ordered from Cammell, Laird, the *Manchester Pioneer* and *Manchester Explorer,* delivered in 1952. The Lakes trade made a good start, and a third vessel was bought from Norwegian owners and was renamed *Manchester Prospector*. My first trip to the Great Lakes was in November 1958 as master on the *Manchester Pioneer*. The St. Lawrence Seaway was still under construction, and only the top half was open to shipping. Sailing from Montreal we had to go through the Lachine Canal to Lake St. Louis, and then through the Soulanges Canal to Lake St. Francis and the new US locks Snell and Eisenhower. Clear of these locks we entered Lake St. Lawrence through the new Iroquois Lock which took us to Lake Ontario and through the Thousand Islands.

For the opening of the St. Lawrence Seaway in 1959, Manchester Liners ordered two ships from Austin and Pickersgill, *Manchester Faith* (1) and *Manchester Fame* (1). The former was the first British ship through the Seaway. I was in Montreal on the *Manchester Port* (3) the

A peacetime view of *Manchester Progress* (1), 9th August 1947.

From *Manchester Commerce* (4) in heavy ice. *[Captain Eric Askew]*

day it was opened and watched Canadian Coast Guard ships and icebreakers going through the St. Lambert Lock, followed by a Dutch ship and then the *Manchester Faith*, which, if I remember rightly, was the ninth ship into the Seaway. It was not long before some of the Montreal ships were transferred to the Lakes, the *Manchester Progress* (1), *Manchester Shipper* (2), *Manchester Regiment* (2), and *Manchester Miller* (2), whilst the smaller ships were phased out or, in the case of the *Manchester Pioneer*, being lengthened. Some ships on the Great Lakes trade appeared with light green hulls. This was to keep them as cool as possible, as at the time cartons of lard were loaded in Chicago and heat caused problems in summer. We also painted the decks aluminium, and while we were above Montreal kept water running on the deck to give a cooling effect.

In the 1960s Manchester Liners decided to containerise; one of the first British companies to do so. After the conventional cargo ships had been sold, I was appointed to the container ships. While on *Manchester Crusade* in December 1972, and approaching Belle Isle Strait outward bound, we encountered broken ice which was quite thick in places, and Belle Isle Radio informed us that the *Susan Constant* (3,385/1958) was fast in ice off the Labrador coast. When we arrived in the area we found the wind and ice had pushed her over to the Newfoundland Coast near Flowers Ledges. On the radio, the *Susan Constant's* captain confirmed that he would like me to cut him out of the ice. I went over and took a position ahead of her and she was able to follow me into clear water and resume her voyage.

Susan Constant in the ice. *[Captain Eric Askew]*

Early next morning in the Gulf of St. Lawrence we suffered steering problems. The helm would not go over to starboard due to a small round plate on the rudder. It was secured by six bolts, five of which had sheared off causing the plate to slew round against the rudder post, preventing the rudder going over to starboard. I informed the Montreal office of our agents of our predicament, and they got in touch with *Manchester Concept*, which was in the St. Lawrence River and came and towed us into Seven Islands. Here, a diver went down and shackled a wire on to the plate, the other end of the wire being secured to a large dumper truck. Despite slipping and sliding on the ice, this vehicle managed to pull the plate free, and we were able to continue our voyage to Montreal.

My next ship was the *Manchester Concorde*, on which I did a spell of three and a half years, sharing with Captain Fielding on a basis of two trips on and two off in the summer, and one on and one off in the winter. Whilst on *Manchester Concorde* I sailed from Manchester on

The icebreakers *Simon Fraser* and *Ernest Lapointe* clearing ice at Yamachiche Bend. *[Captain Eric Askew]*

An iced-up *Manchester Concorde* in the Gulf of St. Lawrence. *[Captain Eric Askew]*

22nd November 1977 and berthed in Montreal on 1st January 1978, thereby winning the Gold-Headed Cane for the first ship arriving in the New Year.

In 1974 two new container ships arrived from Smith's Dock, the *Manchester Renown* (2) and *Manchester Reward*. They were immediately renamed *Asian Renown* and *Asian Reward* for charter to Swires of Hong Kong who, with Nedlloyd, started the Hong Kong to Australia container service known as Asian Australian Express. The route was from Hong Kong to Sydney, Melbourne, Brisbane, then north to Manila, Keelung, Kaohsiung, and back to Hong Kong. It was agreed that the crews would stay on this run for four months, being flown out to Hong Kong for three round trips.

In 1977 the last two ships built for Manchester Liners arrived, again built by Smith's Dock and too big to get up to their home port, the *Manchester Vanguard* (2) and *Manchester Venture* (2). They were built for charter to Swires for the Asian Australian Express, but Swires decided to build two ships in Japan and the Manchester liners were no longer required. I brought the *Asian Reward* home light ship in October 1978, with the *Asia Renown* following a month later. I returned to the Montreal route.

By coincidence, I was to see Greenland's mountains again, almost forty years after glimpsing them from *Manchester Progress* (1). This time it was from an aircraft, whose pilot had flown north to avoid bad weather. I had just finished a trip in *Manchester Concorde* on which I had taken my wife to join our daughter in Toronto. On returning to Manchester, I took my leave and flew back to Toronto to join my wife for three weeks. On arriving home in the UK a letter was on the mat waiting for me. It read 'Your services are no longer required. You will be paid up to 31st December 1980.'

In the ice above Quebec Bridge. *[Captain Eric Askew]*

The short-lived *Manchester Enterprise* with stalls erected on deck for carrying cattle (top). *[Edward Gray collection]*

Manchester Trader (1) (middle) and as *Ferdinand Melsom* (right). *[Glasgow University Archives DC101/1151]*

Manchester City (1) in the Mersey (opposite).

Fleet list

1. MANCHESTER ENTERPRISE 1898-1899

O.N. 96394 3,878g 2,514n 360.0 x 46.0 x 29.0 feet
T. 3-cyl. by Gourlay Brothers and Co., Dundee; 430 NHP, 11½ knots.
26.6.1889: Launched by Gourlay Brothers and Co., Dundee (Yard No. 138).
1.1890: Completed for the Steamship Queensmore Ltd. (William Johnston and Co. Ltd., managers), Liverpool as QUEENSMORE.
10.1896: Sold to Elder, Dempster and Co., Liverpool.
5.5.1898: Acquired by Manchester Liners Ltd., Manchester (Furness, Withy and Co. Ltd., West Hartlepool, managers).
1898: Renamed MANCHESTER ENTERPRISE.
1899: Managers became Manchester Liners Ltd., Manchester.
14.11.1899: Foundered in the North Atlantic in position 50.25 north by 42.25 west whilst on a voyage from Liverpool and Manchester to Montreal with general cargo. The crew was rescued by the steamer LAKONIA (4,686/1899).

MANCHESTER ENTERPRISE and MANCHESTER TRADER were the subject of a rare error by Lloyd's Register, which transposed their ex names in the 1898 Register. The identity of MANCHESTER TRADER was corrected by the 1900 edition.

2. MANCHESTER TRADER (1) 1898-1912

O.N. 97829 3,318g 2,136n 340.0 x 42.7 x 27.0 feet
T. 3-cyl. by McIlwaine and MacColl Ltd., Belfast; 354 NHP, 12 knots. The engines had been begun by Forrester and Co., Liverpool.
16.8.1890: Launched by Charles J. Bigger, Londonderry (Yard No. 17).

28.11.1890: Registered in the ownership of the Steamship Parkmore Ltd. (William Johnston and Co. Ltd., managers), Liverpool as QUEENSMORE.
12.1890: Completed.
1.1897: Sold to Elder, Dempster and Co., Liverpool.
5.5.1898: Acquired by Manchester Liners Ltd., Manchester (Furness, Withy and Co. Ltd., West Hartlepool, managers).
18.7.1898: Renamed MANCHESTER TRADER.
1899: Managers became Manchester Liners Ltd., Manchester.
1912: Sold to Akties. Ferdinand Melson (Johan Johanson and Co., managers), Christiania, Norway and later renamed FERDINAND MELSOM.
1914: Sold to H. Westfal Larsen, Bergen, Norway and renamed KAUPANGER.
1915: Owners became Dampskipsinterressentskap Akties. (H. Westfal Larsen, manager), Bergen.
13.12.1916: Torpedoed by the German submarine U 38 off Cartagena, Spain in position 37.18 north by 00.52 west whilst on a voyage from Cardiff to Spezia with a cargo of coal.

3. MANCHESTER CITY (1) 1898-1929

O.N. 108835 5,833g 3,727n 445.4 x 52.0 x 30.0 feet
T. 3-cyl. by Sir Christopher Furness, Westgarth and Co. Ltd., Middlesbrough; 541 NHP, 3,500 IHP, 11½ knots.
6.6.1898: Launched by Sir Raylton Dixon and Co. Ltd., Middlesbrough (Yard No. 450). She had been ordered by Furness, Withy and Co. Ltd., West Hartlepool.
10.1898: Completed.
27.10.1898: Registered in the ownership of Manchester Liners Ltd., Manchester as MANCHESTER CITY.
6.1929: Broken up by the Stavanger Shipbreaking Co., Stavanger, Norway.
10.6.1929: Register closed.

4. MANCHESTER PORT (1)   1899-1900

O.N. 108840   5,658g   3,630n   452.0 x 52.2 x 28.2 feet
T. 3-cyl. by Palmers' Shipbuilding and Iron Co. Ltd., Newcastle-on-Tyne; 750 NHP, 3,500 IHP, 12 knots.
26.4.1899: Launched by Palmers' Shipbuilding and Iron Co. Ltd., Newcastle-on-Tyne (Yard No. 740). She had been ordered by Furness, Withy and Co. Ltd., West Hartlepool.
6.1899: Completed.
17.6.1899: Registered in the ownership of Manchester Liners Ltd., Manchester as MANCHESTER PORT.
2.8.1900: Sold to Robert P. Houston, London.
14.8.1900: Sold to the British and South American Steam Navigation Co. Ltd. (Robert P. Houston and Co., managers), Liverpool.
18.8.1900: Renamed HYDASPES.
1.1930: Broken up by Luigi Pittaluga, Genoa, Italy.
12.4.1930: Register closed.

5. MANCHESTER IMPORTER   1899-1927

O.N. 108842   4,028g   2,538n   370.0 x 48.0 x 26.3 feet
T. 3-cyl. by W. Allan and Co. Ltd., Sunderland; 379 NHP, 2,000 IHP, 10½ knots.
29.5.1899: Launched by Irvine's Shipbuilding and Dry Dock Co. Ltd., West Hartlepool (Yard No. 107).
8.1899: Completed.
24.8.1899: Registered in the ownership of Manchester Liners Ltd., Manchester as MANCHESTER IMPORTER.
9.1927: Sold to Paul Negroponte, Syra, Greece and renamed ALEXANDRA.
1933: Broken up at Venice.

6. MANCHESTER CORPORATION   1899-1929

O.N. 108844   5,467g   3,457n   430.5 x 48.1 x 30.8 feet
T. 3-cyl. by Sir Christopher Furness, Westgarth and Co. Ltd., Middlesbrough; 357 NHP, 3,000 IHP, 12 knots.
8.6.1899: Launched by Furness, Withy and Co. Ltd., West Hartlepool (Yard No. 243).
9.1899: Completed.

21.9.1899: Registered in the ownership of Manchester Liners Ltd., Manchester as MANCHESTER CORPORATION.
7.1929: Broken up by T.W. Ward Ltd. at Barrow-in-Furness.
16.7.1929: Register closed.

7. MANCHESTER COMMERCE (1)   1899-1914

O.N. 108846   5,363g   3,444n   430.7 x 48.2 x 30.8 feet
T. 3-cyl. by Sir Christopher Furness, Westgarth and Co. Ltd., Middlesbrough; 498 NHP, 2,600 IHP, 12¼ knots.
21.8.1899: Launched by Furness, Withy and Co. Ltd., West Hartlepool (Yard No. 244).
11.1899: Completed.
18.11.1899: Registered in the ownership of Manchester Liners Ltd., Manchester as MANCHESTER COMMERCE.
27.10.1914: Mined 20 miles north by a quarter east of Tory Island whilst on a voyage from Manchester to Montreal with general cargo. The mine had been laid by SMS BERLIN.
7.11.1914: Register closed.

8. MANCHESTER MERCHANT (1)   1900-1903

O.N. 108849   5,657g   3,635n   452.0 52.2 x 28.3 feet
T. 3-cyl. by Palmers' Shipbuilding and Iron Co. Ltd., Newcastle-on-Tyne; 750 NHP, 3,500 IHP, 10 knots.
2.12.1899: Launched by Palmers' Shipbuilding and Iron Co. Ltd., Newcastle-on-Tyne (Yard No. 743). She had been ordered by Furness, Withy and Co. Ltd., West Hartlepool.
2.1900: Completed.
7.2.1900: Registered in the ownership of Manchester Liners Ltd., Manchester as MANCHESTER MERCHANT.
15.1.1903: Scuttled to extinguish fire in Dingle Bay, Ireland whilst on a voyage from New Orleans to Manchester with a cargo of cotton, lumber and maize.
11.5.1903: Register closed.

Manchester Commerce (1) with the tug *Partington.* [Peter Newall collection]

Hydaspes, ex-Manchester Port (1). *[National Maritime Museum N43242]*

Manchester Importer.

Manchester Corporation (1).

Manchester Shipper (1) (top).

Manchester Exchange (middle).
[Edward Gray collection]

Manchester Market (bottom).

Manchester Engineer (1). *[Edward Gray collection]*

9. MANCHESTER SHIPPER (1) 1900-1930
O.N. 108850 4,038g 2,542n 370.0 x 48.0 x 26.3 feet
T. 3-cyl. by W. Allan and Co. Ltd., Sunderland; 379 NHP, 2,000 IHP, 10½ knots.
18.11.1899: Launched by Irvine's Shipbuilding and Dry Dock Co. Ltd., West Hartlepool (Yard No. 110).
2.1900: Completed.
26.2.1900: Registered in the ownership of Manchester Liners Ltd., Manchester as MANCHESTER SHIPPER.
17.7.1930: Arrived at Briton Ferry to be broken up by T.W. Ward Ltd.
22.7.1930: Demolition began.
21.2.1931: Register closed.

10. MANCHESTER EXCHANGE 1901-1925
O.N. 113113 4,115g 2,665n 360.5 x 48.2 x 20.3 feet
T. 3-cyl. by Richardsons, Westgarth and Co. Ltd., Hartlepool; 374 NHP, 1,750 IHP, 10 knots.
15.8.1901: Launched by Furness, Withy and Co. Ltd., West Hartlepool (Yard No. 257).
6.11.1901: Registered in the ownership of Manchester Liners Ltd., Manchester as MANCHESTER EXCHANGE.
16.11.1901: Delivered.
27.11.1925: Sold to A/B Finland-Amerika Linjen O/Y (Erik Tötterman, managers), Helsinki, Finland and renamed EQUATOR.
30.1.1939: Sold to S.A. Cantiere di Porto Venere, La Spezia, Italy and renamed CAPORTO for the voyage to La Spezia where she was broken up by this company.

11. MANCHESTER MARKET 1902-1903
O.N. 113115 4,091g 2,650n 360.6 x 48.2 x 28.2 feet
T. 3-cyl. by Richardsons, Westgarth and Co. Ltd., Hartlepool; 374 NHP, 1,750 IHP, 10 knots.
30.9.1901: Launched by Furness, Withy and Co. Ltd., West Hartlepool (Yard No. 259).
13.1.1902: Registered in the ownership of Manchester

Liners Ltd., Manchester as MANCHESTER MARKET.
23.1.1902: Delivered.
26.4.1903: Wrecked on the Gipsy Rock, Tuskar, whilst on a voyage from Manchester to Philadelphia with general cargo.
11.5.1903: Register closed.

12. MANCHESTER ENGINEER (1) 1902-1916
O.N. 113116 4,302g 2,813n 360.4 x 48.0 x 28.1 feet
T. 3-cyl. by Richardsons, Westgarth and Co. Ltd., Sunderland; 372 NHP, 1,850 IHP, 10 knots.
25.2.1902: Launched by the Northumberland Shipbuilding Co. Ltd., Newcastle-on-Tyne (Yard No. 95).
4.1902: Completed.
24.4.1902: Registered in the ownership of Manchester Liners Ltd., Manchester as MANCHESTER ENGINEER.
27.3.1916: Torpedoed and sunk by the German submarine U 44 in St. George's Channel 20 miles west by south of the Coningbeg Lighthouse whilst on a voyage from Philadelphia to Manchester with general cargo.
4.4.1916: Register closed.

13. MANCHESTER INVENTOR (1) 1902-1917
O.N. 113117 4,247g 2,775n 360.4 x 48.0 x 28.1 feet
T. 3-cyl. by Richardsons, Westgarth and Co. Ltd., Sunderland; 372 NHP, 1,850 IHP, 10 knots.
25.2.1902: Launched by the Northumberland Shipbuilding Co. Ltd., Newcastle-on-Tyne (Yard No. 98)
4.1902: Completed.
2.6.1902: Registered in the ownership of Manchester Liners Ltd., Manchester as MANCHESTER INVENTOR.
18.1.1917: Captured and sunk by gunfire by the German submarine U 57 in the North Atlantic 50 miles north west of Fastnet in position 51.36 north by 10.56 west whilst on a voyage from St. John, New Brunswick to Manchester with general cargo.
31.1.1917: Register closed.

Manchester Spinner (1) (above). [Edward Gray collection]
Manchester Merchant (2) making a very unusual visit to an Australian port.

14. MANCHESTER SPINNER (1) 1903-1918
O.N. 113123 4,227g 2,760n 360.0 x 48.0 x 28.1 feet
T. 3-cyl. by Richardsons, Westgarth and Co. Ltd.,
Sunderland; 372 NHP, 1,850 IHP, 10 knots.
28.5.1903: Launched by the Northumberland Shipbuilding
Co. Ltd., Newcastle-on-Tyne (Yard No. 105).
11.7.1903: Delivered.
8.7.1903: Registered in the ownership of Manchester
Liners Ltd., Manchester as MANCHESTER SPINNER.
22.1.1918: Torpedoed and sunk by the Austro-Hungarian
submarine U 27 33 miles south by half east of Malta whilst
on a voyage from Java to the United Kingdom with a cargo
of sugar.
12.3.1918: Register closed.

15. MANCHESTER MILLER (1) 1903-1905/1908-1917
O.N. 113125 4,234g 2,760n 360.0 x 48.0 x 28.1 feet
T. 3-cyl. by Richardsons, Westgarth and Co. Ltd.,

Sunderland; 372 NHP, 1,850 IHP, 10 knots.
11.7.1903: Launched by the Northumberland Shipbuilding
Co. Ltd., Newcastle-on-Tyne (Yard No. 106).
20.8.1903: Registered in the ownership of Manchester
Liners Ltd., Manchester as MANCHESTER MILLER.
22.8.1903: Delivered.
14.7.1905: Sold to the Britain Steamship Co. Ltd. (Watts,
Watts and Co., managers), London.
29.7.1905: Renamed FULHAM.
14.2.1908: Re-acquired by Manchester Liners Ltd.,
Manchester.
21.2.1908: Renamed MANCHESTER MILLER.
5.6.1917: Torpedoed and sunk by the German submarine
U 66 in the North Atlantic 190 miles north west by half
north from Fastnet in position 52.49 north by 14.7 west
whilst on a voyage from Philadelphia to Manchester with
general cargo. Eight members of the crew were lost.
13.6.1917: Register closed.

Manchester Port (2) in peace (upper) and dressed overall in grey, possibly at the Armistice in 1918. (lower). *[Both: Edward Gray collection]*

16. MANCHESTER MERCHANT (2) 1904-1933
O.N. 113129   4,152g 2,707n   360.0 x 48.0 x 28.1 feet
T. 3-cyl. by Richardsons, Westgarth and Co. Ltd., Sunderland; 400 NHP, 2,400 IHP, 11 knots.
22.10.1903: Launched by Northumberland Shipbuilding Co. Ltd., Howden-on-Tyne (Yard No. 108).
1.1904: Completed.
12.1.1904: Registered in the ownership of Manchester Liners Ltd., Manchester as MANCHESTER MERCHANT.
1.6.1920: Owners became Manchester Ocean Services Ltd., Manchester.
2.3.1930: Owners became Manchester Liners Ltd., Manchester.
9.10.1933: Register closed after sale to shipbreakers.
26.11.1933: Arrived at Genoa to be broken up.

17. MANCHESTER PORT (2) 1904-1925
O.N. 113130   4,093g 2,662n   360.0 x 48.0 x 28.1 feet
T. 3-cyl. by Richardsons, Westgarth and Co. Ltd., Sunderland; 400 NHP, 2,200 IHP, 10½ knots.
21.10.1903: Launched by Furness, Withy and Co. Ltd., West Hartlepool (Yard No. 269).
5.1.1904: Registered in the ownership of Manchester Liners Ltd., Manchester as MANCHESTER PORT.
11.1.1904: Completed.
1.6.1920: Owners became Manchester Ocean Services Ltd., Manchester.
16.3.1925: Registered in the ownership of H. Vogemann, Hamburg, Germany as VOGESEN.
6.5.1940: Mined west of Vinga Lighthouse, Sweden. The mine had been laid by HM Submarine SEAL.

18. MANCHESTER MARINER (1) 1904-1925

O.N. 119582 4,106g 2,672n 360.0 x 48.0 x 28.1 feet
T. 3-cyl. by Richardsons, Westgarth and Co. Ltd., West Hartlepool; 403 NHP, 1,830 IHP, 10 knots.
19.12.1903: Launched by Furness, Withy and Co. Ltd., West Hartlepool (Yard No. 270).
28.1.1904: Delivered.
25.2.1904: Registered in the ownership of Manchester Liners Ltd., Manchester as MANCHESTER MARINER.
1.6.1920: Owners became Manchester Ocean Services Ltd., Manchester.
6.11.1925: Sold to A/B Finland-Amerika Linjen O/Y (Erik Tötterman, manager), Helsinki, Finland and renamed MERCATOR.
1.12.1939: Torpedoed and sunk by the German submarine U 31 off Peterhead, Scotland in position 57.39 north by 00.36 east whilst on a voyage from Rio de Janeiro to Finland with general cargo including coffee. One member of the crew was lost.

19. MANCHESTER CITIZEN (1) 1912-1917

O.N. 124299 4,251g 2,725n 380.1 x 49.0 x 26.4 feet
T. 3-cyl. by Richardsons, Westgarth and Co. Ltd., Sunderland; 372 NHP, 1,850 IHP, 10 knots.
18.6.1912: Launched by Northumberland Shipbuilding Co. Ltd., Howden-on-Tyne (Yard No. 196).
8.1912: Completed.
7.8.1912: Registered in the ownership of Manchester Liners Ltd., Manchester as MANCHESTER CITIZEN.
26.4.1917: Torpedoed and sunk by the German submarine U 70 north west of Fastnet in position 52.30 north by 15.47 west whilst on a voyage from St. John, New Brunswick to Manchester with general cargo.
24.5.1917: Register closed.

20. MANCHESTER CIVILIAN 1913-1933

O.N. 135359 4,706g 2,927n 385.0 x 52.0 x 27.0 feet
T. 3-cyl. by by Richardsons, Westgarth and Co. Ltd., Hartlepool; 376 NHP, 1,700 IHP, 9¾ knots.
8.7.1913: Launched by Irvine's Shipbuilding and Dry Dock Co. Ltd., West Hartlepool (Yard No. 519).
8.1913: Completed.

26.8.1913: Registered in the ownership of Manchester Liners Ltd., Manchester as MANCHESTER CIVILIAN.
5.1933: Sold to S.G. Razis, Argostoli, Greece and renamed TASIS.
1935: Sold to the Myrtoon Steamship Co. Ltd., Piraeus, Greece (Vergottis Ltd., London, managers).
6.1940: Seized at Dakar by the Vichy French Government (Société Navale Caennaise, Caen, managers) and renamed EQUATEUR.
1942: Transferred to the Italian Government, Rome (Italia S.A. di Navigazione, Genoa, managers) and renamed BARI.
1.8.1943: Beached in sinking condition in Naples Roads following an Allied air attack.

21. MANCHESTER HERO 1916-1937

O.N. 135366 5,738g 3,672n 400.0 x 53.0 x 32.3feet
T. 3-cyl. by Blair and Co. Ltd, Stockton; 465 NHP, 2,300 IHP, 10¾ knots.
10.9.1915: Launched by Northumberland Shipbuilding Co Ltd, Howden-on-Tyne (Yard No. 226).
She had been laid down for Lloyd Austriaco, Trieste, Austria-Hungary.
1.1916: Completed.
3.1.1916: Registered in the ownership of Manchester Liners Ltd., Manchester as MANCHESTER HERO.
10.6.1937: Sold to the Barry Shipping Co. Ltd. (B. and S. Shipping Co. Ltd., managers), Barry and renamed ST WINIFRED.
5 and 6.1938: Bombed by Nationalist aircraft at Alicante during Spanish Civil War.
*17.8.1938:*Towed to Marseilles, where she was later declared a constructive total loss.
21.10.1938: Register closed.
1938: Sold to Compagnia Genovese di Navigazione a Vapore S.A., Genoa, Italy and renamed CAPO VITA.
9.3.1941: Torpedoed and sunk by HM Submarine UTMOST west of Lampedusa Island, 25 miles north of Kuriat, Tunisia in position 36.9 north by 11.7 east whilst on a voyage from Naples to Tripoli with a cargo of munitions.

Manchester Mariner (1) outward bound at Boston 3rd September 1921. (1) (opposite top). *[R. Hildebrand (Johnson collection) courtesy William Schell]*
Manchester Civilian in grey (opposite middle) and in regulation black (opposite bottom). *[Ted Gray collection and George Scott collection]*
Manchester Hero (above).

Craigvar which very briefly ran as *Manchester Engineer* (2). *[Glasgow University Archives DC101/1076]*

22. MANCHESTER TRADER (2) 1916-1917

O.N. 115722 3,985g 2,597n 344.8 x 49.9 x 25.7 feet
T. 3-cyl. by Rankin and Blackmore, Greenock; 1,500 IHP, 9¹/₄ knots
1.10.1902: Launched by Russell and Co, Port Glasgow (Yard No. 498).
23.10.1902: Registered in the ownership of Auchenblae Steam Shipping Co. Ltd. (Purdie, Glen and Co., managers), Glasgow as AUCHENBLAE.
11.1902: Completed.
14.3.1916: Acquired by Manchester Liners Ltd., Manchester.
20.3.1916: Renamed MANCHESTER TRADER.
4.6.1917: Captured by the German submarine U 65 and sunk by gunfire eight miles south east of Pantellaria, Italy whilst on a voyage from Suda Bay to Algiers in ballast. One member of the crew was lost and one taken prisoner.
21.6.1917: Register closed.

23. MANCHESTER COMMERCE (2) 1916-1917

O.N. 123988 4,144g 2,687n 385.0 x 50.0 x 24.9 feet
T. 3-cyl. by Dunsmuir and Jackson Ltd., Glasgow; 453 NHP, 2,200 IHP, 11 knots.
19.6.1906: Launched by Russell and Co., Port Glasgow (Yard No. 560).
8.1906: Completed.
8.8.1906: Registered in the ownership of the State Steamship Co. Ltd. (William Thomas, Sons and Co. Ltd., managers), Liverpool as KING.
13.7.1916: Acquired by Manchester Liners Ltd., Manchester.
2.8.1916: Renamed MANCHESTER COMMERCE.
29.6.1917: Torpedoed and sunk by the German submarine U 39 15 miles west by north half north of Cape Spartel whilst on a voyage from Cardiff to Gibraltar with a cargo of coal and Government stores. One member of the crew was lost.
16.8.1917: Register closed.

24. MANCHESTER ENGINEER (2) 1916-1917

O.N. 121260 4,415g 2,874n 378.1 x 50.1 x 26.0 feet
T. 3-cyl. by D. and W. Henderson and Co. Ltd., Glasgow; 370 NHP, 2,150 IHP, 11 knots.
4.9.1905: Launched by D. and W. Henderson and Co. Ltd., Glasgow (Yard 444).
9.1905: Completed.
22.9.1905: Registered in the ownership of the West of Scotland Steamship Co. Ltd. (Alex L. Biggart and John F. Fulton, managers), Glasgow as CRAIGVAR.
6.10.1913: Sold to the Treasury Steamship Co. Ltd. (William Thomas, Sons and Co. Ltd., managers), Liverpool.
23.1.1914: Renamed NATION.
25.5.1916: Acquired by Manchester Liners Ltd., Manchester.
5.5.1917: Renamed MANCHESTER ENGINEER.
16.8.1917: Torpedoed and sunk by the German submarine UC 16 four and a half miles south east of Flamborough Head whilst on a voyage from the Tyne to St Nazaire with a cargo of coal.
28.8.1917: Register closed.

25. MANCHESTER INVENTOR (2) 1917

O.N. 124079 4,112g 2,576n 382.1 x 51.2 x 24.5 feet
T. 3-cyl. by Dunsmuir and Jackson Ltd., Glasgow; 400 NHP, 2,200 IHP, 11 knots.
6.7.1907: Launched by A. MacMillan and Son Ltd., Dumbarton (Yard No. 416).
8.1907: Completed.
16.8.1907: Registered in the ownership of the Celtic Shipping Co. Ltd. (Robert Hughes-Jones and Co., managers), Liverpool as CELTIC KING.
5.3.1917: Acquired by Manchester Liners Ltd., Manchester.
13.3.1917: Renamed MANCHESTER INVENTOR.
30.7.1917: Captured and sunk by gunfire from the German submarine U 94 north east of Muckle Flugga in position 62.10 north by 00.45 west whilst on a voyage from Archangel to Belfast with a cargo of flax.

The First World War brought military names: this is *Manchester Brigade*, seen in the lower photograph leaving the landing stage which served the lairage at Birkenhead.

26. MANCHESTER BRIGADE 1918-1940

O.N. 135368 6,021g 3,771n 418.0 x 53.5 x 33.4 feet
T. 3-cyl. by Richardsons, Westgarth and Co. Ltd., Hartlepool; 691 NHP, 3,500 IHP, 12 knots.
11.2.1918: Launched by Irvine's Shipbuilding and Dry Docks Co. Ltd, West Hartlepool (Yard No. 561).
8.1918: Completed.
26.7.1918: Registered in the ownership of Manchester Liners Ltd., Manchester as MANCHESTER BRIGADE.
26.9.1940: Torpedoed and sunk by the German submarine U 137 west of Malin Head in position 54.53 north by 10.22 west, whilst in convoy OB 218 on a voyage from Manchester to Montreal with general cargo and Government stores. There were four survivors from the 62 crew and gunners on board.
28.11.1940: Register closed.

Manchester Division (opposite).   Manchester Producer (above).   Manchester Spinner (2) (below).

27. MANCHESTER DIVISION 1918-1953
O.N. 135369 6,027g 3,774n 418.0 x 53.5 x 33.4 feet
T. 3-cyl. by Richardsons, Westgarth and Co. Ltd., Hartlepool; 691 NHP, 3,500 IHP, 12 knots.
10.6.1918: Launched by Irvine's Shipbuilding and Dry Docks Co. Ltd., West Hartlepool (Yard No. 562).
10.1918: Completed.
24.9.1918: Registered in the ownership of Manchester Liners Ltd., Manchester as MANCHESTER DIVISION.
2.12.1953: Arrived at Briton Ferry to be broken up by T.W. Ward Ltd.
28.12.1953: Register closed.

28. MANCHESTER PRODUCER 1921-1939
O.N. 137512 6,576g 4,162n 420.3 x 53.5 x 36.3 feet
T. 3-cyl. by Richardsons, Westgarth and Co. Ltd., Sunderland; 681 NHP, 3,560 IHP, 13 knots.
5.1916: Completed by Sir James Laing and Sons Ltd., Sunderland (Yard No. 653).
1.6.1916: Registered in the ownership of the Norfolk and North American Steam Shipping Co. Ltd. (Furness, Withy and Co. Ltd., managers), London as START POINT.
1.4.1921: Acquired by Manchester Liners Ltd., Manchester.
14.5.1921: Renamed MANCHESTER PRODUCER.
11.8.1939: Sold to the Board of Trade (later the Ministry of War Transport), London (P. Henderson and Co., Glasgow,

managers).
14.9.1939: Renamed BOTWEY.
26.7.1941: Torpedoed and sunk by the German submarine U 141 north west of St. Kilda in position 55.42 north by 09.50 west whilst in convoy OS 1 on a voyage from Ellesmere Port to Port Sulphur in ballast. The crew of 53 was rescued.
15.9.1941: Register closed.

29. MANCHESTER SPINNER (2) 1921-1944
O.N. 140506 4,767g 2,968n 385.0 x 52.0 x 27.0 feet
T. 3-cyl. by Richardsons, Westgarth and Co. Ltd., Hartlepool; 372 NHP, 1,650 IHP, $10^{1}/_{4}$ knots.
28.12.1917: Launched by Irvine's Shipbuilding and Dry Docks Co. Ltd., West Hartlepool (Yard No. 551).
16.3.1918: Registered in the ownership of the Neptune Steam Navigation Co. Ltd. (Furness, Withy and Co. Ltd., managers), London as GRAMPIAN RANGE.
5.4.1921: Acquired by Manchester Liners Ltd., Manchester.
2.5.1921: Renamed MANCHESTER SPINNER.
25.3.1944: Sold to the Ministry of War Transport, London.
7.6.1944: Scuttled as part of Gooseberry Harbour No. 4 off Juno Beach during the Normandy landings.
11.7.1944: Register closed.

Manchester Regiment (1) in the Manchester Ship Canal (upper) and at the other end of her route, in ice (lower). *[Upper: George Scott collection; lower: National Maritime Museum P16575]*

30. MANCHESTER REGIMENT (1)   1922-1939
O.N. 146830   7,930g   4948n   450.4 x 58.1 x 38.3 feet
Steam turbines by Richardsons, Westgarth and Co. Ltd.,
Middlesbrough; 977 NHP, 4,600 SHP, 14½ knots.
29.9.1921: Launched by the Furness Shipbuilding Co. Ltd.,
Haverton Hill-on-Tees (Yard No. 18).
3.1922: Completed.
11.8.1922: Registered in the ownership of Manchester
Liners Ltd., Manchester as MANCHESTER REGIMENT.
4.12.1939: Sunk in a convoy collision with the steamer
OROPESA (14,118/1920) south west of Cape Race in
position 44.50 north by 55.30 west whilst on a voyage from
Manchester to St. John, New Brunswick with general
cargo. Seven members of the crew were lost.
10.1.1940: Register closed.

Manchester Commerce (3) (upper).   Manchester Citizen (2) (lower).

31. MANCHESTER COMMERCE (3) 1925-1952
O.N. 147408 5,328g 3,002n 417.7 x 57.0 x 27.7 feet
T. 3-cyl. by Richardsons, Westgarth and Co. Ltd.,
Hartlepool; 3,800 IHP, 13 knots.
23.3.1925: Launched by the Furness Shipbuilding Co. Ltd.,
Haverton Hill-on-Tees (Yard No. 79).
26.7.1925: Completed for Manchester Liners Ltd.,
Manchester as MANCHESTER COMMERCE.
1.1952: Sold to Camel Lines Ltd., London and renamed
CORBITA.
1952: Sold to East and West Steam Ship Co., Karachi,
Pakistan and renamed FAKIRJEE COWASJEE.
11.2.1967: Laid up at Karachi.
12.1967: Breaking up began by Hardware Manufacturing
Corporation Ltd. at Karachi, Pakistan.

32. MANCHESTER CITIZEN (2) 1925-1943
O.N. 147409 5,328g 3,003n 417.7 x 57.0 x 27.7 feet
T. 3-cyl. by Richardsons, Westgarth and Co. Ltd.,
Hartlepool; 453 NHP, 3,800 IHP, 13 knots.
21.5.1925: Launched by Furness Shipbuilding Co. Ltd.,
Haverton Hill-on-Tees (Yard No. 80).
8.1925: Completed.
18.8.1925: Registered in the ownership of Manchester
Liners Ltd., Manchester as MANCHESTER CITIZEN.
9.7.1943: Torpedoed and sunk by the German submarine
U 508 south east of Accra in position 5.50 north by 2.22
east whilst on a voyage from Freetown to Lagos in ballast.
Fifteen of the 67 aboard were lost.
13.12.1943: Register closed.

The meat carrier *El Argentino* was jointly owned by a Houlder subdsidiary and Manchester Liners.

Manchester Exporter (1).

33. EL ARGENTINO 1928-1934

O.N. 160405 9,501g 6,023n 431.3 x 64.5 x 35.4 feet
Two Fairfield-Sulzer 6-cyl. 2SCSA oil engines by the Fairfield Shipbuilding and Engineering Co. Ltd., Govan driving twin screws; 1,710 NHP, 6,400 BHP, 14½ knots.
11.1.1928: Launched by the Fairfield Shipbuilding and Engineering Co. Ltd., Govan (Yard No. 629).
4.1928: Completed.
5.4.1928: Registered in the ownership of the British and Argentine Steam Navigation Co. Ltd., London and Manchester Liners Ltd., Manchester (Houlder Brothers and Co. Ltd., London, managers) as EL ARGENTINO.
24.1.1934: Owners became Furness, Withy and Co. Ltd., London.
26.7.1943: Bombed and sunk by German aircraft north west of Lisbon in position 39.50 north by 13.36 west whilst in convoy OS 52KM on a voyage from Glasgow to Montevideo and Buenos Aires in ballast. Four of the 88 on board were lost.
23.12.1943: Register closed.

34. MANCHESTER EXPORTER (1) 1929-1947

O.N. 140584 5,277g 2,897n 420.3 x 55.0 x 27.9 feet
T. 3-cyl. by Richardsons, Westgarth and Co. Ltd., Middlesbrough; 457 NHP, 3,500 IHP, 12 knots.
12.2.1918: Launched by Sir James Laing and Sons Ltd., Deptford, Sunderland (Yard No. 644).
6.1918: Completed.
20.6.1918: Registered in the ownership of Johnston Line Ltd. (Furness, Withy and Co. Ltd., managers), London as REXMORE.
19.12.1928: Owners became Furness, Withy and Co. Ltd., London.
3.10.1929: Renamed MANCHESTER EXPORTER.
7.10.1929: Acquired by Manchester Liners Ltd., Manchester.
1.1947: Sold to Cargueros Panamenos S.A. (Oscar E. Bertin) (Wallem and Co., managers), Hong Kong and renamed NICARAGUA under the Panama flag.
1948: Sold to the Yu Chang Steam Ship Co. Ltd., Shanghai, China and renamed YU TUNG.
1950: Sold to Wallem and Co. Ltd., Hong Kong and

Manchester Port (3) with stalls on deck for cattle, in the Mersey 25th April 1936 (top), and postwar in the Manchester Canal (middle and bottom). *[Middle: John Slavin; bottom: Peter Wynne]*

renamed RIO BAMBA under the Panama flag.
1952: Sold to T.Y. Chao (Wallem and Co. Ltd., managers), Hong Kong and renamed PRECILA.
18.5.1958: Arrived at Osaka, Japan to be broken up by the Sakaguchi Trading Co., Osaka..
6.1958: Work began.

35. MANCHESTER PORT (3)   1935-1964
O.N. 147428   5,649g 3,287n   422.2 x 56.7 x 27.1 feet
Steam turbines by David Rowan and Co. Ltd., Glasgow; 3,800 SHP, 13½ knots.
30.7.1935: Launched by Blythswood Shipbuilding Co. Ltd., Glasgow (Yard No. 38).
10.1935: Completed for Manchester Liners Ltd., Manchester as MANCHESTER PORT.
29.9.1964: Arrived at Bilbao, Spain to be broken up by Revalorizacion de Materiales S.A.
1.1965: Work began.

45

Manchester City (2) (above).

Manchester Trader (3) (below).

36. MANCHESTER CITY (2)   1937-1964
O.N. 147429 5,600g 3,329n 430.7 x 57.0 x 27.0 feet
Steam turbines by David Rowan and Co. Ltd., Glasgow;
800 NHP, 13½ knots.
23.6.1937: Launched by Blythswood Shipbuilding Co.
Ltd., Glasgow (Yard No. 46).
8.1937: Completed for Manchester Liners Ltd.,
Manchester as MANCHESTER CITY.
15.5.1964: Arrived at Faslane to be broken up by
Shipbreaking Industries Ltd.
23.5.1964: Work began.

37. MANCHESTER PROGRESS (1)   1938-1966
O.N. 147432 5,620g 3,343n 430.7 x 57.0 x 27.0 feet
Steam turbines by David Rowan and Co. Ltd., Glasgow;
3,800 SHP, 13½ knots.
28.6.1938: Launched by Blythswood Shipbuilding Co.
Ltd., Glasgow (Yard No. 51).
9.1938: Completed for Manchester Liners Ltd.,
Manchester as MANCHESTER PROGRESS.
15.1.1966: Arrived at Split, Yugoslavia to be broken up by
Brodospas.
2.1966: Work began.

38. MANCHESTER MERCHANT (3)   1940-1943
O.N. 147439 7,264g 4,408n 432.0 x 57.0 x 35.2 feet
Steam turbines by David Rowan and Co. Ltd., Glasgow;
4,300 SHP, 13¾ knots.
10.2.1940: Launched by Blythswood Shipbuilding Co.
Ltd., Glasgow (Yard No. 58).
5.1940: Completed.
30.4.1940: Registered in the ownership of Manchester
Liners Ltd., Manchester as MANCHESTER MERCHANT.
25.2.1943: Torpedoed and sunk by the German submarine
U 628 east of Cape Race in position 45.10 north by 43.23
west in convoy ON 166 on a voyage from Manchester to
Halifax and St John, New Brunswick in ballast. Thirty six
of the 65 on board were lost.
22.4.1943: Register closed.

39. MANCHESTER TRADER (3)   1941-1963
O.N. 168551 5,671g 3,373n 432.0 x 57.0 x 27.0 feet
Steam turbines by David Rowan and Co. Ltd., Glasgow;
4,300 SHP, 13¾ knots.
15.2.1941: Launched by Blythswood Shipbuilding Co.
Ltd., Glasgow (Yard No. 59).
5.1941: Completed for Manchester Liners Ltd.,
Manchester as MANCHESTER TRADER.
5.1963: Breaking up began by Brodospas at Split,
Yugoslavia.

Manchester Progress (1) on trials (above), landing Canadian cattle at Birkenhead on 9th August 1947 (right), and with modified bridge front (below). _[Top: Roy Fenton collection]_

Views of *Manchester Shipper* (2), again showing changes to the superstructure (top and middle) and in green livery (bottom). *[Top: Roy Fenton collection; middle: M.J. Dobson; bottom: Peter Wynne]*

40. MANCHESTER SHIPPER (2) 1943-1969
O.N. 169066   7,881g   4,638n   444.3 x 58.1 x 351/2 feet
Steam turbines by David Rowan and Co. Ltd., Glasgow;
4,350 SHP; 14 knots.
30.6.1943: Launched by Blythswood Shipbuilding Co. Ltd., Glasgow (Yard No. 71).
10.1943: Completed for Manchester Liners Ltd., Manchester as MANCHESTER SHIPPER.
10.7.1969: Arrived at Trieste, Italy to be broken up by SIDEMAR.
4.1970: Work began.

41. MANCHESTER REGIMENT (2) 1947-1968
O.N. 169069   5,825g   3,476n   444.3 x 58.0 x 27.2 feet
Steam turbines by David Rowan and Co. Ltd., Glasgow;
4,350 SHP, 14 knots.
16.10.1946: Launched by Blythswood Shipbuilding Co. Ltd., Glasgow (Yard No. 84).
2.1947: Completed for Manchester Liners Ltd., Manchester as MANCHESTER REGIMENT.

1967: Sold to Astro Tropico Compania Naviera S.A., Panama (P.B. Pandelis Ltd., London, managers) and renamed AZURE COAST II.

1970: Sold to Li-Ho Shipping (Singapore) Co. Private Ltd., Singapore (Associated Maritime Investment Co. Ltd., Taipei, Taiwan, managers).

1971: Sold to United Maritime Management Co. (Private) Ltd., Singapore and renamed PU GOR.

22.12.1971: Breaking up began by Shin Keun Yung Steel and Iron Co. Ltd. at Kaohsiung, Taiwan.

42. MANCHESTER MERCHANT (4) 1951-1967
O.N. 182613 7,651g 4,621n 9,790d 446.5 x 59.2 x 35.3 feet
Steam turbines by David Rowan and Co. Ltd., Glasgow; 5,000 SHP, 14$\frac{1}{4}$ knots.

27.9.1950: Launched by Blythswood Shipbuilding Co. Ltd., Glasgow (Yard No. 95).

1.1951: Completed for Manchester Liners Ltd., Manchester as MANCHESTER MERCHANT.

1967: Sold to Clio Shipping Company, Monrovia (Ionian Sea Operators Inc., New York, USA, managers) and renamed CLIO.

13.2.1972: Caught fire about 700 miles off the west coast of Angola in approximate position 10.18 south by 1.45 west whilst on a voyage from Chittagong to Rotterdam and Hamburg with a cargo of jute and cattle cake.

14.2.1972: Abandoned and presumed sunk about 22.2.1972 in approximate position 5.21 south by 5.7 west.

Manchester Regiment (2) (top). [John Slavin]

Manchester Merchant (4) (middle) and as Clio (bottom). [Middle: M.J. Dobson]

Manchester Pioneer shown in black when new (opposite top), in grey just after lengthening by Manchester Dry Docks (opposite bottom) and visiting Preston (top left), and at Manchester with a light green hull (top right). *[Opposite: Peter Newall collection; this page: World Ship Photo Library].*
Manchester Explorer in the Great Lakes (above) and in green with 'Manchester Liners Ltd.' on her hull (right). *[Above: Peter Kenyon collection; right: World Ship Photo Library]*

43. MANCHESTER PIONEER   1952-1963
O.N. 184857   1,805g   707n   250.0 x 43.1 x 16.9 feet
1960: 2,074g 1,044n 290.0 x 43.1 x 16.9 feet
Two steam turbines by Cammell, Laird and Co. Ltd., Birkenhead geared to a single shaft; 1,500 SHP, 11½ knots.
30.1.1952: Launched by Cammell, Laird and Co. Ltd., Birkenhead (Yard No. 1222).
4.1952: Completed for Manchester Liners Ltd., Manchester as MANCHESTER PIONEER.
1960: Lengthened by Manchester Dry Docks Co. Ltd., Manchester.
1963: Sold to United Maritime Enterprises S.A., Panama (D. Th. Petropoulos, London, manager) and renamed CYPRIAN MED under the Greek flag.
1969: Sold to Spanline Compania Naviera S.A., Panama (M. Scufalos, Piraeus, manager) and renamed SAN ANTONIO under the Greek flag, although she appears not to have traded under this name.
30.7.1971: Breaking up began by Naftem S.A. at Piraeus, Greece.

44. MANCHESTER EXPLORER   1952-1963
O.N. 184858   1,805g   707n   250.0 x 43.1 x 16.9 feet
Two steam turbines by Cammell, Laird and Co. Ltd., Birkenhead geared to a single shaft; 1,500 SHP, 11½ knots.
14.3.1952: Launched by Cammell, Laird and Co. Ltd., Birkenhead (Yard No. 1223).
5.1952: Completed for Manchester Liners Ltd., Manchester as MANCHESTER EXPLORER.
1963: Sold to Chimo Shipping Ltd. (Crosbie and Co. Ltd., managers), St. John's, Newfoundland and renamed C.A. CROSBIE.
1965: Renamed P.M. CROSBIE.
1968: Sold to Panagos Shipping Co. Ltd., Nicosia (Lyras Brothers, Piraeus, Greece, managers) and renamed PANAGOS L.
1971: Sold to Sylvia Shipping Co. Ltd., Nicosia and renamed YPERMACHOS.
1973: Sold to Argolis Shipping Co. Ltd., Nicosia (Agen Naviera S.A., Piraeus, Greece, managers) and renamed EMILIA.
6.2.1974: Laid up near Piraeus.
1980: Renamed TASSOS.
12.1980: At Salamis, Greece for breaking up.

Manchester Spinner (3) leaving Eastham (top).

Manchester Prospector (above and right).
[Above: E. N. Taylor; right: Keith Byass]

Manchester Mariner (2) at a Canadian port in winter (right) and in the Manchester Ship Canal in summer (below). *[Right: Rene Beauchamp]*

45. MANCHESTER SPINNER (3) 1952-1968
O.N. 184861 7,815g 4,580n 447.0 x 60.1 x 27.0 feet
Steam turbines by Cammell, Laird and Co. Ltd., Birkenhead; 6,000 SHP, 15 knots.
30.1.1952: Launched by Cammell, Laird and Co. Ltd., Birkenhead (Yard No. 1217).
7.1952: Completed for Manchester Liners Ltd., Manchester as MANCHESTER SPINNER.
1968: Sold to Estia Compania Naviera S.A., Panama (Stravelakis Brothers Ltd., Piraeus, managers) and renamed ESTIA under the Greek flag.
25.11.1971: Sank following an engine room explosion off Paramaribo in position 6.11 north by 53.49 west whilst on a voyage from the Gulf of Mexico to Brazil with a cargo of phosphate.

46. MANCHESTER PROSPECTOR 1953-1960
O.N. 184865 1,400g 665n 251.2 x 41.7 x 14.7 feet
C. 2-cyl. with low pressure turbine by Langesund Mekaniske Verkstads A/S, Langesund, Norway; 1,200 IHP, 11 knots.
12.10.1947: Launched by Langesund Mekaniske Verkstads A/S, Langesund, Norway (Yard No. 19) for S. Ugelstads Rederi A/S (S. Ugelstad, manager), Oslo, Norway as VIGØR.
1953: Acquired by Manchester Liners Ltd., Manchester and renamed MANCHESTER PROSPECTOR.

1960: Sold to Chr. M. Sarlis and Co., Piraeus, Greece and renamed GEORGIOS.
1971: Reported broken up, but in 1972 sold to Lassea Special Shipping S.A, Piraeus and renamed AGHIOS NEKTARIOS L.
1976: Sold to Nicolau Nikolaos, Piraeus.
1991: Deleted from *Lloyd's Register*, continued existence in doubt.

47. MANCHESTER MARINER (2) 1955-1968
O.N. 185817 7,580g 4,571n 447.0 x 60.1 x 35.2 feet
Steam turbines by Cammell, Laird and Co. (Shipbuilders and Engineers) Ltd., Birkenhead; 6,400 SHP, 15½ knots.
20.10.1954: Launched by Cammell, Laird and Co. (Shipbuilders and Engineers) Ltd., Birkenhead (Yard No. 1244).
3.1955: Completed for Manchester Liners Ltd., Manchester as MANCHESTER MARINER.
1968: Sold to Mira Compania Naviera S.A., Panama (Stravelakis Brothers Ltd., Piraeus, Greece, managers) and renamed IRA.
1974: Sold to National Steel Corporation, Manila, Philippines (Reyes and Lim Co. Inc., Rizal, Philippines, managers) and renamed PANDAY IRA.
5.1977: Broken up at Iligan, Manila, Philippines.

Manchester Vanguard (1) (top). [George Scott collection]

Manchester Venture (1) in the Manchester Ship Canal in black (above) and green (right). [Above: John Slavin; right: World Ship Photo Library]

Manchester Faith (1) as built (above), and anchored above Sorel waiting to become the first British merchant ship to enter the St. Lawrence Seaway in April 1959 (right). *[Top: George Scott collection; right: Captain Eric Askew collection]*

48. MANCHESTER VANGUARD (1)   1956-1963

O.N. 185822 1,662g 704n 2,670d 258.0 x 42.8 x 18.4 feet
Two Deutz 8-cyl. 4SCSA oil engines by Klockner-Humboldt-Deutz, Koln, West Germany; 2,000 BHP, 12½ knots.
27.1.1956: Launched by A.G. Weser, Bremerhaven (Yard No. 808).
4.1956: Completed for Manchester Liners Ltd., Manchester as MANCHESTER VANGUARD.
1963: Sold to the General Steam Navigation Co. Ltd., London and renamed SHELDRAKE.
1968: Sold to Bat-Golan Mediterranean Lines Ltd. (Mediterranean Lines Ltd., and later Ofer Brothers (Holdings) Ltd.), Haifa, Israel, managers) and renamed BAT GOLAN.
1974: Sold to Woodchuck Shipping Corporation Inc., Panama (Fui-Yong Wood Products (Private) Ltd., Singapore, managers) and renamed WOODCHUCK.
1974: Sold to South Wind Shipping Co. (Private) Ltd., Singapore and renamed SELATAN MAJU.
1981: Sold to Hai Lee Shipping and Trading Co. (Private) Ltd. (Madam Dolly Seah, Singapore, manager) and renamed WIHAR I under the Panama flag.
16.3.1985: Arrived at Junk Bay, Hong Kong to be broken up by Fu Mow and Co. Ltd., Hong Kong.
6.6.1985: Work began.

49. MANCHESTER VENTURE (1)   1956-1961

O.N. 185824 1,662g 704n 2,670d 258.0 x 42.8 x 18.4 feet
Two Deutz 8-cyl. 4SCSA oil engines by Klockner-Humboldt-Deutz, Koln, West Germany; 2,000 BHP, 12½ knots.
27.1.1956: Launched by A.G. Weser, Bremerhaven, West Germany (Yard No. 809).
5.1956: Completed for Manchester Liners Ltd., Manchester as MANCHESTER VENTURE.
1961: Sold to the General Steam Navigation Co. Ltd., London and renamed PHILOMEL.
1968: Sold to Bat-Tiran Mediterranean Lines Ltd. (Mediterranean Lines Ltd. and later Ofer Brothers (Holdings) Ltd., managers), Haifa, Israel and renamed BAT TIRAN.

5.8.1972: Caught fire in number 1 hold off Strofadhes Island in the Ionian Sea whilst on a voyage from Rijeka to Haifa with a cargo of chemicals, timber and newsprint. One member of her crew was lost. Beached three miles east of Katakolo Harbour by the salvage tug VERNICOS DIMITRIOS (1,136/1945).

50. MANCHESTER FAITH (1)   1959-1970

O.N. 300142 4,459g 2,456n 6,228d 378.2 x 50.4 x 31.0 feet
Two Sulzer 5TAG48 5-cyl. 2SCSA oil engines by George Clark and North Eastern Marine (Sunderland) Ltd., Sunderland; 7,050 BHP, 14½ knots.
26.11.1958: Launched by Austin and Pickersgill Ltd., Sunderland (Yard No. 435).
3.1959: Completed for Manchester Liners Ltd., Manchester as MANCHESTER FAITH.
1965: Chartered to Cairn Line Ltd., Newcastle-on-Tyne and renamed CAIRNESK.
1966: Renamed MANCHESTER FAITH on completion of charter.
1970: Sold to Marlineas Oceanicas S.A., Panama (Aharnai Shipping Inc. (Ilias Konstantinou), New York, USA, managers) and renamed ILKON TAK under the Liberian flag.
1978: Ultimate owners became Ilkon Shipping Co. S.A. (Ilias Konstantinou), Sarasota, Florida, USA.
1978: Sold to Yakinthai Shipping Co. S.A., Panama (Chrimar Shipping Co. Ltd., Piraeus, managers) and renamed CHRYSEIS.
3.6.1983: Breaking up began by the Jilani Corporation, Gadani Beach, Pakistan.

51. MANCHESTER FAME (1) 1959-1970

O.N. 300145 4,462g 2,459n 6,228d 378.2 x 50.4 x 31.0 feet

Two Sulzer 5TAG48 5-cyl. 2SCSA oil engines by George Clark and North Eastern Marine (Sunderland) Ltd., Sunderland; 7,050 BHP, 14½ knots.

22.7.1959: Launched by Austin and Pickersgill Ltd., Sunderland (Yard No. 436).

10.1959: Completed for Manchester Liners Ltd., Manchester as MANCHESTER FAME.

1965: Chartered to Cairn Line Ltd., Newcastle-on-Tyne and renamed CAIRNGLEN.

1966: Renamed MANCHESTER FAME on completion of charter.

1970: Sold to Marcaminos Surenos Navegacion S.A., Panama (Aharnai Shipping Inc. (Ilias Konstantinou), New York, USA, managers) and renamed ILKON NIKI under the Liberian flag.

1978: Ultimate owners became Ilkon Shipping Co. S.A. (Ilias Konstantinou), Sarasota, Florida, USA.

1979: Sold to Tranquil Marine Inc., Panama (Spenco Shipping Co. Ltd., Piraeus, Greece, managers) and renamed EFI.

1980: Sold to Seatime Shipping Inc., Piraeus and renamed PANAGIS K.

23.1.1981: Damaged in collision with the motor vessel NORTH WAVE (7,848/1954) whilst laid up at Alexandria.

10.1986: Broken up at Alexandria, Egypt.

52. MANCHESTER MILLER (2)/MANCHESTER QUEST 1959-1976

O.N. 300143 9,297g 5,184n 9,660d 467.8 x 62.3 x 39.5 feet

1970: 10,149g 5,625n following conversion to a container ship.

Steam turbines by Harland and Wolff Ltd., Belfast; 7,000 SHP, 17 knots.

12.12.1958: Launched by Harland and Wolff Ltd., Belfast (Yard No. 1582).

3.1959: Completed for Manchester Liners Ltd., Manchester as MANCHESTER MILLER.

1970: Converted to cellular container ship by Smith's Dock Co. Ltd., Middlesbrough and renamed MANCHESTER QUEST.

1976: Sold to Mitsui and Co. Ltd.

29.1.1976: Arrived at Kaohsiung.

24.2.1976: Breaking up began by the Tung Chen Steel Co. Ltd., Kaohsiung, Taiwan.

Manchester Fame (1) (opposite middle). *[A. Duncan]*

Manchester Miller (2) as delivered with plain black hull and with uptakes in mast colours (opposite lower) and as repainted in Manchester Liners funnel colours (this page top). At Manchester the company's ships were loaded under the supervision of shore-based staff rather than the ships' officers. To help them there was a Ralston stability appliance in the office at No. 9 Dock. This method of supervision was extended to some other Furness Group vessels loading at Manchester, including the North Pacific Line. *[Opposite lower: Roy Fenton collection; this page top: World Ship Photo Library]*

When rebuilt as a containership, *Manchester Miller* became *Manchester Quest* (below). *[Middle: John Slavin]*

Manchester Commerce (4) (upper). [Roy Fenton collection]

Manchester City (3) (lower). [M.J. Dobson]

53. MANCHESTER COMMERCE (4)   1963-1971
O.N. 303114   8,724g   4,998n   11,829d   502.2 x 62.4 x 37.0 feet
Sulzer 6RD76 6-cyl. 2SCSA oil engines by George Clark (Sunderland) Ltd., Sunderland; 17 knots.
12.3.1963: Launched by Smith's Dock Co. Ltd., Middlesbrough (Yard No. 1268).
6.1963: Completed for Manchester Liners Ltd., Manchester as MANCHESTER COMMERCE.
1971: Sold to Yick Fung Shipping and Enterprises Co. Ltd., Hong Kong and renamed BER SEA under the Somali flag.
1975: Sold to Government of the People's Republic of China, Peking and renamed YANGCHUN.

4.9.1980: Arrived Khorramshahr with general cargo from China.
7.10.1980: Gutted by fire following shelling in Shatt-el-Arab, Khorramshahr, during the Iran/Iraq War and later declared a constructive total loss

54. MANCHESTER CITY (3)   1964-1971
O.N. 303116   8,734g   5,014n   153.07 x 19.03 x 11.28 metres
Sulzer 6RD76 6-cyl. 2SCSA oil engines by George Clark (Sunderland) Ltd., Sunderland; 9,600 BHP, 17 knots.
15.5.1964: Launched by Smith's Dock Co. Ltd., Middlesbrough (Yard No. 1270).
7.1964: Completed for Manchester Liners Ltd.,

Manchester Renown (upper). [Roy Fenton collection]

Manchester Exporter (2) (lower).

Manchester as MANCHESTER CITY.
1971: Sold to Korea Shipping Corporation Ltd., Seoul, South Korea and renamed KOREAN WINNER.
1978: Sold to Jin Yang Shipping Co. Ltd., Seoul and renamed ONE WEST NO 8.
9.6.1985: Arrived at Pusan, South Korea to be broken up by the Seo Heung Salvage Co.
4.11.1985: Work began.

55. MANCHESTER RENOWN (1) 1964-1971
O.N. 303115   8,742g   5,017n   153.07 x 19.03 x 11.28 metres
Sulzer 6RD76 6-cyl.   2SCSA oil engine by George Clark (Sunderland) Ltd., Sunderland; 9,600 BHP, 17 knots.
31.10.1963: Launched by Smith's Dock Co. Ltd., Middlesbrough (Yard No. 1269).
4.1964: Completed for Beaver Industries Ltd., London (Smith's Dock Co. Ltd., Middlesbrough) and demise chartered to Manchester Liners Ltd., Manchester as MANCHESTER RENOWN.
1971: Acquired by Manchester Liners Ltd., Manchester.
1971: Sold to Korea Shipping Corporation Ltd., Seoul, South Korea and renamed KOREAN CHALLENGER.
1978: Sold to Witney Shipping Corporation, Panama

(Alandis (London) Ltd., London, managers) and renamed EDESSA under the Greek flag.
4.2.1984: Engine room and accommodation badly damaged by fire whilst laid up at Trincomalee.
5.2.1984: Towed out of harbour and fire extinguished.
1.5.1984: Arrived at Kaohsiung, Taiwan to be broken up by the Shyeh Sheng Huat Steel and Iron Co.
6.5.1984: Work began, and was completed on 13.5.1984.

56. MANCHESTER EXPORTER (2) 1965-1969
O.N. 169236   7,506g   4,637n   428.5 x 60.2 x 24.25 feet
Steam turbines by Parsons Marine Steam Turbine Co. Ltd., Wallsend-on-Tyne; 4,650 SHP, 13 knots.
9.4.1952: Launched by William Gray and Co. Ltd., West Hartlepool (Yard No. 1249).
9.1952: Completed for Cairn Line Ltd., Newcastle-on-Tyne as CAIRNDHU.
1965: Acquired by Manchester Liners Ltd., Manchester and renamed MANCHESTER EXPORTER.
1969: Sold to Halieto Oceanica Naviera S.A., Panama (N. and J. Vlassopulos Ltd., London, managers) and renamed GEMINI EXPORTER under the Greek flag.
17.5.1971: Breaking up began by the Lunk Yung Steel and Iron Works, Kaohsiung, Taiwan.

57. MANCHESTER PORT (4) 1966-1971
O.N. 307319 8938g 5,817n 153.04 x 19.03 x 11.28 metres
Two Pielstick 14-cyl. 4SCSA V oil engines by Crossley
Brothers Ltd., Manchester; 11,480 BHP, 17 knots.
5.5.1966: Launched by Smith's Dock Co. Ltd.,
Middlesbrough (Yard No. 1281).
11.1966: Completed for Manchester Liners Ltd.,
Manchester as MANCHESTER PORT.
1971: Sold to Jadranska Slobodna Plovidba, Split,
Yugoslavia and renamed BIOKOVO.
1980: Sold to Vroulidia Compania Naviera S.A., Panama
(A. Halcoussis and Co., Piraeus, Greece, managers) and
renamed YDRA under the Greek flag.
20.1.1983: Fire in engine room in position 37.32 north by
10.05 east whilst on a voyage from Piraeus to Sweden, and
beached one mile east of Bizerta.
21.1.1983: Fire extinguished but later declared a
constructive loss.

**58. MANCHESTER PROGRESS (2)/MANCHESTER
CONCEPT 1967-1980**
O.N. 307321 8,176g 5,093n 153.02 x 19.03 x 11.28 metres
1971: 11,228g 7,361n 11,921d
Two Pielstick 14-cyl. 4SCSA V oil engines by Crossley
Brothers Ltd., Manchester; 11,480 BHP, 17½ knots.
11.9.1966: Launched by Smith's Dock Co. Ltd.,
Middlesbrough (Yard No. 1282).
2.1967: Completed for Manchester Liners Ltd.,
Manchester as MANCHESTER PROGRESS.
1971: Converted to a cellular container ship at Amsterdam.
1972: Renamed MANCHESTER CONCEPT.

1973: Sold to Mercantile Leasing Co. Ltd., London
(Manchester Liners Ltd., Manchester, managers).
1980: Sold to Peninsular Shipping Co. (Private) Ltd.
(Madam Dolly Seah, manager), Singapore and renamed
CHERRY BUNGA.
2.5.1985: Breaking up began by Desguaces Vige S.A. at
San Esteban, Spain.

59. MANCHESTER CHALLENGE (1) 1968-1979
O.N. 334288 12,039g 7,338n 12,319d 161.47 x 19.44
x 14.64 metres
Two Pielstick 18PC2V 18-cyl. 2SSCA V oil engines by
Crossley Premier Engines Ltd., Manchester; 16,380 BHP,
19½ knots.
11.6.1968: Launched by Smith's Dock Co. Ltd.,
Middlesbrough (Yard No. 1294).
10.1968: Completed for Manchester Liners Ltd.,
Manchester as MANCHESTER CHALLENGE.
1978: Sold to Hong Kong Ocean Shipping Co. Ltd.,
Monrovia (Hong Kong Islands Shipping Co. Ltd., Hong
Kong, managers) and renamed OCEAN CONTAINER
under the Panama flag.
1984: Owners became the Hong Kong Champion Shipping
Co. S.A., Panama (Hong Kong Islands Line Ltd., Hong
Kong, managers).
1989: Renamed HANG FU.
1989: Sold to Glavish International Corporation, Panama
(Mediterranean Shipping Co. S.A., Geneva, Switzerland,
managers) and renamed MSC SUSANNA.
1992: Renamed SWAN 1.
12.2.1993: Arrived at Alang, India to be broken up.

Manchester Port (4) (opposite upper). *[George Scott collection]*

Manchester Progress (2) (opposite lower).

When rebuilt as a containership, *Manchester Progress* (2) became *Manchester Concept* (above and in No. 9 Dock, Manchester ,right). *[Above: World Ship Photo Library; right: M.J. Dobson].*

Manchester Challenge (1) in ice at Montreal on 9th December 1976 (below). *[Rene Beauchamp]*

Manchester Courage leaving Eastham (above) and on 7th May 1978 (right). *[Right: John Slavin]*

Manchester Concorde (below).

Manchester Merit at Malta (above) and at Manchester (right). *[Right: Peter Wynne]*

60. MANCHESTER COURAGE 1969-1979
O.N. 334289 12,039g 7,341n 12,319d 161.47 x 19.44 x 14.64 metres
Two Pielstick 18PC2V 18-cyl. 4SCSA V oil engines by Crossley Premier Engines Ltd., Manchester; 16,380 BHP, 19½ knots.
23.9.1968: Launched by Smith's Dock Co. Ltd., Middlesbrough (Yard No. 1295).
2.1969: Completed for Manchester Liners Ltd., Manchester as MANCHESTER COURAGE.
1979: Sold to Carolina Leasing Ltd., London (Hong Kong Islands Shipping Co. Ltd., Hong Kong, managers) and renamed PACIFIC CONTAINER.
1984: Owners became the Hong Kong Excellent Shipping Co. S.A., Panama (Hong Kong Islands Line Ltd., Hong Kong, managers).
1989: Sold to Ginza International Corporation, Panama (Mediterranean Shipping Co. S.A., Geneva, Switzerland, managers) and renamed MSC MARINA.
1992: Renamed CITY OF LIMASSOL.
28.4.1992: Arrived at Alang, India to be broken up by Nickson Export Private Ltd.
21.5.1992: Work began.

61. MANCHESTER CONCORDE 1969-1982
O.N. 337261 12,040g 7,341n 12,319d 161.47 x 19.44 x 14.64 metres
Two Pielstick 18PC2V 18-cyl. 4SCCA V oil engines by Crossley Premier Engines Ltd., Manchester; 16,380 BHP, 19½ knots.
20.1.1969: Launched by Smith's Dock Co. Ltd., Middlesbrough (Yard No. 1296) for the Nile Steam Ship Co. Ltd., London.
5.1969: Completed and demise chartered to Manchester Liners Ltd., Manchester as MANCHESTER CONCORDE.

1982: Sold to Furness, Withy (Shipping) Ltd.
1982: Sold to Char Lian Marine (Panama) S.A., Panama (Char Ching Marine Co. Ltd., Taipei, Taiwan, managers) and renamed CHAR LIAN.
14.12.1983: Arrived at Kaohsiung, Taiwan to be broken up by Chih I Enterprise Co. Ltd..
18.12.1983: Work began, and was completed by 27.12.1983.

62. MANCHESTER MERIT 1970-1975
O.N. 339463 3,414g 2,499n 6,533d 99.73 x 15.21 x 7.70 metres
Deutz RBV12M350 12-cyl. 4SCSA V oil engines by Hijos de J. Barreras S.A., Vigo, Spain; 4,000 BHP, 14½ knots.
31.7.1969: Launched by Basse Sambre-Corcho S.A., Santander, Spain (Yard No. 108) as CATALINA DEL MAR.
9.1970: Completed for Manchester Liners Ltd., Manchester as MANCHESTER MERITO.
1970: Renamed MANCHESTER MERIT.
1972: Demise chartered to Plumbton Shipping Corporation, Bermuda and renamed FORTUNA.
1975: Sold to Chelwood Shipping Ltd., Monrovia (Equimar Maritima S.A., Bilbao, Spain, managers) and renamed KATHLEEN.
1987: Renamed KUDU.
1990: Sold to Societa Italiana di Navigazione S.r.l., Naples, Italy, converted to a cement carrier and renamed CEMENT TWO.
1996: Sold to Jukingor Marine Corporation, Panama (Pan Nautic S.A., Lugano, Switzerland, managers) and renamed FORTUNE R.
1999: Owners became Cement Trading Inc., Panama (Pan Nautic S.A., Lugano, Switzerland, managers) and renamed LIBERA.
9.2000: Still in service.

Manchester Crusade (above, right upper and middle). *[Top: Peter Kenyon collection; others John Slavin]*

Manchester Vigour (this page bottom and opposite bottom). *[This page: John Slavin; opposite: Peter Kenyon collection]*

63. MANCHESTER CRUSADE   1971-1982

O.N. 339473   12,039g 7,337n 12,319d   161.27 x 19.44 x 14.64 metres

Two Pielstick 18PC2V 18-cyl. 4SCSA V oil engines by Crossley Premier Engines Ltd., Manchester; 16,380 BHP, $19\frac{1}{2}$ knots.

31.10.1970: Launched by Smith's Dock Co. Ltd., Middlesbrough (Yard No. 1315) for the Nile Steam Ship Co. Ltd., London.

3.1971: Completed and demise chartered to Manchester Liners Ltd., Manchester as MANCHESTER CRUSADE.

1982: Sold to Furness Withy (Shipping) Ltd., London.

1982: Sold to Char Che Marine (Panama) S.A., Panama (Char Ching Marine Co. Ltd., Taipei, Taiwan, managers) and renamed CHAR CHE.

14.11.1983: Arrived at Kaohsiung, Taiwan to be broken up by Swie Horng Steel Enterprise.

14.12.1983: Work began, and was completed on 24.12.1983.

Condrons (Manchester) Ltd. and Manchester Liners (Freighting) Ltd.

64. FRONTIER 1972-1979

O.N. 358674   3,621g 2,250n 6,533d   99.73 x 15.30 x 7.70 metres

Deutz 12-cyl. 4SCSA V oil engine by Hijos de J. Barreras S.A., Vigo, Spain; 4,000 BHP, 14 knots.

16.3.1972: Launched by Astilleros del Atlantico, Santander, Spain (Yard No. 116).

10.1972: Completed for Condrons (Manchester) Ltd. Manchester as FRONTIER.

1975: Owners became Manchester Liners (Freighting) Ltd., Manchester.

1979: Sold to Bayworth Shipping Corporation, Monrovia (Manta Line Inc. of Liberia, Piraeus, Greece, managers) and renamed BOX TRADER under the Greek flag.

1984: Sold to Wexford Shipping Co. Ltd., Limassol, Cyprus and renamed HARIS.

15.2.1985: Fire broke out in engine room in position 36.49 north by 01.47 east whilst on a voyage from Cyprus to Algiers in ballast. Later declared a constructive total loss.

20.4.1985: Arrived at Cartagena, Spain to be broken up by Desguaces Mastia S.A. (DEMASA).

3.5.1985: Work began, and was completed in June.

Frontier

Manchester Liners (Transport) Ltd.

65. MANCHESTER VIGOUR   1973-1980
O.N. 358130   5,310g 3,357n 5,579d   112.10 x 15.63 x 10.65 metres
Pielstick 12PC2V-400 12-cyl. 4SCSA V oil engines by Crossley Premier Engines Ltd., Manchester; 6,000 BHP, 15½ knots.
17.3.1973: Launched by Appledore Shipbuilders Ltd., Appledore (Yard No. AS92).
4.4.1973: Completed for Manchester Liners (Transport) Ltd., Manchester as MANCHESTER VIGOUR.
1976: Chartered to Cargo Liners S.A., Chiasso, Italy and renamed CARGO VIGOUR.
1976: Charterer failed and renamed MANCHESTER VIGOUR.
1980: Sold to Compagnie Maritime d'Affretement,

Marseilles, France and renamed VILLE D'ORIENT.
1984: Sold to Islamic Development Bank, Abu Dhabi, United Arab Emirates (Turkish-Libyan Joint Maritime Transport Stock Co., Istanbul, managers) and renamed BENWALID under the Turkish flag.
7.1985: Converted into a livestock carrier by Meyer Werft, Papenburg, West Germany.
1997: Sold to Pollux Shipping Lines Inc. (Sistrin Services Ltd., Lugano, Switzerland, managers) (Accord Ship Management (Private) Ltd., Mumbai, India, managers) and renamed POLLUX under the Panama flag.
1998: Sold to Luhum International Ltd. (Sistrin Services Ltd., Lugano, Switzerland, managers), Tortola, British Virgin Islands and registered in Panama.
1999: Sold to Winnerwald Inc., Panama (Gestioni Maritime e Finanziarie, Lugano, Switzerland, managers).
9.2000: Still in service.

Manchester Zeal at Malta (top) and in the Manchester Ship Canal on 23rd August 1980 (middle). *[Top: World Ship Photo Library; middle: John Slavin]*

66. MANCHESTER ZEAL 1973-1981
O.N. 358134 5,310g 3,357n 5,589d 112.10 x 15.63 x 10.65 metres
Pielstick 12PC2V-400 12-cyl. 2SCSA V oil engines by Crossley Premier Engines Ltd., Manchester; 6,000BHP, 15½ knots.
19.6.1973: Named MANCHESTER ZEAL.
7.1973: Completed by Appledore Shipbuilders Ltd., Appledore (Yard No. AS93) for Manchester Liners (Transport) Ltd., Manchester.
1975: Chartered to Cargo Liners S.A., Chiasso, Italy and renamed CARGO ZEAL.
1976: Charterers failed and renamed MANCHESTER ZEAL.
1981: Sold to Pacific International Lines (Private) Ltd. (Y.C. Chang, manager), Singapore and renamed SEA HAWK.
1990: Sold to Tanto Intim Lines P.T., Surabaya and renamed SEA LEOPARD.
1991: Renamed KURNIA SAMUDERA.
1993: Sold to Pacific Lady Inc., Surabaya (New Ocean Ltd., Hong Kong, managers) and renamed PACIFIC LADY.
1996: Renamed HUB USAHA.
9.2000: Still in existence.

Manchester Liners (Intermodal) Ltd.

67. MANCHESTER RENOWN (2) 1974-1982
O.N. 358139 12,577g 7,755n 12,126d 161.27 x 19.44 x 14.64 metres
Two Pielstick 18PC2V 18-cyl. 4SCSA V oil engines by Crossley Premier Engines Ltd., Manchester; 16,380 BHP. 18½ knots.
11.1.1974: Launched by Smith's Dock Co. Ltd., Middlesbrough (Yard No. 1326).
5.1974: Completed for Manchester Liners (Intermodal) Ltd., Manchester as MANCHESTER RENOWN.
1974: Chartered to China Navigation Co. Ltd., London and renamed ASIAN RENOWN.
1978: Renamed MANCHESTER RENOWN on completion of charter.
1982: Sold to P.T. Perusahaan Pelayaran Samudera Karana Line, Djakarta, Indonesia and renamed RATIH.
1990: Renamed OOCL AMITY.
1993: Renamed RATIH.
1.1995: Breaking up began at Djakarta, Indonesia.

68. MANCHESTER REWARD 1974-1982
O.N. 364712 12,577g 7,752n 161.27 x 19.44 x 14.64 metres
Two Pielstick 18PC2V 18-cyl. 4SCSA V oil engines by Crossley Premier Engines Ltd., Manchester; 16,380 BHP, 20 knots.
6.5.1974: Launched by Smiths' Dock Co. Ltd., Middlesbrough (Yard No. 1327) as MANCHESTER REWARD.
10.1974: Completed for Manchester Liners (Intermodal) Ltd., Manchester as ASIAN REWARD and chartered to China Navigation Co. Ltd., London.
1978: Renamed MANCHESTER REWARD.
1979: Renamed SEATRAIN NORFOLK.
1979: Renamed TFL REWARD.
1980: Renamed MANCHESTER REWARD.
1982: Sold to Famous Steamship S.A., Monrovia (C.Y. Tung, Hong Kong, manager) and renamed R. R. RATNA.
1991: Sold to Greenford Shipping Ltd., Monrovia (C.Y. Tung, Hong Kong, manager) and renamed OOCL AWARD.
1997: Renamed AWARD 1.
2.8.1897: Arrived at Chittagong, Bangladesh to be broken up by Taher and Co. Ltd., work commencing the next day.

Manchester Renown (2) (top and middle left) on the Manchester Ship Canal 6th June 1979 and as *Asian Renown* (middle right). *[Top: Peter Kenyon collection; middle left: John Slavin]*
Manchester Reward at Liverpool 18th April 1981 (bottom). *[John Slavin]*

Manchester Vanguard (2) (this page above) and laid up on the Fal (right). *[Above: [Fotoflite incorporating Skyfotos; right: World Ship Photo Library]*

Manchester Venture (2) as *Seatrain Bennington* (opposite page top). *[Fotoflite incorporating Skyfotos]*

Manchester Challenge (opposite page lower). *[Fotoflite incorporating Skyfotos]*

Golden Cross Line Ltd.

69. MANCHESTER VANGUARD (2) 1977-1983

O.N. 364729   17,385g 9,231n   168.87 x 25.20 x 15.73 metres
Sulzer 7RND90 7-cyl.   2SCSA oil engines by Scotts' Engineering Co. Ltd., Greenock; 20,300 BHP, 19 knots.
26.4.1977: Named MANCHESTER VANGUARD.
5.1977: Completed by Smiths' Dock Co. Ltd., Middlesbrough (Yard No. 1335) for Golden Cross Line Ltd., and demise chartered for 15 years to Manchester Liners Ltd., Manchester.
1977: Chartered to Seatrain Lines Inc., Monrovia, Liberia and renamed SEATRAIN TRENTON.
1978: Returned MANCHESTER VANGUARD.
1979: Chartered to Gold Star Line, Hong Kong and renamed KEELUNG.
1980: Renamed MANCHESTER VANGUARD.
1980: Bareboat chartered to the C.Y. Tung Group, but the charter was cancelled and the intended name, ORIENTAL VANGUARD, was not carried.
1982: Chartered to United Arab Shipping Co. (S.A.G.), Kuwait and renamed IBN MAJID.
1983: Sold to Express Tanker Services (Bermuda) Ltd., Bermuda (Manchester Liners Ltd., Manchester, managers) and renamed ORIENTAL EXPERT.
1983: Sold to Chinese Maritime Transport Ltd., Taipei (C.Y. Tung, Hong Kong, manager).
1991: Sold to Wellway Shipping Ltd. (C.H. Tung, manager), Hong Kong and renamed OOCL APPLAUSE.
1994: Renamed EAGLE RESPECT.
1998: Renamed OOCL APPLAUSE.
3.4.2000: Sold to Da Ling Shipping Ltd., Belize (Fortune Glory Private Ltd., Singapore, managers).
9.2000: Still in service.

Gough and Crosthwaite Ltd.

70. MANCHESTER VENTURE (2) 1977-1980

O.N. 364731   17,385g 9,231n 17,607d   168.87 x 25.20 x 15.70 metres
Sulzer 7RND90 7-cyl. 2SCSA oil engines by Scotts' Engineering Co. Ltd., Greenock; 20,300 BHP, 19 knots.
13.10.1977: Named MANCHESTER VENTURE.
10.1977: Completed by Smiths' Dock Co. Ltd., Middlesbrough (Yard No. 1336) for Gough and Crosthwaite Ltd., Manchester.
1977: Chartered to Seatrain Lines Inc., Monrovia, Liberia and renamed SEATRAIN BENNINGTON.
1979: Renamed MANCHESTER VENTURE.
1979: Chartered to Gold Star Line, Hong Kong and renamed MARSEILLE.
1980: Reverted to MANCHESTER VENTURE.
1980: Sold to Kalten Shipping Ltd. (C.H. Tung, manager), Hong Kong and renamed ORIENTAL VENTURE.
1981: Renamed RHEIN EXPRESS.
1984: Renamed ORIENTAL AMBASSADOR.
1989: Renamed OOCL ALLIANCE.
1992: Sold to Chinese Maritime Transport Ltd. (C.H. Tung, manager), Hong Kong.
1996: Sold to Pacific Union Container Carriers Ltd. (C.H. Tung, manager), Hong Kong.
1999: Renamed STAR ALLIANCE.
1999: Renamed OOCL ALLIANCE.
9.3.2000: Sold to Da Sheng Shipping Ltd., Belize (Fortune Glory Private Ltd., Singapore., managers) and renamed DA SHENG.
9.2000: Still in service.

Tynedale Shipping Co. Ltd.

MANCHESTER CHALLENGE (2) 1981-1988
O.N. 337546   31,036g 17,658n 28,482d   231.55 x 30.64
x 15.60 metres
Sulzer 10RND90 10-cyl. 2SCSA. oil engines by G. Clark
and North Eastern Marine Ltd., Wallsend-on-Tyne; 29,000
BHP, 23 knots.
5.5.1970: Launched by Swan Hunter Shipbuilders Ltd.,
Newcastle-on-Tyne (Yard No. 14).
11.1970: Completed for Tynedale Shipping Co. Ltd.,
London (Charles Hill and Sons, Bristol, managers) as

DART AMERICA.
1974: Managers became Bibby Line Ltd., Liverpool.
1979: Manager became C.Y. Tung, Hong Kong.
1981: Renamed MANCHESTER CHALLENGE.
1988: Renamed OOCL CHALLENGE.
1995: Sold to the Tolmi Shipping Co. Ltd., Nicosia, Cyprus
(Tsakos Shipping and Trading S.A., Piraeus, Greece)
(Orient Overseas Container Line Ltd., Hong Kong,
managers).
19.2.1996: Arrived at Gadani Beach, Pakistan to be broken
up.
25.2.1996: Work began.

Steamship Knutsford Ltd.

The outbreak of war in 1914 had an immediate and on-going effect on ship values and prices. Typical was the steamer *Knutsford*, managed by R.B. Stoker of Manchester Liners. Senior staff of Furness, Withy were permitted private ventures like this, with the understanding that Furness, Withy offices were employed to provide services. Built in 1903, she was sold in December 1913 to a company managed by Roth Brothers for £28,000, being renamed *Gripwell*. Roth's ventures failed and a few days after arriving at Cardiff on 3rd August 1914 she was re-possessed by Steamship Knutsford Ltd. as mortgagees. In April 1916 the Leeds Fireclay Co. Ltd. paid £78,000 and then received £100,000 from the Woolston Steamship Co. Ltd. for her in June 1916. The effect of wartime demand can clearly be seen in the way these prices spiralled in a short time. But she only survived another month, being captured and sunk by gunfire from an Austro-Hungarian submarine in July 1916. At the time she was in the Government War Risk Insurance Scheme for £30,200.

KNUTSFORD 1903-1915
O.N. 113124   3,842g 2,489n 6,250d   340.0 x 47.1 x 27.1 feet
T. 3-cyl. by Richardsons, Westgarth and Co. Ltd., Middlesbrough; 314 NHP, 1,600 IHP, 9 knots.

15.6.1903: Launched by Robert Stephenson and Co. Ltd., Hebburn-on-Tyne (Yard No. 79).
7.1903: Completed.
30.7.1903: Registered in the ownership of Robert B. Stoker, Manchester as KNUTSFORD.
8.9.1903: Owners became Steamship Knutsford Ltd. (Robert B. Stoker, manager), Manchester.
29.12.1913: Sold to Gripwell Steamship Co. Ltd. (Roth Brothers (London) Ltd., managers), London.
30.12.1913: Renamed GRIPWELL.
5.8.1914: Re-possessed by Steamship Knutsford Ltd. (Robert B. Stoker, manager), Manchester as mortgagees.
21.12.1914: Renamed KNUTSFORD.
28.4.1916: Sold to the Leeds Fireclay Co. Ltd. (T.H. Evans and Co., managers), London.
26.6.1916: Sold to the Woolston Steamship Co. Ltd. (S. Instone and Co. Ltd., managers), Cardiff.
22.7.1916: Sunk by gunfire from the Austro-Hungarian submarine U 39 12 miles north west of Cape Corbelin in position 37.3 north by 4.17 east whilst on a voyage from Tunis to Baltimore with a cargo of zinc ore.
16.8.1916: Register closed.

Knutsford in bound Boston 27th July 1913. *[R. Hildebrand (Johnson collection) courtesy William Schell]*

Managed for the Park Steamship Co. Ltd. (Government of Canada)
The Montreal office of Furness, Withy and Co. Ltd. was appointed managers of ten ships built in Canada during the Second World War. Three were manned and handled by Manchester Liners Ltd. on behalf of Furness, Withy, Montreal.

1. WESTMOUNT PARK 1943-1946
O.N. 174806   7,133g 4,241n   424.5 x 57.2 x 34.9 feet
T. 3-cyl. by Dominion Engineering Works Ltd., Montreal, Canada.
10.7.1943: Launched by United Shipyards Ltd., Montreal, Canada (Yard No. 13) for the Park Steamship Co. Ltd., Montreal as WESTMOUNT PARK.
9.1943: Completed and chartered to the Ministry of War Transport, London (Manchester Liners Ltd., Manchester, managers).
1946: Charterers became the Ministry of Transport, London (John Morrison and Son, Newcastle-on-Tyne,

managers).
28.2.1947: Managers became Andrew Crawford and Co. Ltd., Glasgow.
1949: Managers became G. Heyn and Sons Ltd., Belfast.
1950: Sold to Fairview Overseas Freighters Ltd., Halifax (Counties Ship Management Co. Ltd., London). It was intended to rename her LILAC HILL, but instead managers became C.M. Lemos and Co. Ltd., London and she was renamed NORDICSTAR.
17.12.1956: Sailed from Philadelphia for Le Havre with a cargo of coal.
27.12.1956: Last reported west of Ushant in approximate position 44 north by 38 west.
23.1.1957: Posted missing.
23.5.1957: Lifeboat found at Machri Bay, Eire.

2. RIVERDALE PARK 1943-1946
O.N. 174807   7,132g 4,244n   424.6 x 57.2 x 34.9 feet
T. 3-cyl. by Dominion Engineering Works Ltd., Montreal, Canada.

9.1943: Completed by Davie Shipbuilding and Repairing Co. Ltd., Lauzon, Canada (Yard No. 547) for the Park Steamship Co. Ltd., Montreal as RIVERDALE PARK and chartered to the Ministry of War Transport, London (Manchester Liners Ltd., Manchester, managers).

1946: Sold to Triton Steamship Co. Ltd. (March Shipping Agency Ltd., managers), Montreal and renamed TRIDALE.

1957: Sold to Bahia Salinas Compania Naviera S.A., Panama (Goulandris Brothers Ltd., London, managers) and renamed HARRIER under the Liberian flag.

1964: Sold to Steering Line Co. S.A., Panama (Power Navigation Ltd., Hong Kong, managers) and renamed JAVA STEER under the Liberian flag.

1965: Confiscated by Government of Indonesia and renamed JAVA STAR.

1968: Sold to Sun Life Marine Industries Inc., Monrovia (Skyview Shipping Enterprises Ltd., Hong Kong, managers) and renamed TRIUMPH under the Panama flag.

10.5.1968: Breaking up began at Onomichi, Japan by Koshin Sangyo K.K.

3. BELWOODS PARK   1943-1946
O.N. 175359   7,149g 4,227n   424.7 x 57.2 x 34.9 feet
T. 3-cyl. by Dominion Engineering Works Ltd., Montreal, Canada.

6.12.1943: Launched by Marine Industries Ltd., Sorel, Canada (Yard No. 126) for the Park Steamship Co. Ltd., Montreal as FORT CHIMO.

12.1943: Completed as BELWOODS PARK and bareboat chartered to the Ministry of War Transport, London (Manchester Liners Ltd., Manchester, managers)

1946: Charterers became the Ministry of Transport, London (James Chambers and Co., Liverpool, managers).

12.8.1946: Managers became the South American Saint Line Ltd., London.

2.1950: Managers became G. Heyn and Sons Ltd., Belfast.

5.1950: Sold to Rex Shipping Co. Ltd. (Hadjilias and Co. Ltd., managers), London and renamed BROOKHURST.

1957: Owners became Asturias Shipping Co., Panama (Hadjilias and Co. Ltd., London, managers) and renamed GALICIA under the Liberian flag.

25.2.1967: Arrived at Mihara, Japan to be broken up by Seibu Kogyo K.K.

4.1967: Work completed.

Belwoods Park (above) *[World Ship Photo Library]* and *Westmount Park* (below).

JOSEPH FISHER AND SONS
Roy Fenton and Seán Patterson

Over almost a century of independent shipowning, the Fishers of Newry were, if not the largest, certainly the best-established and longest-lived of the Irish coal merchant-shipowners. They also pursued the most consistent new building policy, producing a series of steamers whose somewhat frugal design evolved, albeit slowly, during a period of over sixty years.

The port of Newry and Joseph Fisher

Newry, where Joseph Fisher and Sons were to become by far the largest steamship owners, orginally had a tidal harbour on the Newry River. Newry's importance was greatly enhanced in 1742 by the completion of a canal to Portadown and hence to Lough Neagh, a summit canal which predated the far better-known Bridgewater Canal by some twenty years. The Newry River and the canal provided a trading artery which made Newry one of, if not the, most important ports in the province of Ulster. A further improvement was the first Newry Ship Canal, opened in 1769 with a sea lock at Upper Fathom, which allowed access for vessels up to 120 feet in length. But silting began as soon as the lock was opened, reducing the draft from an initial ten feet to five. The Newry River was deepened in 1830, but real improvement only came with the building of a new Newry Ship Canal between 1842 and 1850. The new sea lock at Lower Fathom, opened on 18th April 1850, could accommodate vessels of 205 feet by 50 feet, drawing up to 14 feet. The harbour at Newry was vastly enlarged by the building of Albert Basin, at the time claimed to be Europe's second largest 'floating dock', so called because ships could remain afloat in it at all states of the tide. But Newry did not long benefit from the advantages of its new Ship Canal. By 1852 a railway was completed between Belfast and Dublin and, with the city of Belfast expanding quickly, its trade fast overtook that of Newry.

The sea lock at Lower Fathom.

Joseph Fisher came from a farming background, his family having the freehold of a farm near Kilkeel on the coast of County Down. Joseph Fisher was born in 1836, the first of three sons. He did not go into farming, possibly because of the Irish potato famine, and instead was apprenticed to a shipbroker in Newry. In 1852, shortly after the completion of the second Newry Ship Canal, he started his own shipbroking business. By the nature of their business, shipbrokers are aware of the opportunities for ships, and when the time is right many who can raise or borrow the necessary capital make the move to shipowning. Fisher followed the usual practice of taking small numbers of shares in locally-owned ships. His career as a shipowner really dates from 1867, when in March he acquired 32 shares in the brigantine *Brothers* and in May took a minority holding in another brigantine, *Edith*.

Albert Basin at Newry with a collier to the right and to the left the *Iveagh* (533/1892) of the Dundalk and Newry Steam Packet Co. Ltd. *[National Library of Ireland]*

Brothers was wrecked in 1870, but Fisher maintained and increased his interest in ships by purchasing *Flora* and *Guitar*, both products of the immensely productive shipbuilding industry of Prince Edward Island. Although *Flora* foundered within a year, sail was to remain a part of the Fisher fleet for many years, the registry of *Edith* not being closed until 1903.

Steam and coal

By Irish Sea standards, Joseph Fisher was relatively early into steam, buying the virtually-new *Kilkeel* in November 1882. Although steam colliers had been running down the east coast of the UK in increasing numbers since 1852, only isolated examples worked on the Irish Sea over the next 30 years, despite Ireland's almost total reliance on coal imports from England, Wales and Scotland. In the early 1880s, pioneers such as William Robertson and the Hay family from Glasgow, and Liverpool's Mack family and Richard Hughes began building up fleets, and Fisher was undoubtedly watching their example.

The Newry Steamship Co. Ltd. was set up to provide the additional finance required by steamers compared with sailing vessels, and to its ownership was delivered the newly-built *Clanrye* in 1884, with the *Kilkeel* (1) transferred in 1885. The Newry company was perhaps under-capitalised, or possibly damaged by the tragic loss of *Clanrye* and her entire crew when the steamer was only two years old, and the company was reconstituted on 13th December 1886 as the Newry and Kilkeel Steamship Co. Ltd.

Joseph Fisher added coal importing to his shipowning and shipbroking businesses at a relatively early date. It was a logical addition, meaning that in summer months when freights were fewer and rates low, Fisher's ships could be employed bringing in coal for the company to stockpile and sell in the coming winter.

Fishers and Fullertons

Joseph Fisher and his wife Margaret had seven sons and one daughter, but only the two eldest sons, Frank (1867-1951) and Joseph junior (1871-1899), entered the shipping business. The others became solicitors, a doctor, a captain in the Royal Navy, and a minister of the Church of Scotland: family reunions must have been interesting occasions with so many talented and ambitious offspring. Frank and Joseph junior appear to have encouraged their father in the transition from sail to steam, as acquisition of steamers gathered pace from about 1890. Additional companies were also set up to own these steamers. The Carlingford Lough Steamship Co. Ltd. was formed in 1891, with Frank Fisher designated manager of its ships until it was wound up in 1912. The Frontier Town Steamship Co. Ltd. was set up in April 1897 and Joseph junior was designated manager of its ships, at least until his untimely death from tuberculosis on the last day of December 1899. The Frontier Town company was wound up when its last ship, the *Balsa*, was sold to the Newry and Kilkeel company in 1956. Joseph Fisher senior remained manager of the ships of the latter company until his death at the turn of the century, from when Frank Fisher managed the business on his own for many years.

The foundering of *Clanrye* in 1886 can have done nothing to bolster Fisher's confidence in Workman, Clark's products, but the nearly-new *Kilkeel* established the reputation of its builders, Fullertons of Paisley. Fishers were to go to Fullertons no fewer than 28 times for new steamers, beginning with the *Rostrevor* of 1890, and ending with the *Palm* of 1927, built shortly before Fullertons themselves gave up shipbuilding. The size of the Fullerton ships grew, from 120 feet for the *Rostrevor* of 1890, to 140 feet for the *Frontier Town* of 1898. A larger ship, *Cloughmore* of 170 feet, was built at Paisley in 1897 and then in 1899 came a solitary ship from Ayr, the 175-feet *Seapoint*, ordered as an improved *Cloughmore*. Length settled at 142 feet, the usual length for Irish Sea colliers, which allowed them access to the locks at Ringsend Basin, Dublin, an important destination for colliers. A beam of 23 feet was specified for most Fisher colliers, slightly narrower than other company's coasters, to allow two vessels to be simultaneously locked through at Victoria Locks at Newry, which were just 50 feet wide.

The Ayr-built *Seapoint* on trials. *[Glasgow University Archives DC101/1549]*

The 'long backs'

Many of Fullerton's early products for Fishers - certainly including *Carlingford Lough* and *Mourne* - were built to a standard, 125-foot design. The bridge, such as it was, was aft, there was a half-height forecastle below in which the seamen and firemen slept, and a mast with two derricks stepped about one third of the way back along the well deck. A further, stubbier mast was mounted on the superstructure aft. Examples built to this design for other owners include the *Emily* of 1893 (Fullerton's yard number 111) and *Eller* of 1896 (yard number 129). The *Joseph Fisher* of 1892 was a larger vessel, with the same layout and half-height forecastle, but with a higher bridge. The next design advance was a full-height forecastle, and this can be seen in photographs of *Orior*, *Ivytown* as *Abbot* became, and *Dromore*. This particular design became known amongst local seamen as the 'long back', possibly because, in contrast to later vessels with a bridge almost amidships and a raised quarter deck, they had a long, uninterrupted well deck. Although the sample is small, the 'long backs' seem to have suffered a number of losses which, it is presumed, were due to stress of weather. The *Clonallon* disappeared in 1904, the *Orior* in 1908, the second *Rostrevor* foundered in 1917, the *Mourne* foundered in 1933 (she had been sold after a collision in 1898) and the *Abbot* - after sale and renaming *Ivytown* and then *Kentbrook* - disappeared in 1935. All were laden with coal or, in the case of *Kentbrook*, stone. With these ships, such dense bulk cargoes tended to be heaped up amidships in the hold, leaving loose surfaces at either end – surfaces which could shift in heavy weather. The company certainly learned its lesson: in 1946 they refused to purchase the motor vessel *Empire Albany*, which had been managed on behalf of the Ministry of War Transport, because of her long single hold. This decision was vindicated when *Albany* disappeared in the Irish Sea soon afterwards.

Raised quarter decks

The loss of *Clonallon* in 1904 may have persuaded Fishers to build a different type of ship with better sea-keeping properties, the bridge-amidships, raised quarter deck design. The first of these for Fisher, the *Yews*, emerged a year after the disappearance of *Clonallon*, and showed improvements in seaworthiness and, more modestly, in accommodation. The raised quarterdeck,

A contrast in 'long backs'. Seen above in later owner-ship, *Carlingford Lough* has the low forecastle of the earlier group, whilst *Ivytown*, ex-*Abbot*, seen right has a full height forecastle. *[Right: A. Duncan]*

The *Yews* on trials. *[Glasgow University Archives DC101/1647]*

about 80 feet long, gave increased freeboard aft and extra protection from seas sweeping from astern. The lines at both bow and stern were fuller, helping the ship ride over seas rather than slice through them and flood the decks. Hatches were wider, making it easier to trim a coal cargo, and ballast capacity was increased to improve handling on light passages. *Yews* was wider by two feet, meaning that - although the machinery space was moved forward - cubic capacity was increased by over 20 per cent. The twin-cylinder compound machinery was unchanged, despite the ships' greater size, but bunker space was increased to allow for a higher coal consumption. The amidships bridge structure gave room for a saloon for the master and mate, and in some ships at least the galley was moved from the forecastle to a more conventional position in the after superstructure.

The new raised-quarter deck design also marked a change in nomenclature. Local place names had previously been favoured, but the *Yews* introduced tree names, an attractive and distinctive naming style which lasted for the rest of the company's existence.

Founderings and disappearances amongst the raised quarter deck vessels were almost as great as amongst the 'long backs' which preceded them, but this requires further consideration. In 1910 the almost-new *Maple* foundered and in 1915 so did the *Upas*, considered to be very tender, and not a good seaboat. Both were carrying particular dense cargoes; iron ore in the case of *Maple* and Ayrshire coal in that of *Upas*, and with these cargoes a ship was down to its marks well before the hold was full. There was thus space for the cargo to shift in bad weather, and both founderings are ascribed to this cause. Two further steamers which disappeared, the *Privet* in 1940 and the *Walnut* (1) in 1941, were carrying less dense coal loaded on Merseyside, and with these cargoes it was usual to insist on careful trimming to ensure the holds were evenly filled, so there was less chance of the cargo shifting. The master of the *Privet*, Captain Parry, was valued by the company as an experienced skipper, and is likely to have taken seriously the words of Frank Fisher to each new skipper on his appointment: 'It is not necessary to take risks.' The loss of both *Privet* and *Walnut* (2) were considered by the company to be due to enemy action, possibly through hitting mines, and others are of the same opinion: the names of their crews are inscribed on the Merchant Marine

War Memorial at Tower Hill in London. However, there are also suggestions that their stability was adversely affected by wartime alterations. With just two losses due to heavy cargoes shifting in many years of trading the raised quarter deck vessels, the Fisher family themselves feel that this design was much safer than the 'long backs.'

The arrival of new raised quarter deck steamers allowed the disposal of the 'long backs', and most of those which were not wrecked or otherwise lost were sold. Only the *Portadown* remained after 1917, because her size made her useful for serving the section of the Newry Ship Canal from the Albert Basin past Merchants Quay through the town of Newry. The decline in use of this section of canal led to *Portadown* being sold in 1935.

Like most steam coasters of the day, the hulls and engines of the long raised quarter deck ships were sturdy and built to last - those ships that survived marine hazards worked for upwards of 40 years. But the owners were clearly very cost conscious and their vessels had few frills. All the Paisley and Ayr-built vessels, including the 175-foot examples, had two-cylinder compound engines, which were less efficient than the triple-expansion versions, but were cheaper to construct and took up less space. No steam anchor windlass or steam capstans were fitted, only two steam winches for operating the cargo gear. A messenger chain was used to drive the anchor windlass from the steam winch, a procedure which could put those on the forecastle at risk if a chain broke. Work normally carried out by the capstan was done by connecting a wire hawser to the forward winch. There was no double bottom to provide additional ballast capacity, and this could make the ships difficult to handle during windy passages when running light. A flying bridge was fitted to aid visibility.

A total of 13 raised-quarter deck steamers were built by Fullertons for Fisher between 1905 and 1927 and, although dimensionally similar, they did gradually incorporate minor improvements. For instance, the *Alder* of 1909 had berths for extra hands in the forecastle. Changes were made to the positions of bulkheads, the fore bulkhead being moved aft slightly to make the space under the forecastle usable, and to increase ballast capacity. The later ships also had the foremast and winch moved from the well deck onto the forecastle, allowing a longer derrick and a better view for the winch operator. The last two Fullerton completions, *Palm* and *Poplar* of 1927, had no mizzen masts. Abandoned because it gave trouble under the coal tips at Garston, the mizzen was by now something of an anachronism, as after the First World War steam coasters mostly lost the sails with which they were invariably equipped in earlier years. Many seamen regretted this, however, as the mizzen sail helped to steady the ship when headed into the wind.

The accompanying table summarises what is known about the prices paid for Fisher's vessels. No account has been taken of inflation, so comparing costs needs to be done cautiously. However, it is clear that larger colliers such as *Seapoint* and *Cloughmore* cost a great deal more than smaller contemporaries, partly reflecting a higher standard of equipment. The fall in costs in the mid-1900s is also notable, and was probably due to the prolonged and deep slump which affected shipping. This explains why the *Yews*, despite a better cargo capacity than the 'long backs' which preceded her, was actually cheaper to build. A sister ship to *Aspen* was ordered in January 1915, but Fullertons were unable to start because the Admiralty had first call on their building berths. Wisely, Fishers ordered no new ships from then until 1927, for most of which period prices were inflated by wartime shortages. Their business shows the great truism, also exemplified in this book by Edward Nicholl, that prospering in shipping was largely a matter of buying ships at a time when low freight rates depressed the price of new tonnage. Looking back over the company's history, Mr. John D.F. Fisher, great grandson of the founder, concluded that shipowning, if well managed, did produce a positive but not generous return on capital provided the market was judged correctly and the vessel sold at a good price.

Deep-sea foray

Fisher's sole deep-sea vessel was delivered from South Shields in 1903; the *Ulidia*, owned by the newly-established Mercantile Steamship Co. of Ulster Ltd. (1903). She was by far the largest vessel ever registered in Newry, not surprising as she was far too big to enter the port. She was employed in deep sea tramping, which in the early years of the twentieth century meant coal out, usually from South Wales to either South America or the Mediterranean, followed by grain home from Argentina to Europe or from the Black Sea. For example, the crew agreements and other papers for *Ulidia* for 1908 indicate that she left Penarth on 12th December 1907 with coal for Buenos Aires, then loaded grain for Genoa, where she arrived on 26th March 1908. A later voyage that year took her again from Penarth on 24th August to Genoa, where she sailed for Mariupol to load grain for Rotterdam. During her Fisher career she also visited the eastern seaboard of the USA. Local men were in command of *Ulidia*: Captain Robert McClenaghan of Dundalk and Hugh O'Neill of Killowen as mate, who later died when the *Dundalk* of the Dundalk and Newry Steam Packet Co. Ltd. was torpedoed in October 1918. The latter part of the first decade of the century saw low freight rates, and *Ulidia*

Costs of Fisher's newbuildings

Date	Name	Price	Length
1894	*Mourne*	£4,000	125 feet
1896	*Joseph Fisher*	£5,000	140 feet
1897	*Cloughmore*	£8,000	170 feet
1898	*Frontier Town*	£5,700	142 feet
1899	*Seapoint*	£9,250	175 feet
1899	*Rostrevor* (1)	£6,300	142 feet
1899	*Clonallon*	£6,100	142 feet
1900	*Portadown*	£6,300	142 feet
1903	*Abbot*	£6,208	142 feet
1903	*Dromore*	£6,335	142 feet
1905	*Yews*	£6,000	142 feet
1905	*Oak* (1)	£6,500	142 feet
1906	*Elm*	£6,500	142 feet
1907	*Pine*	£6,500	142 feet
1909	*Alder*	£6,000	142 feet
1910	*Walnut* (1)	£6,000	142 feet
1912	*Mango*	£6,500	142 feet
1914	*Aspen*	£7,300	142 feet
1927	*Poplar*	£11,700	142 feet
1927	*Palm*	£11,700	142 feet
1932	*Jasmine*	£10,750	142 feet
1934	*Rowan*	£14,750	173 feet
1934	*Broom*	£10,360	142 feet
1936	*Bamboo*	£11,850	142 feet
1936	*Karri*	£25,000	147 feet
1947	*Balsa*	£46,000	148 feet
1947	*Ebony*	£46,000	148 feet
1953	*Oak* (2)	£95,000	190 feet

was sold in 1912, after which she survived one serious stranding to be wrecked in the Far East in 1948.

Secondhand tonnage

Secondhand acquisitions were the exception in the Fisher fleet, in contrast to almost all other Irish Sea collier and tramp coaster owners - even such large, well-established owners as John Kelly and William Robertson had a significant proportion of second-hand vessels in their fleets. The second-hand steamers which came into the Fisher fleet were, with one exception, almost new. The *Celtic* was only two months old, and the big collier *Moygannon* acquired in 1924 had been built in 1921 for another Newry coal company and was bought by Fishers from her mortgagees after the owners had gone bankrupt in 1924. At £10,500, *Moygannon* was a bargain, considerably bigger than the Fullerton ships, with a triple-expansion engine rather than a two-cylinder compound, and better facilities for the crew, including a substantially larger galley, which made her particularly popular. The exception to the almost-new rule was the *Shark*. This tiny, 22-year old iron steamer was ashore, damaged when bought in March 1888, the price of £525 suggesting that she was of little value, and repairs cost over £880. Initially, she was owned by a James MacFarland, the manager of Fisher's local bank, suggesting that the bank bought her whilst Fisher's were arranging the finance. She was a poor bargain, however: disabled near Newry in July 1890, she had to be assisted by the *Bessbrook* (485/1877) of the Dundalk and Newry Steam Packet Co. Ltd., which cost Fishers £225 for services rendered. Soon afterwards, Fishers were in correspondence with McLarens, the Glasgow sale and purchase brokers, about selling the

An Italian pierhead painter's impression of *Ulidia*. [J.D.F. Fisher collection]

Antrim Iron Ore Co.'s *Glenaan* in the Avon.

Shark. But it took until June 1892 before a buyer was found who took her for £1,100, it being minuted that 'the directors were pleased to be rid of her.' After *Moygannon*, the only other secondhand vessel was the Dutch-built motor vessel *Walnut* (2) bought almost new in 1956, so that of 47 powered vessels owned in the name of Fishers, 43 had been built for them.

Antrim Iron Ore Co.

The distinction 'owned in the name of Fishers' in the previous paragraph is important, because secondhand vessels were acquired in the name of another company, the Antrim Iron Ore Co. Ltd. This concern could trace its origins back to 1872. Formed to export iron ore from Parkmore, County Antrim, its ships usually loaded at Red Bay, County Antrim where a narrow gauge railway brought ore from the mines. The company became much more than a simple carrier of bulk goods, however, as several of its ships had passenger accommodation. As the Antrim Line they ran from Northern Ireland to the Tyne and Tees with ore, often bringing back steel cargoes. Other, smaller ships brought steam coal from South Wales and elsewhere to Belfast. When the Antrim Iron Ore Company sold out in August 1929, the coal-carrying side of the business passed to Fishers, who ran *Glenaan* under the old company's name. When *Glenaan* was wrecked in 1932, another steamer was bought to replace her and given the name *Glendun* in Antrim style. The two other Antrim vessels, the passenger-carrying *Glentaise* (1,001/ 1905) and the first *Glendun* (1,013/1903), went to Coast Lines Ltd. together with the Belfast to Newcastle service and were given -*Coast* names.

Coal and other cargoes

Cargoes carried by Fisher's vessels were chiefly coal, but loading ports varied considerably: Garston, Partington and other Mersey ports, Preston, Ayr and Irvine on the Clyde, Whitehaven and South Wales. Latterly, the second *Olive* loaded at north east coast ports including Blyth. Much coal was destined for Newry where Fishers' ships berthed along one side of the Albert Basin. Coal would also be consigned to Waterford — where on occasions four or five Fishers ships might be discharging — to Cork, Belfast, Dublin, Dundalk, and, after the closure of the Newry Ship Canal in 1974, Warrenpoint. Return cargoes from Ireland were the exception, but they could include barrels of herrings from the west coast, seaweed loaded from carts brought to a vessel aground in some sandy, sheltered creek, and potatoes from small ports in County Down to south west England. In summer months other trades would be entered: herrings on the east coast of Scotland, French potatoes from ports such as Roscoff (where *Orior* was photographed loading from horse-drawn carts) to English south coast ports, and Portland stone to Belfast.

Orior loading potatoes at Roscoff. [*Courtesy V. Evans*]

The cargo book of *Poplar* for the years following her delivery in July 1927 illustrates the pattern of trade of Fisher's ships. Her maiden voyage was from the Clyde, where she was built, to Newry with coal, and *Poplar* then spent six months almost exclusively in the coal trade across the Irish Sea. On just three occasions she had a back cargo of crushed stone from Newry to Manchester. In May and June 1928 *Poplar* was chartered to load potatoes in Trequier, Roscoff and Loctudy for Cardiff, Swansea and Bristol. At the end of 1930, she had a spell largely away from the coal trade. On 10th November 1930 she left Newry for Garston to load coal for Cork and was not to return to her home port for over three months. She visited Guernsey, probably for strawberries, loaded china clay in Fowey for Runcorn, carried coal to Waterford, and spent two months on charter running with general cargo between London and Dordrecht in Holland. Other cargoes included 360 tons of manure carried from Dublin to Waterford over Christmas 1929, onions and oilcake.

The large collier *Moygannon* spent extended periods carrying salted herrings from Lerwick to Hamburg, calling in at Runcorn on the return voyage to load salt for Lerwick to salt more herrings. After being renamed *Agba* she also carried potatoes, this time between Jersey and Newhaven, and potatoes to Weymouth on charter to the Great Western Railway and wearing their red funnel with black top. Fruit and vegetable carrying in season continued to provide regular employment for the colliers, and in post-war years *Balsa*, *Karri* and *Ebony* were time-chartered for a month at a time to run with strawberries between Brest and Plymouth, and potatoes between Jersey and Portsmouth and Jersey and Liverpool.

The later motorships ranged further. Between 1968 and 1970 the *Walnut* (2) wandered far afield when the coal trade was quiet, often bringing timber home from Finland. The miner's strike of 1972 saw the *Olive* load coal in Gdansk.

Although work was hard for the crews, with long hours, in some ways the pace of life in the steamers was less frantic than in the coastal trade today. On one occasion, the *Broom* arrived at a port in County Kerry on a Friday afternoon, too late for work to begin that day. No work was done on Saturday, and Sunday was a holiday. On Monday there was a local race meeting, to which the entire crew was taken by the receiver of the cargo. On Tuesday discharge finally began, but proceeded slowly because of a number of hangovers. Time seemed to be of lesser importance than today, possibly because wages were lower, and it could be worthwhile waiting several days to load rather than making a ballast passage. John D.F. Fisher believes the slower tempo led to a happier, almost family, atmosphere on board.

The 'tarboat' *Palm* at Dublin: note the spark arrester.
[Pat Sweeney]

Fullertons to Scotts

The frugality of Fishers when it came to equipping their coasters helped ensure the family not only survived the depression of the 1920s and 1930s, but actually expanded their fleet in this period. Sadly, after the *Palm* of 1927 Fullertons delivered no more colliers to Fishers: after completing one other coaster, the *Greta Force* (914/1928) for W.S. Kennaugh and Co., this well-respected Paisley yard closed. It was a victim of the over-building of coasters in the boom years immediately following the First World War, which resulted in a collapse of freight rates and

Jasmine on 18th March 1951, after the fitting of a wheelhouse.
[World Ship Photo Library]

The motorship *Karri*.

Karri also introduced other innovations to Fisher's fleet: a double bottom to improve ballast capacity, and a cruiser rather than a counter stern. Probably because of these two changes, she gained an excellent reputation as a sea boat. Forecastle accommodation for seamen was now at deck level.

Karri was the last vessel delivered before the outbreak of the Second World War, and had the misfortune to be the only Fisher vessel which, as far as is known, was directly damaged by enemy action. *Karri* was mined in the Mersey during 1942 and, although her hull survived to sail for many another day, her German diesel had to be replaced by a new British Polar unit.

With the *Karri* apparently successful, it could be expected that Fishers would replace their wartime losses with further motorships. But no, Scotts were asked to build two new steamers to a design which dated back virtually to 1911. Although not quite the last of the traditional steam coasters built (that dubious honour belongs to Zillah's *Hazelfield* completed at Lytham in April 1948), the *Balsa* and *Ebony* of 1947 even had counter sterns which, years later, had observers refusing to believe they were post-war craft. James S. Fisher, grandson of the founder, proposed that the two ships should be diesel powered, but was overruled by other members of the board, who cited the restricted availability of diesel engines and engineers to run them, and the cheapness of bunker coal and steam engineers. Comparison of the cost of the motor vessel *Karri* and the steamer *Bamboo* in 1936 shows that motor coasters certainly did cost more. However, ordering obsolescent steamers cannot have been anything but a short-sighted step, and this is reflected by the brief service of *Balsa* and *Ebony* with Fishers: just ten years with a fleet in which ships could survive for over 45.

In 1953, Scotts did deliver a relatively modern motor coaster, the *Oak* (2), which had a carrying capacity of 850 tons of coal, twice that of the steamers she replaced. Crew accommodation was aft, below decks, and each man had his own cabin: 'we're all officers!' exclaimed one seaman on seeing this. But Fishers had not quite deserted steam technology, and *Oak* had a steam donkey engine to power her deck machinery, probably specified because of the unreliability of the deck machinery on the motor vessel *Karri*. *Oak* gained a bad reputation for rolling, a propensity possibly due to a combination of a wheelhouse and a relatively narrow beam, and at times she would roll her sidelights under. In 1955 came one of Fisher's rare secondhand acquisitions, the Dutch-built *Walnut* (2). Her bridge was aft - the first Fisher vessel in 52 years to have such an arrangement. But in some ways she was still old-fashioned, and Fishers later replaced the wood and canvas covers on her after hatch with MacGregor patent steel covers, at the same time raising the after hatch to improve trim. *Walnut's* accommodation was attractively panelled in wood, but was rather cramped - Dutch builders had a reputation for using every inch of space. She was also considered under-powered, and her hand-operated capstan would not have endeared her to crews.

with it coaster values. Once Fullertons had closed, Fishers transferred their loyalty to Scotts of Bowling, building eight steamers and three motor vessels there over the period from 1932 to 1963.

Scott's first delivery, *Jasmine* of 1932, was almost a repeat of *Palm*, and not greatly different from *Yews* of 1911 except for her triple expansion engine, steam windlass and capstan. There was still no enclosed wheelhouse and no electricity, and the crew's accommodation was still below decks in the forecastle. *Rowan* of 1932 was a bigger collier of 173 feet overall, making her the largest in the fleet by a small margin. Further deliveries from Bowling were 'Dublinmax' vessels of 142 feet. These came in pairs: *Broom* and *Thorn* in 1934, *Privet* and *Bamboo* in 1936, and the singular *Opepe* in 1937, the first Fisher coaster with a wheelhouse and with electricity, although the latter was only available when at sea. The dynamo was driven directly from the main engine, and so did not work when the ship was in dock and the furnaces banked down.

After building to a design which was, arguably, not even state-of-the-art in 1911, Fishers and Scotts then took a big leap forward in 1938 by building a motor coaster. The Dutch had successfully applied the diesel engine to small coasters very soon after the end of the First World War, aided by German engine builders who had benefited from the experience of developing engines for submarines. British coaster owners were a lot slower in seeing the benefits of the diesel in terms of reduced engine room space, lower manning costs and fuel economy, but in the mid-1930s many well-established owners such as Coast Lines and William Robertson took a deep breath and embraced motor ships. J.S. Fisher visited Holland to investigate Dutch coaster building, but gave the contract to Scotts who made a very competitive bid. In *Karri* of 1938 Fishers and Scotts produced a ship which successfully blended the proven, raised-quarter deck design with a German diesel installation. This gave a reduction in draft from 10.5 to 8.8 feet which was a positive benefit in the coastal trade where berths were often tidal or shallow.

Balsa outward bound off Clarence Dock, Liverpool on 30th May 1953.

Olive (2) with her original masts. *[A. Duncan]*

In December 1963, the last vessel built for Fishers made her maiden voyage from Ayr to Newry, the *Olive* (2). Again, Scotts had been told not to fit any frills, and this went for a radar set, which had to be added later. Steering was manual, although with hydraulic assistance. However, MacGregor hatch covers were fitted. Unlike *Oak* (2), she was regarded as being very stable, which was all to the good as she was to make many voyages around the north of Scotland, loading coal in Blyth for Northern Ireland. *Oak* was sold the next autumn after the arrival of *Olive* (2).

Fisher's fortunes

Surviving minute books show that Fisher steamers were financed through issuing shares in the owning companies, by loans from banks, with cash raised through debentures or, in some cases with loans from Joseph Fisher and Co., the managing company. Others were financed with money from reserves and, undoubtedly, with insurance money from lost ships which they replaced. The managing company, which had been a simple partnership for many years, became Joseph Fisher and Sons Ltd. in 1919. This may have reflected the arrival in the business of James S. Fisher, Frank Fisher's son. Although the owning companies were public ones, much of the capital came from the Fisher family. By the 1950s, for instance, the relatively modest £14,000 capital of the Frontier Town Steamship Co. Ltd. was almost all in the hands of Fishers.

After the Second World War, trading conditions remained good for British and Irish coastal shipowners for a decade, explaining why many who had clung to the romantic but outdated steam coaster could survive. After 1955, conditions became much more competitive, and the wholesale clear out of steam from many fleets including

Fishers dates from mid-decade. Fisher's last steamer clung on until 1963, the *Palm* which was fitted with tanks and latterly was engaged almost exclusively in carrying tar and creosote from Ardrossan to Belfast and to the Royal Canal in Dublin. By now, with a fleet reduced to just three ships, Fishers must have wondered about the wisdom of continuing in shipowning, especially as their staple business, coal carrying, must have seemed in almost terminal decline, and the port of Newry was itself under threat of closure. Other factors were the increased economy of land transport, meaning fewer transhipments to coasters from ocean-going vessels, and the steady growth in the numbers of container and roll-on, roll-off vessels, which reduced turnrounds and meant fewer coasters were needed. Fishers also felt that the tax position of British shipping companies was not as favourable as that for their competitors in continental Europe.

On 10th November 1966, a year short of their centenary as shipowners, Joseph Fishers and Sons Ltd. was sold to Cawood Holdings Ltd. However, the ships continued to trade as before, running to Warrenpoint after Newry closed in 1974. The new owner seemed to value Fisher's goodwill, just as Fishers had themselves maintained the independence of the Antrim Iron Ore Co. Ltd. through the 1930s. But, as so often happens, the new owner - or more likely, his accountants - eventually decided that the old identity was unnecessary. *Olive* (2) adopted Cawood's colours in July 1979, but - according to the owners - had been put under Cawood management a year earlier. But the new arrangement was short-lived, and *Olive* was sold on 1st May 1981, bringing to a close just under a century of Fisher powered craft.

Accidents

For almost a century, the fleet carried coal across the Irish Sea, with only occasional changes to the management as one generation of Fishers replaced another. But if board room dramas were largely absent, there was excitement and tragedy in good measure on the sea. For a relatively modest fleet, Fisher's colliers suffered a surprisingly large number of accidents. The accompanying table summarises the major casualties in chronological order, and the entries in the fleet list provide further detail, but some accidents deserve a few more words.

The foundering of the *Cloughmore* in 1902 was the subject of a legal action by some of its surviving crew. At 170 feet, the 1897-built steamer was one of the larger colliers in the fleet, and differed from the contemporary 'long backs' in having a bridge amidships. On 14th June 1902, *Cloughmore* left Liverpool for Galway with a cargo

of maize. Grain such as this was a notoriously difficult cargo, prone to shifting unless precautions were taken, such as filling bags and using these to stabilise the ends of the heap in the hold. By the time *Cloughmore* reached Lough Swilly, she had taken a list of 7-8 degrees, but she proceeded onwards to Galway. Three to four hours later the list increased to 45 degrees and off Tory Island she foundered stern first. Two boats were launched, but only the one which contained the master, his sister and two members of the crew reached the Bloody Foreland - the other boat containing seven crew members was lost. The subsequent Board of Trade Enquiry found that bags for the grain were available to the crew, but had not been used. The families of four of those lost on *Cloughmore* took Fishers to court, alleging that the owners were negligent for not ensuring that the vessel was seaworthy, and especially that Captain McClenaghan had left Lough Swilly with a

Summary of major casualties to Fisher steamers

Further details will be found in the fleet list and the accompanying text.

1886	*Clanrye*	Foundered
1892	*Kilkeel* (1)	Sank
1898	*Rostrevor* (1)	Wrecked
1898	*Mourne*	Collision
1902	*Cloughmore*	Foundered
1904	*Clonallon*	Disappeared
1908	*Warrenpoint*	Collision
1908	*Orior*	Missing
1909	*Elm*	Stranded
1910	*Maple*	Foundered
1910	*Yews*	Collision
1915	*Upas*	Foundered
1917	*Rostrevor* (2)	Foundered
1932	*Glenaan*	Wrecked
1933	*Mango*	Wrecked
1936	*Pine* and *Olive* (1)	Collision
1937	*Alder*	Collision
1940	*Privet*	Disappeared
1940	*Agba*	Collision
1940	*Glendun* (2)	Wrecked
1941	*Walnut* (1)	Disappeared
1942	*Karri*	Mined
1942	*Poplar*	Wrecked

list. McClenaghan claimed that he considered the list due to taking more coal from one of the side bunkers, a common reason for coasters to assume a slight list. A stevedore involved in loading *Cloughmore* said that he had warned of the risk of the cargo shifting and had advised the use of shifting boards. The company was judged liable, and the plaintiffs were awarded a sum of £650. Fishers appealed to overturn this judgement, on the grounds that the negligence - if any - was down to the mate of *Cloughmore*, George Townley. The appeal was dismissed, and the families got their money, Lord Justice Fitzgibbons commenting that the loss arose from 'taking a chance of a summer voyage from Liverpool to Galway in the hope that they would have summer weather.'

Fishers lost no ships during the First World War through enemy action, although a submarine fired a torpedo at the *Mango* off the Scottish coast on 26th April 1918. However, marine hazards continued to take their toll. On 17th March 1915, the *Upas*, another big collier, left Ayr for Warrenpoint with coal. Approaching the South Rock Lightship off Portavogie, winds had reached gale force, with driving snow making it virtually impossible to see the foremast from the bridge. Before leaving the bridge at 4.00 am, mate Samuel Hanna had set a course to pass the Lightship to starboard. However, Captain William McFerran, fearing that *Upas* might slip inside the South Rock and go ashore, decided to heave to and await improved weather. But as he attempted to bring the *Upas* round, she rolled and her cargo of dense, Ayrshire coal shifted. Lying at an angle of 45 degrees, she was unsteerable and rapidly filling with water. The list made it impossible to launch the starboard boat, and attempts to launch the port boat, which was almost in the water, failed when it capsized after being hit by a davit rolling on top of it, throwing those on board into the sea. Washed off the deck of *Upas*, Hanna and the second mate James McShane had lifebelts and managed to stay afloat. At 10.30 am, the Belfast-registered steamer *Ailsa Craig* (641/1906) came upon the *Upas* which was lying on her beam ends. She could not get alongside because of the proximity of the rocks, but launched a boat with three crew members which succeeded in picking up Hanna and McShane. However, the boat began to take in water, and the wind made it impossible for it to return to *Ailsa Craig*. Hanna watched *Upas* sink from the boat, presumably wondering if he would be saved. However, the Donaghadee lifeboat arrived shortly and took all five on board. Hanna and McShane were the only survivors from *Upas*; Hanna's brother

Joe - on his first voyage - being one of those lost.

Two of Fisher's steamers were involved in an accident in 12th November 1936. *Pine* had put into Carlingford Lough to shelter during a voyage from Garston to Dundalk. Early in the morning a crash awoke the crew when the *Olive*, bound for Kilkeel to load potatoes, ran into her. *Pine* sank within ten minutes, but fortunately all the crew were rescued by *Olive* (1), which limped into Warrenpoint. Less than five months later, Captain Robert Campbell who had command of the *Olive* during the collision, experienced a repeat of the accident, but with far more tragic results. He was now in command of *Alder*, and on 4th April 1937 had anchored her off Greencastle in Carlingford Lough waiting for fog to clear before proceeding to Newry. At 4.00 am, *Alder* was rammed amidships by the *Lady Cavan* (602/1906), a regular trader between Newry and Liverpool. According to the survivors, those on board did not realise the immediate danger, and decided to remain on board, but *Alder* quickly heeled over and sank. Six persons were lost, including Campbell and his wife Catherine, three survivors being picked up by a boat launched by the *Lady Cavan*. One who survived by clinging to an oar, William Cahoon, went on to skipper *Karri* and *Walnut* (2). In 1968 he was instrumental in saving life when he picked up six fishermen washed overboard in a North Sea gale.

Both *Pine* and *Alder* were raised by Samuel Gray of Belfast, who won a reputation for salvage work in northern Irish waters. Gray himself traded *Pine* for a couple of years, but the hulk of *Alder* was sold for scrap.

As in the previous conflict, no Fisher ships are known to have been lost through enemy action in the Second World War. However, *Karri* was seriously damaged and had one crew member killed by a mine in the Mersey in 1942, returning to service after being laid up and then re-engined in Glasgow. However, during the war five of the fleet foundered, disappeared or were wrecked, partly as a result of hostilities. The fate of neither *Privet* nor *Walnut* (1) is known for certain, although the position of the *Privet* is marked on local fishermen's charts as lying about ten miles west of the Chickens. To ensure that two could fit into the sea lock to the Newry Ship Canal, Fisher's ships had a relatively narrow beam of 23 feet, and there are suspicions that their stability may have been affected by wartime additions. Some coasters carried guns on their poops, and their wheelhouses were often protected by concrete. There is some doubt as to whether Fisher's coasters were protected in this way: John Fisher has no evidence that concrete was fitted, but there are stories that *Aspen's* wheelhouse was protected with concrete and that she once almost capsized when entering Carlingford Lough.

1940 was a bad year, the worst in Fisher's history, with the disappearance of *Privet*, the sinking of *Agba* after a collision with a ship in convoy in the Clyde, and the wreck of Antrim Iron Ore's *Glendun* on the coast of the Isle of Man after lighthouses and other navigation lights had been extinguished as a wartime measure. There may be a similar explanation for the wreck of *Poplar* off Harrington in October 1942. This was to be the last serious casualty to a vessel in Fisher's ownership.

Oak (1) in trouble at Cemaes Bay, Anglesey in 1924. *[Seán Patterson, courtesy M. O'Rourke]*

Derivations of Fisher names

Fishers used two distinct naming schemes: places near Newry and trees. After accidents to *Clanrye*, *Cloughmore* and *Clonallon*, names including the letter C were avoided, which meant many familiar tree names were not used, and some rather unusual ones commemorated. Two place names and three tree names were used twice.

Place names

Abbot Newry was founded by Cistercian monks in 1144, and this name may refer to the Abbot of their monastery.

Ashton An eighteenth century house overlooking Victoria Locks on the Newry Canal. Probably owned by an associate or shareholder.

Carlingford Lough A deep arm of the sea, with Greenore on its southern bank and Warrenpoint near its head, forming part of the boundary between Northern Ireland and the Republic of Ireland.

Clanrye A local river.

Clonallon Townland near Warrenpoint.

Cloughmore Irish for 'large stone', the stone in question being in Rostrevor.

Dromore A town about 20 miles north of Newry, and a diocese.

Frontier Town Refers to Newry, situated just north of the border of Ulster. The '*Frontier Sentinel*' was a local newspaper.

Kilkeel A village on the coast of County Down, just north of Carlingford Lough.

Mourne A range of hills to the north west of Newry, giving their name to a district of Northern Ireland, Newry and Mourne.

Orior A small but ancient group of townlands adjacent to Newry.

Portadown One of the largest towns in County Armagh, north of Newry.

Rostrevor A town just below Warrenpoint on Carlingford Lough.

Seapoint A house owned by James McFarland, manager of the Belfast Bank in Newry, who was Joseph Fisher's bank manager and financial adviser.

Ulidia Latinisation of Uladh, an ancient kingdom of Ulster, occupying approximately the area of present-day County Down, with its capital at Downpatrick. The name is still used in the Spanish army, which has a Regimento de Ulidia.

Warrenpoint The point where the Newry River enters Carlingford Lough, and the port for Newry since the closure of the Ship Canal.

Tree names

Agba Pink mahogany, a valuable wood which comes from a large west African tree of the same name.

Alder A tree of wet places whose wood was formerly used for making clogs, and the charcoal for gunpowder.

Aspen A very hardy type of poplar found in a wide range of localities from wet lowland woods to high mountain ledges.

Balsa A remarkably light wood from a tropical American tree used originally for building rafts, and now beloved of modelmakers.

Broom Grows throughout the British Isles on light, sandy soil and was once used for making brooms. Now much planted to stabilize steep road banks.

Bamboo A few members of this grass family, which originates from south-east Asia, are now naturalized in the British Isles.

Ebony An exceptionally dark and hard tropical wood used in cabinet making.

Elm The whole aspect of the countryside of lowland Britain has been changed by the loss of the distinctive hedgerow elms to Dutch elm disease.

Jasmine This name may refer to yellow winter-flowering jasmine, introduced from western China, or to fragrant white jasmine, an old cottage-garden favourite.

Karri A durable wood which is used in construction work and comes from some forms of Australian eucalyptus.

Mango Large tropical trees best known for their sweet juicy fruits which are also rich in vitamin A.

Maple A big family of trees. This name may refer to the American sugar maple whose sap is used for making maple syrup. Or to fine-grained maple wood used for high-quality turned work and for musical instruments.

Oak Wonderfully strong, attractive and versatile constructional timber found in old church roofs, timber-framed buildings, and wooden ships. The heavy lower branches of oaks once provided the curved timbers essential for wooden shipbuilding.

Olive A small, slow-growing tree which originated in the Mediterranean and often lives to a great age.

Opepe An African mahogany which is in high demand. Uses include dock and marine work, boatbuilding, railway sleepers, flooring and furniture.

Palm These economically important tropical trees include oil, coconut, date, sago and sugar palms. Oil palms yield more edible oil per acre than any other crop.

Palm [R. Fenton collection]

Pine Another group of trees which are of economic importance. The softwood of our only native pine, the Scots pine, has many everyday uses.

Poplar Handsome trees which can grow very large and are best kept to the fields and riversides. In an urban setting they can draw moisture from the surrounding soil causing it to shrink and thereby endangering the foundation of buildings.

Privet Most commonly planted as a garden hedging shrub in Europe, privet comes originally from Japan. Its white flowers are fragrant, but the shiny purple-black berries are poisonous.

Rowan Known also as the mountain ash, rowan was formerly planted to protect dwellings from witches.

Thorn Common hawthorn is our most familiar hedgerow shrub, but it has long been regarded as unlucky to bring hawthorn blossom into a house.

Upas A large Javanese tree which has poisonous milky sap that is used as an arrow poison.

Walnut A fine tree valued both for its timber and its nuts. Walnuts have also been used for centuries in the preparation of artist's paints.

Yews Although the leaves, bark and seeds of this evergreen are poisonous to man and animals, its new young leaves contain a substance called taxol which seems to be effective in the treatment of some cancers.

Fleet list

1. BROTHERS 1867-1870 Wooden brigantine
O.N. 82g 63.0 x 18.4 x 10.4 feet
1826: Built at Maryport as BROTHERS.
21.7.1847: Registered at Maryport.
15.3.1867: Registered at Newry in the ownership of Joseph Fisher, Newry (32/64) and Edward Toomby (32/64), Omeath, County Louth.
18.10.1870: Wrecked near Dumfries.
2.11.1870: Register closed.

2. EDITH 1867-1903 Wooden two-masted schooner
O.N. 47140 89g 81n 67.7 x 21.0 x 9.9 feet
Built by unknown foreign builders as EDITH.
4.9.1866: Registered at Newry in the ownership of James Hunter, Newry.
21.5.1867: Sold to James Hunter (16/64), Moses Hunter (12/64), Alex Gordon (16/64), William Galloway (12/64), Joseph Fisher (8/64), Newry.
11.5.1903: Wrecked at Bannow Bay, County Wexford.
15.6.1903: Register closed.

Although there were at least four schooners of the name registered in UK ports at the turn of the century, the location - Kilkeel Harbour - suggests this is Joseph Fisher's *Edith. [National Library of Ireland]*

3. FLORA 1871-1872 Wooden brigantine
O.N. 18341 100g 91n 74.1 x 19.4 x 11.5 feet
1848: Built at Launching, Prince Edward Island as FLORA.
21.5.1853: Registered at Drogheda.
11.4.1859: Registered at Irvine.
28.3.1867: Registered in the ownership of James Skimming, Castleblaney, County Monaghan.
2.6.1871: Registered at Newry in the ownership of Christopher Toomby, Omeath, County Louth (22/64), Joseph Fisher, Newry (21/64) and James Savage junior, Newry (21/64).
28.3.1872: Foundered
9.4.1872: Register closed.

4. GUITAR 1873-1896 Wooden brigantine
O.N. 33895 110g 95n 85.0 x 20.6 x 11.0 feet
1853: Built at Charlottetown, Prince Edward Island as GUITAR.
4.10.1867: Registered in the ownership of Dionisio G.F. Mancini (32/64), Newry and John Halligan (32/64), Carlingford.
16.8.1873: Sold to Moses Hunter (48/64) and Joseph Fisher (16/64), Newry.
15.1.1896: Register closed after conversion to a hulk.

5. KILKEEL (1) 1882-1895 Iron
O.N. 86707 192g 84n 120.0 x 20.0 x 9.4 feet
C. 2-cyl. by William King and Co., Glasgow; 40 HP.
16.10.1882: Launched by John Fullerton and Co., Paisley (Yard No. 53) for J. and J. Macfarlane, Glasgow as CELTIC.
20.12.1882: Acquired by Joseph Fisher (15/64) and others, Newry.
4.6.1883: Renamed KILKEEL.
3.2.1885: Owners became the Newry Steamship Co. Ltd. (Joseph Fisher and Sons, managers), Newry.
7.3.1887: Owners became the Newry and Kilkeel Steamship Co. Ltd. (Joseph Fisher and Sons, managers), Newry.
8.3.1892: Sank at Greenore in Carlingford Lough. Raised and taken to Ayr for repairs.
5.3.1895: Sold to John Coppack, trading as Coppack, Carter and Co., Connah's Quay.
7.3.1904: Owners became Thomas and John Coppack, Connah's Quay.
5.6.1905: Wrecked near Skomer whilst on a voyage from Queensferry to Swansea with a cargo of pitch.
20.7.1905: Register closed.

6. CLANRYE 1884-1886 Iron
O.N. 83012 239g 115n 138.0 x 20.5 x 10.3 feet
C. 2-cyl. by V. Coates and Co., Belfast; 55 HP, 280 IHP.
5.4.1884: Launched by Workman, Clark and Co., Belfast (Yard No. 23).
12.5.1884: Registered in the ownership of the Newry Steamship Co. Ltd. (Joseph Fisher and Sons, managers), Newry as CLANRYE.
9.4.1886: Foundered in the Irish Sea whilst on a voyage from Swansea to Newry with a cargo of coal. Her crew of nine was lost.

7. SHARK 1888-1892 Iron
O.N.55240 163g 72n 119.4 x 19.9 x 9.5 feet
I. 2-cyl. by Macnab and Co., Greenock; 40 HP.
1866: Launched by Walpole, Dublin for the Irish Sea Fishery Co. Ltd., Dublin as SHARK.
1869: Sold to the Berwick and London Steam Ship Co., Berwick and renamed TWEED.
1870: Sold to William Johnston, Liverpool, and renamed SHARK.
1871: Sold to John Miller, Liverpool.
1873: Sold to James Teulon, London.
1874: Sold to E. and J. Philips, Swansea.
1876: Sold to H.L. Worthington, London.
1876: Sold to Frank C. Strick, Swansea.
1879: Sold to Martin L. Moore, Dublin.
1879: Sold to Stephen B. Walsh, Kilmallock,County Limerick.
1880: Sold to W.L. Moore, Dublin.
1880: Sold to the Aston Steamship Co. Ltd., Connah's Quay.
1882: Sold to the Solway Steamship Co. Ltd., Whitehaven.
1888: Sold to James McFarland, Newry.
21.3.1888: Acquired by the Newry Steamship Co. Ltd., (Joseph Fisher and Sons, managers), Newry.
9.8.1888: Owners became the Newry and Kilkeel Steamship Co. Ltd.
3.5.1892: Sold to the Boston and Hull Steam Shipping Co. Ltd. (Vicars H. Walker, manager), Hull.
6.12.1899: Left North Queensferry for Hull with a cargo of granite and disappeared.
23.1.1900: Register closed.

8. ROSTREVOR (1) 1890-1898 Iron

O.N. 83020   192g 84n   120.0 x 20.1 x 9.4 feet
T. 3-cyl. by William Kemp. Glasgow; 45 NHP, 220 IHP.
23.1.1890: Launched by John Fullerton and Co., Paisley (Yard No. 88).
2.1890: Completed.
7.3.1890: Registered in the ownership of the Newry and Kilkeel Steamship Co. Ltd. (Joseph Fisher and Sons, managers), Newry as ROSTREVOR.
8.12.1898: Wrecked on Horse Rock, Ramsey Sound whilst on a voyage from Newport, Monmouthshire to Belfast with a cargo of coal. Her crew was rescued by the steamer WARRENPOINT (228/1892).
12.1.1899: Registry closed.

9. CARLINGFORD LOUGH 1891-1901

O.N. 98271   219g 87n   125.2 x 20.1 x 9.5 feet
C. 2-cyl. by Ross and Duncan, Govan; 52 NHP, 350 IHP, 10½ knots.
23.7.1891: Launched by John Fullerton and Co., Paisley (Yard No. 98).
18.8.1891: Registered in the ownership of the Carlingford Lough Steamship Co. Ltd. (Joseph Fisher and Sons, managers), Newry as CARLINGFORD LOUGH.
19.1.1901: Sold to the Wilson Brothers Bobbin Co. (1900) Ltd. (Edward W. Turner, manager), Garston.
13.10.1904: Owners became Wilson Brothers Bobbin Co. Ltd. (Edward W. Turner, manager), Garston.
7.10.1910: Sold to John T. Staples, Liverpool.
23.9.1911: Sold to the Ribble Shipping Co. Ltd. (John S. Sellers, manager), Liverpool.
12.5.1913: Wrecked on the north side of Curachan Island whilst on a voyage from Weston Point to Castlebay, Barra with a cargo of salt.
23.7.1913: Register closed.

10. WARRENPOINT 1892-1902

O.N. 98273   228g 72n   125.2 x 20.1 x 9.5 feet
C. 2-cyl. by Ross and Duncan, Govan; 51 NHP, 390 IHP.
24.6.1892: Launched by John Fullerton and Co., Paisley (Yard No.108).
7.1892: Completed.
5.8.1892: Registered in the ownership of the Carlingford Lough Steamship Co. Ltd. (Joseph Fisher and Sons, managers), Newry as WARRENPOINT.
29.5.1902: Sold to Robert Rix, Hull.
28.2.1908: Sank following a collision with the German steamer SCHWALBE (1,178/1898) about fifteen miles off the Sunk Lightvessel whilst on a voyage from Boston to Dunkirk with a cargo of beans.
10.3.1908: Register closed.

11. MOURNE 1894-1898

O.N. 102021   228g 70n   125.0 x 20.1 x 9.5 feet
C. 2-cyl. by Hall-Brown, Buttery and Co., Govan; 45 NHP, 330 IHP, 10 knots.
10.4.1894: Launched by John Fullerton and Co., Paisley (Yard No.118).
4.1894: Completed.
7.5.1894: Registered in the ownership of the Newry and Kilkeel Steamship Co. Ltd., (Joseph Fisher and Sons, managers), Newry as MOURNE.
17.12.1898: Sank following a collision with the Norwegian bargue MORGENRY (611/1888) in Penarth Roads whilst on a voyage from Cardiff to Dublin with a cargo of coal.
Later raised and rebuilt by the Channel Dry Dock Company, Passage West, Cork.
23.7.1900: Register closed.
23.7.1900: Re-registered in the ownership of the Mourne Steamship Co. Ltd. (William T. Ferris, manager), Newry.
8.10.1901: Sold to Thomas Coppack, trading as Coppack Brothers and Co., Connah's Quay.
1909: Owners became Thomas Coppack and Co., Connah's Quay.
1926: Owners became Coppack Brothers and Co., Connah's Quay.
21.9.1933: Foundered six miles south-east of St. Anthony's Lighthouse whilst on a voyage from Par to Runcorn with a cargo of china clay.
7.10.1933: Register closed.

Mourne in Coppack's ownership. *[World Ship Photo Library]*

12. KILKEEL (2) 1895-1903

O.N. 102022 252g 56n 135.0 x 21.0 x 9.4 feet
C. 2-cyl. by Hall-Brown, Buttery and Co., Glasgow; 39 NHP, 325 IHP, 10 knots.

8.6.1895: Launched by John Fullerton and Co., Paisley (Yard No.126).
10.7.1895: Registered in the ownership of the Carlingford Lough Steamship Co. Ltd. (Joseph Fisher and Sons, managers), Newry as KILKEEL.
8.9.1903: Sold to Walter B. Niven, Parrsboro, Nova Scotia.
3.5.1906: Sold to the Kilkeel Co. Ltd., Toronto, Canada.
8.1.1915: Wrecked on Bald Rock, Canso, Nova Scotia whilst on a voyage from Port Hastings to Halifax with a cargo of coal.
29.1.1915: Register closed.

13. JOSEPH FISHER 1896-1912

O.N. 102023 286g 64n 140.0 x 21.1 x 9.6 feet
C. 2-cyl. by Hall-Brown, Butttery and Co., Glasgow; 45 NHP, 400 IHP, 9½ knots.

25.7.1896: Launched by John Fullerton and Co., Paisley (Yard No.133).
14.9.1896: Registered in the ownership of the Newry and Kilkeel Steamship Co. Ltd. (Joseph Fisher and Sons, managers), Newry as JOSEPH FISHER.
2.3.1912: Sold to Duncan and Leith, Aberdeen and renamed DUNLEITH.
1915: Sold to the Ferrum Steamship Co. Ltd. (G.T. Gillie and Co., managers), Newcastle-on-Tyne.
1918: Owners became G.T. Gillie and Co., Newcastle-on-Tyne.
1919: Sold to the Harrissmith Steam Shipping Co. Ltd. (Thomas S. Jones, manager), Cardiff.
1920: Sold to the Kirk Shipping Co. Ltd. (P. and F. Atkins, managers), Cardiff.
1922: Sold to William Thomas and Sons, Amlwch.
1936: Sold to Eric C. Burden, Poole.
1938: Sold to Emlyn S. Philips, London.
1939: Sold to David Chalmers, Stronsay, Orkney.
1946: Sold to the Tay Sand Co. Ltd. (John Neilson, manager), Dundee.
4.11.1960: Breaking up began in the Dundee area.

14. CLOUGHMORE 1897-1902

O.N. 102025 547g 172n 170.0 x 26.6 x 10.0 feet
C. 2-cyl. by Hall-Brown, Buttery and Co., Govan; 66 NHP, 500 IHP.

31.8.1897: Launched by John Fullerton and Co., Paisley (Yard No.135).
28.9.1897: Registered in the ownership of the Frontier Town Steamship Co. Ltd. (Joseph Fisher and Sons, managers), Newry as CLOUGHMORE.
14.6.1902: Foundered off Tory Island whilst on a voyage from Liverpool to Galway with a cargo of maize. Seven of the 11 on board were lost.
9.9.1902: Register closed.

Joseph Fisher on trials (below) and as *Dunleith* in William Thomas's ownership (above). *[Below: P.N. Thomas collection; above: World Ship Photo Library]*

15. FRONTIER TOWN 1898-1906
O.N. 108641 294g 64n 142.5 x 21.3 x 10.4 feet
C. 2-cyl. by Hall-Brown, Buttery and Co., Govan; 47 NHP, 400 IHP, 9½ knots.
4.10.1898: Launched by John Fullerton and Co., Paisley (Yard No.144).
11.1898: Completed.
4.11.1898: Registered in the ownership of the Frontier Town Steamship Co. Ltd. (Joseph Fisher and Sons, managers), Newry as FRONTIER TOWN.
22.5.1906: Sold to James W. Little and Robert P. Little, trading as James Little and Co., Barrow-in-Furness.
19.6.1906: Renamed RIVER LUNE.
19.10.1908: Owners became James W. Little and Angus A.G. Tulloch, Manchester.
3.12.1917: Owners became James W. Little and Robert P. Little, London.
15.2.1921: Sold to Robert Brockbank, Barrow-in-Furness.
17.1.1927: Owners became James Little and Co. Ltd. (Robert Brockbank, manager), London.
27.9.1927: Sold to the St. Baldred Shipping Co. Ltd. (Arthur Tate and Co., managers), Newcastle-on-Tyne.
19.5.1930: Register closed, sold for breaking up.
6.1930: Sold to Malcolm Brechin for demolition at Granton.

16. SEAPOINT 1899-1911
O.N. 108642 593g 205n 175.0 x 26.6 x 10.5 feet
C. 2-cyl. by McKie and Baxter, Govan; 100 NHP, 500 IHP, 9 knots.
25.3.1899: Launched by S. McKnight and Co. Ltd., Ayr (Yard No.56).
4.1899: Completed.
24.4.1899: Registered in the ownership of the Frontier Town Steamship Co. Ltd. (Joseph Fisher and Sons, managers), Newry as SEAPOINT.
4.12.1911: Sold to John Stewart and Walter Fulton, trading as John Stewart and Co., Glasgow.
18.4.1912: Sold to Ernest and Arthur B. Johnson, trading as Johnson and Co., Goole.
25.10.1916: Sold to Ernest Sutcliffe (32/64) and Tom Sutcliffe (32/64), Healing and later Grimsby, Lincolnshire.
11.3.1917: Sold to the London Transport Co. Ltd. (Frank Newsom, trading as Brown, Jenkinson and Co., manager), London.
29.12.1917: Foundered off the Seven Stones whilst on a voyage from Newport, Monmouthshire to Rouen with a cargo of coal.
16.3.1918: Register closed.

17. ROSTREVOR (2) 1899-1917
O.N. 108644 298g 82n 142.5 x 21.3 x 10.4 feet
C. 2-cyl. by Hall-Brown, Buttery and Co., Govan; 61 NHP, 400 IHP, 9½ knots.
25.8.1899: Launched by John Fullerton and Co., Paisley (Yard No.150).
9.10.1899: Registered in the ownership of the Newry and Kilkeel Steamship Co. Ltd. (Joseph Fisher and Sons, managers), Newry as ROSTREVOR.
12.4.1917: Foundered 25 miles north west of the Skerries whilst on a voyage from Newry to Manchester with a cargo of granite setts.
17.4.1917: Register closed.

18. CLONALLON 1899-1904
O.N. 108645 295g 80n 142.5 x 21.3 10.4 feet
C. 2-cyl. by Hall-Brown, Buttery and Co., Govan; 61 NHP, 400 IHP, 9½ knots.
6.10.1899: Launched by John Fullerton and Co., Paisley (Yard No.151).
21.12.1899: Registered in the ownership of the Frontier Town Steamship Co. Ltd. (Joseph Fisher and Sons, managers), Newry as CLONALLON.
8.12.1904: Left Swansea for Dublin with a cargo of coal and disappeared.
23.1.1905: Register closed.

19. PORTADOWN 1900-1935
O.N. 108646 291g 78n 142.5 x 21.3 x 10.4 feet
C. 2-cyl. by Hall-Brown, Buttery and Co., Govan; 61 NHP, 500 IHP, 9½ knots.
13.2.1900: Launched by John Fullerton and Co., Paisley (Yard No.152).
12.3.1900: Registered in the ownership of the Newry and Kilkeel Steamship Co. Ltd. (Joseph Fisher and Sons, managers), Newry as PORTADOWN.
27.7.1935: Sold to Samuel Gray, Belfast.
12.1935: Broken up at Dalmuir by W.H. Arnott, Young Ltd.
29.1.1936: Register closed.

20. ASHTON 1901-1912
O.N. 108649 283g 77n 142.2 x 21.2 x 10.5 feet
C. 2-cyl. by A. Rodgers and Co., Govan; 61 NHP, 400 IHP, 9½ knots.
13.11.1901: Launched by John Fullerton and Co., Paisley (Yard No. 162).
12. 1901: Completed.
11.2.1901: Registered in the ownership of the Carlingford Lough Steamship Co. Ltd. (Joseph Fisher and Sons, managers), Newry as ASHTON.
16.8.1912: Sold to Richard Penberthy Care, Cardiff.
21.6.1915: Owners became the Care and Young Shipping Co. Ltd. (Richard P. Care, manager), Cardiff.
27.2.1917: Sold to William A. Jenkins and Co., Swansea.
26.2.1920: Sold to Edward T. Lindley, London.
9.11.1921: Sold to Thomas W. Barnett (Clifford Jenks, manager, trading as Barnett, Jenks and Co.), Cardiff.
21.12.1921: Sold to Edward G. Willis trading as Guernsey Coasters Ltd., Guernsey.
4.12.1925: Sank near Boompje in Austruweel Roads, River Scheldt following a collision with the United States steamer FEDERAL (6,868/1918) whilst on a voyage from Fremington to Antwerp with a cargo of china clay. Four of her crew of ten were lost.
1.2.1926: Register closed.

21. ORIOR 1903-1908
O.N. 115632 284g 75n 142.7 x 21.3 x 10.5 feet
C. 2-cyl. by by A. Rodger and Co., Govan; 61 NHP, 400 IHP, 9½ knots.
25.2.1903: Launched by John Fullerton and Co., Paisley (Yard No.171).
3.1903: Completed.
24.3.1903: Registered in the ownership of the Carlingford Lough Steamship Co. Ltd. (Joseph Fisher and Sons, managers), Newry as ORIOR.
7.3.1908: Left Newport, Monmouthshire for Belfast with a cargo of coal and disappeared.
3.4.1903: Register closed.

Clonallon at Dublin Dockyard, where much of Fishers' repair work was carried out. *[P.N. Thomas collection]*

Portadown, the last surviving 'long back'. *[World Ship Photo Library]*

22. ABBOT 1903-1915

O.N. 115631 282g 73n
142.5 x 21.3 x 10.5 feet
C. 2-cyl. by A. Rodgers and Co., Govan.; 61 NHP, 400 IHP, 9½ knots.

4.1903: Completed by John Fullerton and Co., Paisley (Yard No.172).

24.4.1903: Registered in the ownership of the Frontier Town Steamship Co. Ltd. (Joseph Fisher and Sons, managers), Newry as ABBOT.

22.4.1915: Sold to Joseph Llewelyn and John T. Evans, Cardiff.

30.6.1915: Sold to the Care and Young Shipping Co. Ltd., Cardiff.

6.10.1916: Sold to William A. Jenkins and Co., Swansea.

23.12.1916: Sold to Ernest Wilford, London.

20.7.1917: Sold to Channel Transports Ltd. (Stone and Rolfe, managers), Llanelly.

30.8.1917: Sold to the Abbot Steamship Co. Ltd. (Robert A. Constantine and Thomas H. Donking, managers), Middlesbrough.

22.6.1918: Stone and Rolfe became managers.

1.11.1918: Sold to Town Line (London) Ltd. (Harrison, Sons and Co., managers), London.

15.2.1919: Renamed IVYTOWN.

9.2.1924: Sold to Norman B. Leslie, Dundee.

12.12.1924: Sold to the Great Yarmouth Shipping Co. Ltd., Yarmouth.

22.2.1927: Sold to Arthur Ogg, Aberdeen.

4.1.1929: Sold to Steam Coasters Ltd. (Alfred B. Wade, manager), Cardiff.

2.7.1934: Sold to Arthur Simpson (Comben, Longstaff and Co. Ltd., managers), London.

4.1935: Sold to J.N. Vlassopoulos, Greece and renamed BALTIKI.

29.7.1935: Registered in the ownership of the Brook Shipping Co. Ltd. (Comben, Longstaff and Co. Ltd., managers), London as KENTBROOK.

27.12.1935: Left Plymouth for Portsmouth with a cargo of stone and disappeared.

12.10.1936: Register closed.

Abbot on trials. *[Glasgow University Archives DC101/0852]*

Dromore in the River Avon whilst in Care and Young ownership.

23. DROMORE 1903-1915
O.N. 115632 286g 77n 142.5 x 21.3 x 10.2 feet
C. 2-cyl. by A. Rodger and Co., Govan; 61 NHP, 400 BHP, 9½ knots.
13.5.1903: Launched by John Fullerton and Co., Paisley (Yard No.173).
6.6.1903: Registered in the ownership of the Frontier Town Steamship Co. Ltd. (Joseph Fisher and Sons, managers), Newry as DROMORE.
7.4.1915: Sold to the Care and Young Shipping Co. Ltd. (Richard P. Care, manager), Cardiff.
27.2.1917: Sold to William A. Jenkin, Swansea.
28.2.1917: Sold to Samuel W. Oakley, London.
18.5.1917: Sunk by the German submarine UC 70 six miles south of St. Martin's Point, Guernsey whilst on a voyage from St. Malo to Swansea in ballast.
29.6.1917: Register closed.

24. ULIDIA 1903-1916
O.N. 115633 3,081g 1,988n 323.0 x 47.1 x 23.8 feet
T. 3-cyl. by John Readhead and Sons, South Shields; 300 NHP, 1,200 IHP, 10 knots.
10.9.1903: Launched by by John Readhead and Sons, South Shields (Yard No. 372).
10.1903: Completed.
15.10.1903: Registered in the ownership of the Mercantile Steam Ship Company of Ulster Ltd. (1903) (Joseph Fisher and Sons, managers), Newry as ULIDIA.
29.8.1912: Owners became the Mercantile Steam Ship Company of Ulster Ltd.
12.2.1916: Sold to the Cliffe Steamship Co. Ltd. (George T. Readhead, manager), Newcastle-on-Tyne.
6.9.1917: Ashore at Soroka in the White Sea whilst loading timber for the United Kingdom.
11.8.1919: Register closed, but subsequently refloated and repaired.

1920: Owner D/S A/S Skaraas (C.K. Gran, manager), Bergen, Norway and renamed SKARAAS.
1924: Sold to A/S Phoenix, (J. Erland, manager), Bergen.
1928: Sold to Skibs. A/S Nansett (Iver Bugge, manager), Larvik.
1935: Sold to the Hwah Sung Steamship Co. Ltd., Shanghai, China and renamed HWAH JANG.
1940: Sold to the Java-China Trading Co., Willemstad, Curacoa and renamed WILHELMINA.
1943: Owners became the United States War Shipping Administration, Washington, U.S.A. and renamed COVENTRY.
5.1945: Stranded off Cuba and later declared a constructive total loss, but subsequently refloated.
1946: Sold to the Hwah Sung Steamship Co. Ltd., Shanghai, China and renamed HWAH JANG.
11.6.1948: Wrecked on Piting Rock in position 29.53 north by 122.31 east whilst on a voyage from Keelung to Shanghai with coal. Subsequently sank.

25. YEWS 1905-1910
O.N. 115634 333g 100n 142.6 x 23.4 x 10.1 feet
C. 2-cyl. by Renfrew Brothers and Co., Irvine; 47 NHP, 400 IHP, 9½ knots.
10.11.1905: Launched by John Fullerton and Co., Paisley (Yard No.186).
13.12.1905: Completed for the Frontier Town Steamship Co. Ltd. (Joseph Fisher and Sons, managers), Newry as YEWS.
20.6.1910: Sank off the Skerries following a collision the previous day with the French steamer LA ROCHELLE (1,360/1883) whilst on a voyage from Harrington to Port Talbot with a cargo of pig iron. The LA ROCHELLE sank; ten of her crew of nineteen and the crew of the YEWS being picked up by the steamers PANMURE (321/1859) and ALDERNEY.
29.6.1910: Register closed.

26. OAK (1)   1906-1951
O.N. 115636   346g 80n   142.5 x 23.3 x 10.1 feet
C. 2-cyl. by Renfrew Brothers and Co., Irvine; 47 NHP,
400 IHP, 10 knots.
20.9.1906: Launched by John Fullerton and Co., Paisley
(Yard No.191).
10.1906: Completed.
22.10.1906: Registered in the ownership of the Newry and
Kilkeel Steamship Co. Ltd.   (Joseph Fisher and Sons,
managers), Newry as OAK.

15.9.1951: Arrived at Llanelli to be broken up by the Rees
Shipbreaking Co. Ltd.
10.1951: Work began.
21.1.1952: Register closed.

Oak with open bridge and mizzen mast (above) and with
wheelhouse and no mizzen in the Mersey post-war (below).
[Both: World Ship Photo Library]

27. ELM 1906-1909

O.N. 115637   349g   81n   142.6 x 23.4 x 10.1 feet
C. 2-cyl. by Fisher and Co., Paisley; 47 NHP, 400 IHP, 10 knots.

29.11.1906: Launched by John Fullerton and Co., Paisley (Yard No.192).

12. 1906: Completed.

29.12.1906: Registered in the ownership of the Frontier Town Steamship Co. Ltd. (Joseph Fisher and Sons, managers), Newry as ELM.

6.7.1909: Stranded on Crow Rock, Linney Head whilst on a voyage from Whitehaven to Briton Ferry with a cargo of pig iron.

30.8.1909: Register closed.

28. OLIVE (1)   1907-1951

O.N. 115639   354g   86n   142.5 x 23.4 x 10.2 feet
C. 2-cyl. by Renfrew Brothers and Co., Irvine; 47 NHP, 400 IHP, 9$\frac{1}{2}$ knots.

21.8.1907: Launched by John Fullerton and Co., Paisley (Yard 197).

9.1907: Completed.

27.9.1907: Registered in the ownership of the Carlingford Lough Steamship Co. Ltd. (Joseph Fisher and Sons, managers), Newry as OLIVE.

14.9.1912: Owners became the Frontier Town Steamship Co. Ltd., Newry.

15.9.1951: Arrived at Llanelli to be broken up by the Rees Shipbreaking Co. Ltd., who began work during October.

21.1.1952: Register closed.

This page: two views of *Olive* with an open bridge arriving at (left) and leaving Preston (below). Her mizzen has a distinct rake to port. *[Below: World Ship Photo Library]*

Opposite: three views of *Pine*. Note that between the upper and middle views the open area below the bridge has been filled, presumably with accommodation. *[Middle and bottom: World Ship Photo Library]*

29. PINE   1907-1936

O.N. 115640   355g 87n   142.7 x 23.4 x 10.2 feet

C. 2-cyl. by Renfrew Brothers and Co., Irvine; 47 NHP, 400 IHP, 10 knots.

25.9.1907: Launched by John Fullerton and Co., Paisley (Yard No. 198).

11.1907: Completed.

6.11.1907: Registered in the ownership of the Frontier Town Steamship Co. (1897) Ltd. (Joseph Fisher and Sons, managers), Newry as PINE.

29.8.1912: Owners became the Frontier Town Steamship Co. Ltd. (Joseph Fisher and Sons, managers), Newry.

12.11.1936: Sunk in collision with the steamer OLIVE (328/1907) whilst at anchor in Carlingford Lough during a voyage from Garston to Dundalk with a cargo of coal. Her crew was rescued by the OLIVE.

5.1937: Refloated by Samuel Gray, Belfast.

12.11.1937: Re-registered in the ownership of Samuel Gray, Belfast.

15.4.1938: 32/64 shares sold to Isaac Stewart, trading as Stewart and Partners, Belfast.

12.11.1939: Owners became Isaac Stewart (64/64), Belfast.

16.2.1940: Renamed SECOND.

14.6.1955: Arrived at Troon for breaking up by the West of Scotland Shipbreaking Co. Ltd.

1.7.1955: Register closed.

30. MAPLE 1909-1910

O.N. 127471 341g 125n 142.7 x 23.6 x 10.4 feet

C. 2-cyl. by Fishers Ltd., Paisley; 47 NHP, 360 IHP.

28.4.1909: Launched by John Fullerton and Co., Paisley (Yard No. 208).

5.1909: Completed.

9.6.1909: Registered in the ownership of the Carlingford Lough Steamship Co. Ltd. (Joseph Fisher and Sons, managers), Newry as MAPLE.

9.12.1910: Foundered ten miles north west of Peel, Isle of Man whilst on a voyage from Belfast to Whitehaven with a cargo of iron ore.

19.12.1910: Register closed.

31. ALDER 1909-1937

O.N. 127472 341g 126n 142.8 x 23.6 x 10.3 feet

C. 2-cyl. by Fishers Ltd., Paisley; 47 NHP, 360 IHP.

3.8.1909: Launched by John Fullerton and Co., Paisley (Yard No. 209).

9.1909: Completed.

11.9.1909: Registered in the ownership of the Newry and Kilkeel Steamship Co. Ltd. (Joseph Fisher and Sons, managers), Newry as ALDER.

4.4.1937: Sunk in collision with the steamer LADY CAVAN (602/1906) in Carlingford Lough whilst on a voyage from Irvine to Newry with a cargo of coal. Only three of the nine on board survived.

7.9.1937: Register closed.

Two views of *Alder*. Accommodation has been added below the bridge.
[Lower: World Ship Photo Library]

3.1938: Raised by Samuel Gray, Belfast and beached at Greenore.

30.5.1938: Sold to T.W. Ward Ltd. for breaking up.

15.6.1938: Arrived at Barrow-in-Furness in tow of the steamer BEN MAY (154/1894) for demolition.

Walnut

32. WALNUT (1) 1910-1941
O.N. 127473 340g 125n 142.6 x 23.6 x 10.4 feet
C. 2-cyl. by Fishers Ltd., Paisley; 50 NHP, 400 IHP, 9 knots.
25.2.1910: Launched by John Fullerton and Co., Paisley (Yard No. 214).
3.1910: Completed.

24.3.1910: Registered in the ownership of the Frontier Town Steamship Co. Ltd. (Joseph Fisher and Sons, managers), Newry as WALNUT.
27.10.1941: Left Birkenhead for Newry with a cargo of coal and disappeared.
10.9.1942: Register closed.

33. MANGO 1912-1933
O.N. 127475 341g 125n
142.8 x 23.6 x 10.4 feet
C. 2-cyl. by Fishers Ltd., Paisley; 47 NHP, 360 IHP.
4.7.1912: Launched by John Fullerton and Co., Paisley (Yard No. 223).
7.1912: Completed.
27.7.1912: Registered in the ownership of the Frontier Town Steamship Co. Ltd. (Joseph Fisher and Sons, managers), Newry as MANGO.
6.2.1933: Wrecked about three miles west of Arranmore Lighthouse, Donegal whilst on voyage from Sligo to Coleraine in ballast.
24.2.1933: Register closed.

Mango at Preston. *[World Ship Photo Library]*

34. UPAS 1913-1915

O.N. 127476   470g   181n   168.1 x 25.7 x 10.0 feet
C. 2-cyl. by Ross and Duncan, Govan; 72 NHP, 750 IHP.
21.2.1913: Launched by John Fullerton and Co., Paisley (Yard No. 226).
3.1913: Completed.
3.4.1913: Registered in the ownership of Joseph Fisher and Sons, Newry as UPAS.
18.3.1915: Foundered off Ballyherbert, County Down whilst on a voyage from Ayr to Warrenpoint with a cargo of coal. There were only two survivors.
27.3.1915: Register closed.

35. ASPEN 1915-1954

O.N. 127477   333g   123n   142.6 x 23.6 x 10.1 feet
C. 2-cyl. by Fishers Ltd., Paisley; 47 NHP, 360 IHP, 8½ knots.
8.12.1914: Launched by John Fullerton and Co., Paisley (Yard No. 237).
1.1915: Completed.
7.1.1915: Registered in the ownership of the Newry and Kilkeel Steamship Co. Ltd. (Joseph Fisher and Sons, managers), Newry as ASPEN.
22.6.1954: Arrived at Llanelli to be broken up by the Rees Shipbreaking Co. Ltd.
2.10.1954: Register closed.

Opposite: *Upas* on trials, 3rd April 1913. *[Glasgow University Archives DC101/1609]*
This page: *Aspen* with three masts, two masts, and a wheelhouse. *[Right: A. Duncan]*

36. MOYGANNON/AGBA 1924-1940

O.N. 127478 498g 193n 164.9 x 25.7 x 9.5 feet

T. 3-cyl. by William Beardmore and Co. Ltd., Coatbridge, Glasgow; 99 NHP, 580 IHP, 9 knots.

27.7.1921: Launched by Dublin Shipbuilders Ltd., Ringsend, Dublin (Yard No.16).

10.1921: Completed.

20.10.1921: Registered in the ownership of the Newry Provincial Coal Co. Ltd. (Frederick Ferris, manager), Newry as MOYGANNON.

16.12.1924: Sold by mortgagees in possession to the Newry and Kilkeel Steamship Co. Ltd. (Joseph Fisher and Sons Ltd., managers), Newry.

24.12.1938: Renamed AGBA.

12.10.1940: Sank in the Firth of Clyde following a collision with the steamer MANO (1,418/1925) whilst on a voyage from Newry to Ayr in ballast.

18.12.1940: Register closed.

37. POPLAR 1927-1942

O.N. 127479 343g 122n 142.7 x 23.6 x 10.3 feet

C. 2-cyl. by Fishers Ltd., Paisley; 52 NHP, 500 IHP, 9.5 knots.

31.5.1927: Launched by John Fullerton and Co., Paisley (Yard No. 277).

7.1927: Completed.

21.7.1927: Registered in the ownership of the Frontier Town Steamship Co. Ltd. (Joseph Fisher and Sons Ltd., managers), Newry as POPLAR.

14.10.1942: Wrecked off Harrington, Cumberland whilst on a voyage from Newry to Whitehaven in ballast. Wreck later sold for scrap.

4.2.1943: Register closed.

Moygannon (above) and *Poplar* (below). [Both: World Ship Photo Library].

38. PALM 1927-1963
O.N. 127477 344g 122n
142.7 x 23.6 x 10.3 feet
C. 2-cyl. by Fishers Ltd.,
Paisley; 52 NHP.
16.8.1927: Launched by
John Fullerton and Co.,
Paisley (Yard No. 278).
9.1927: Completed for the
Newry and Kilkeel
Steamship Co. Ltd. (Joseph
Fisher and Sons Ltd.,
managers), Newry as
PALM.
9.7.1963: Arrived at Preston
to be broken up by T.W.
Ward Ltd.

39. JASMINE 1932-1952
O.N. 160291 353g 124n
142.5 x 23.6 x 10.5 feet
T. 3-cyl. by Aitchison, Blair
Ltd., Clydebank; 60 NHP.
26.11.1931: Launched by
Scott and Sons, Bowling
(Yard No.320).
1.1932: Completed.
Registered in the ownership
of the Newry and Kilkeel
Steamship Co. Ltd. (Joseph
Fisher and Sons Ltd.,
managers), Newry as
JASMINE.
10.1952: Arrived at Troon
for breaking up by W.H.
Arnott, Young and Co.
25.10.1952: Demolition
began.

Palm with open bridge (top)
and after conversion to a tar
carrier, with wheelhouse and
spark arrester (middle).

Jasmine before having a
wheelhouse (bottom) (see
also page 78). *[All: World Ship
Photo Library]*

40. ROWAN   1932-1956

O.N. 160292   500g   188n   173.0 x 25.6 x 10.0 feet
T. 3-cyl. by Aitchison, Blair Ltd., Clydebank; 86 NHP.
26.1.1932: Launched by Scott and Sons, Bowling (Yard No.321).
2.1932: Completed for the Frontier Town Steamship Co. Ltd. (Joseph Fisher and Sons Ltd., managers), Newry as ROWAN.
20.8.1956: Arrived at Dublin to be broken up by the Hammond Lane Foundry Co. Ltd.

Rowan in the River Ribble in August 1945 (above) and a peacetime view of her in Preston (below). *[Top: World Ship Photo Library]*

98

41. BROOM 1934-1954
O.N. 160293   347g 121n   142.8 x 23.6 x 10.5 feet
T. 3-cyl. by Aitchison, Blair Ltd., Clydebank; 62.5 NHP, 500 IHP, 10 knots.
28.5.1934: Launched by Scott and Sons, Bowling (Yard No.335).
6.1934: Completed.
20.6.1934: Registered in the ownership of the Frontier Town Steamship Co. Ltd. (Joseph Fisher and Sons Ltd., managers), Newry as BROOM.

28.10.1954: Arrived at Barrow-in-Furness to be broken up by T.W. Ward Ltd.
2.3.1955: Register closed.

Broom before (above, at Waterford) and after (below, at Preston) fitting a wheelhouse. *[Top: J. Hartery]*

42. THORN 1934-1954

O.N. 160294 347g 121n 142.8 x 23.6 x 10.5 feet

T. 3-cyl. by Aitchison, Blair Ltd., Clydebank; 62 NHP.

31.5.1934: Launched by Scott and Sons, Bowling (Yard No.326).

6.1934: Completed for the Newry and Kilkeel Steamship Co. Ltd. (Joseph Fisher and Sons Ltd., managers), Newry as THORN.

1954: Sold to Hay and Co. (Lerwick) Ltd. (W.N. Lindsay Ltd., Leith, managers), Lerwick and renamed COLUMBINE.

24.12.1957: Ran aground at North Head, Peterhead and broke up in heavy seas, her forepart sinking 30.12.1957. She was on a voyage from Baltasound to Middlesbrough with a cargo of serpentine stone.

Thorn with open bridge (top), in the winter of 1948 (middle), and at Preston (bottom). *[Top: R. Fenton collection; middle: Welsh Industrial and Maritime Museum 1388/1487; bottom: World Ship Photo Library]*

Privet on trials. *[Glasgow University Archives DC101/1471]*

43. PRIVET 1936-1940

O.N. 160295 360g 129n 142.2 x 23.6 x 10.5 feet
T. 3-cyl. by Aitchison, Blair Ltd., Clydebank; 62.5 NHP, 500 IHP, $9^3/4$ knots.
17.9.1936: Launched by Scott and Sons, Bowling (Yard No.339).
10.1936: Completed.
12.10.1936: Registered in the ownership of the Newry and Kilkeel Steamship Co. Ltd. (Joseph Fisher and Sons Ltd., managers), Newry as PRIVET.
5.12.1940: Left Birkenhead for Belfast with a cargo of coal and disappeared.
29.1.1941: Posted missing. She is considered to have been a marine loss rather than a war loss.
19.9.1941: Register closed.

44. BAMBOO 1936-1953

O.N. 160296 360g 129n 142.2 x 23.6 x 10.5 feet
T. 3-cyl. by Aitchison, Blair Ltd., Clydebank; 62.5 NHP, 500 IHP, $9^3/4$ knots.
1953: Oil engne 6-cyl. 4SCDA by A/S Volund, Copenhagen; 395 BHP, 8 knots.
1.10.1936: Launched by Scott and Sons, Bowling (Yard No. 340).
27.10.1936: Registered in the ownership of the Frontier Town Steamship Co. Ltd. (Joseph Fisher and Sons Ltd., managers), Newry as BAMBOO.
11.1936: Completed.
7.1953: Sold to Rederiet Uffe A/S (C.W. Folting, manager), Copenhagen, Denmark, renamed GRANITA and fitted with an oil engine.
1956: Manager became J.P.B. Nielsen.
1958: Managers became Fa. Borge Nielsen and Co., Faaborg.
1959: Renamed PUTTE PAN.
1962: Sold to U.W. Bahnsen, Svendborg, Denmark and renamed KARIN BAHNSEN.
1965: Sold to Andreas B. Kromann Partrederi, Marstal, Denmark and renamed HENRIK.
1970: Sold to the Norwegian-Caribbean Shipping Co. (St. Lucia) Ltd., Panama and renamed MORUKA.
1986: Renamed MORUKA EXPRESS and registered in San Lorenzo, Honduras.
27.3.1988: Towed out of Miami River for Haiti.
11.1997: Deleted from *Lloyd's Register.*

Bamboo in the Mersey in July 1950. *[World Ship Photo Library]*

45. OPEPE 1937-1955

O.N. 160297   362g   131n   148.1 x 23.6 x 10.5 feet
T. 3-cyl. by Aitchison, Blair Ltd., Clydebank; 62 NHP.
8.7.1937: Launched by Scott and Sons, Bowling (Yard No.342).
8.1937: Completed for the Frontier Town Steamship Co. Ltd. (Joseph Fisher and Sons Ltd., managers), Newry as OPEPE.
1955: Sold to the Thorn Line Ltd. (S. William Coe and Co. Ltd., managers), Liverpool and renamed BANNQUEST.
8.4.1958: Arrived at Boom for breaking up by the Boom Shipbreaking Co.

46. KARRI 1938-1957

O.N. 160298   354g   179n   147.0 x 23.9 x 8.8 feet
Oil engine 8-cyl. 4SCSA by Humboldt-Deutz Motoren A.G., Koln-Deutz, Germany; 94 NHP.

5.1942: Oil engine 6-cyl. 2SCSA made by British Auxiliaries Ltd., Glasgow; 520 BHP, 10 knots.
30.6.1938: Launched by Scott and Sons, Bowling (Yard No. 347)
9.1938: Completed for the Newry and Kilkeel Steamship Co. Ltd. (Joseph Fisher and Sons Ltd., managers), Newry as KARRI.
15.1.1942: Caught fire after being damaged by a mine two miles north of the Bar Light Vessel whilst on a voyage from Garston to Dublin with a cargo of coal.
1957: Sold to W.N. Lindsay, Leith.
1967: Sold to M. Gigilinis and D. Kalkasinas, Piraeus, Greece.
1967: Sold to A. Iatridi Brothers, Thessalonika, Greece and renamed ATHANASSIOS 1.
1976: Sold to K.J. Palmos, Greece.
18.5.1977: Sank in position 42.30 north by 06.07 east after her engine failed in heavy weather. Her crew was rescued.

Less than a year separated the building of the *Opepe* (above) and the motorship *Karri* (below). *[Both: World Ship Photo Library]*

Balsa (top) and *Ebony* (bottom). *[Both: World Ship Photo Library]*

47. BALSA 1947-1957

O.N. 180060 405g 146n 148.1 x 24.6 x 10.4 feet
T. 3-cyl. by Aitchison, Blair Ltd., Clydebank; 63 NHP.
21.5.1947: Launched by Scott and Sons, Bowling (Yard No.380).
7.1947: Completed for the Frontier Town Steamship Co. Ltd. (Joseph Fisher and Sons Ltd., managers), Newry as BALSA.
1956: Owners became Newry and Killkeel Steamship Co. Ltd. (Joseph Fisher and Sons Ltd., managers), Newry.
1957: Sold to John S. Monks and Co. Ltd., Liverpool and renamed ROCKVILLE.
3.1963: Broken up by Lacmots Ltd. at Glasson Dock.

48. EBONY 1947-1957

O.N. 180061 405g 146n 148.1 x 24.6 x 10.4 feet
T. 3-cyl. by Aitchison, Blair Ltd., Clydebank; 63 NHP.
1967: Oil engine 6-cyl. 4SCSA made in 1957 by Klockner-Humboldt-Deutz A.G., Koln-Deutz, West Germany; 500 BHP, 12 knots.
20.8.1947: Launched by Scott and Sons, Bowling (Yard No.381).
10.1947: Completed for the Newry and Kilkeel Steamship Co. Ltd. (Joseph Fisher and Sons Ltd., managers), Newry as EBONY.
1957: Sold to John S. Monks and Co. Ltd., Liverpool and renamed MONKSVILLE.
1963: Sold to Athanassios and Petros Callitsis, Piraeus, Greece.
1964: Renamed GEORGE CALLITSIS.
1969: Owners became George A. Callitsis Succesors S.A., Piraeus and renamed SYNERGASIA.
1970: Sold to Loukos Brothers and Phil Mavros, Piraeus and renamed PHILIPPOS.
1983: Sold to Tsagala Brothers, Piraeus and renamed STAVROS T.
1991: Sold to Dimiko Naftiki Eteria, Piraeus.
5.1995: Sank in port and subsequently broken up.

49. OAK (2) 1953-1964

O.N. 183664 709g 358n 189.6 x 31.7 x 10.8 feet

Oil engine 5-cyl. 2SCSA by British Polar Engines Ltd., Glasgow; 850 BHP, 11 knots.

2.2.1953: Launched by Scott and Sons, Bowling (Yard No.397) for the Newry and Kilkeel Steamship Co. Ltd. (Joseph Fisher and Sons Ltd., managers), Newry as OAK.

4.1953: Completed.

1964: Sold to J. and A. Gardner and Co. Ltd., Glasgow and renamed SAINT BRIDGET.

1970: Owners became the Strathpark Shipping Co. Ltd. (J. and A. Gardner and Co. Ltd., managers), Glasgow.

6.12.1972: Whilst her cargo of nitroglycerine was being transhipped to the motor vessel AUTOLYCUS (7,705/1949) in Carrick roads it was discovered that some of the cases were leaking.

14.12.1972: Taken out and deliberately exploded and sunk forty miles south of the Lizard.

Oak (top), *Walnut* (middle) and *Olive* in later condition (bottom, see also page 80) *[Top: A. Duncan; bottom: World Ship Photo Library]*

50. WALNUT (2) 1956-1973
O.N. 186851   539g 282n   185.0 x 28.4 x 12.0 feet
Oil engine 8-cyl. 4SCSA by Maschinenfabriek Deutz, Koln-Deutz, West Germany; 575 BHP.
30.9.1955: Launched by Scheepswerf Hoogezand J. Bodewes, Hoogezand, Holland (Yard No.74).
12.1955: Completed for the Whitehaven Shipping Co. Ltd. (Anthony and Bainbridge Ltd., managers), Newcastle-on-Tyne as WHITEHAVEN.
1956: Acquired by Joseph Fisher and Sons Ltd., Newry and renamed WALNUT.
1973: Sold to Spyros and Filippos Aravinis, Piraeus, Greece and renamed COSTAS A.
1980: Sold to A. Katopodi, Greece.
1.4.1981: Foundered at Dirachion, Albania.

51. OLIVE (2) 1963-1981
O.N. 300518   791g 402n   201.7 x 32.7 x 12.8 feet
Oil engine 8-cyl. 4SCSA by the English Electric Co. Ltd., Vulcan Works, Newton-le-Willows, Lancashire; 900 BHP, 11 knots.
19.9.1963: Launched by Scott and Sons (Bowling) Ltd., Bowling (Yard No.429) for Joseph Fisher and Sons Ltd. Ltd., Newry as OLIVE.
12.1963: Completed
1.7.1978: Managers became Cawood Shipping Services Ltd.
1.5.1981: Sold to the Ulster Steamship Co. Ltd., Belfast.
1983: Registered in the Cayman Islands.
1983: Sold to the Omega Maritime Corporation, Panama and renamed OMEGA LADY.
12.2.1984: Sank after developing leaks three days earlier in bad weather about 70 miles off Puerto Cortes, Honduras in position 16.09 north by 86.46 east whilst on a voyage from Aruba to Puerto Cortes with a cargo of sulphur.

Managed for the Ministry of War Transport

EMPIRE ALBANY 1944-1946
O.N. 166695   306g 135n   137.0 x 24.6 x 7.9 feet
Oil engines 6-cyl. 2SCSA by Crossley Brothers Ltd., Manchester; 330 BHP, 9 knots.
3.10.1944: Launched by Richard's Ironworks Ltd., Lowestoft (Yard No. 337).
28.11.1944: Registered in the ownership of the Ministry of War Transport, London (Joseph Fisher and Sons Ltd., Newry, managers) as EMPIRE ALBANY.
12.1944: Completed.
1946: Owners became Ministry of Transport, London.
8.7.1946: Sold to Mrs. Primrose Dowds, Grangemouth (Arthur Dowds, Dublin, manager).
29.10.1946: Renamed ALBANY.

20.11.1946: Sailed from Port Talbot for Rosslare with a cargo of coal and disappeared. Two boats were washed ashore on the Pembrokeshire coast two days later.
22.7.1947: Register closed.

Antrim Iron Ore Co. Ltd.
Acquired by James Fisher and Sons Ltd. in August 1929

1. GLENAAN 1929-1932 Iron
O.N. 86550   333g 140n   159.2 x 23.1 x 11.3 feet
C. 2-cyl. by McIlwaine and Lewis, Belfast; 60 HP.
3.1884: Launched by McIlwaine and Lewis, Belfast (Yard No.21).
1884: Registered in the ownership of William A. Grainger, Belfast as THEME.
1888: Sold to the Volana Steamship Co. Ltd. (John K. Rogers and Allan H. Bright, managers), Liverpool.
31.10.1889: Renamed VOLANTE.
20.4.1892: Allan H. Bright and Ernest Cook, trading as Rogers and Bright, became managers.
2.3.1905: Manager became Ernest Cook.
30.10.1912: Sold to John Kelly Ltd. (Samuel Kelly, manager), Belfast.
31.10.1912: Renamed CULTRA.
29.5.1914: Sold to William A. Grainger, Belfast.
17.6.1914: Renamed THEME.
7.5.1915: Owner became Mrs. Dorothea A.M. Grainger, Belfast
14.10.1915: Sold to the Antrim Iron Ore Co. Ltd., Belfast.
10.11.1915: Renamed GLENAAN.
21.1.1932: Wrecked on Torlinn Point, South Arran, whilst on a voyage from Belfast to Glasgow in ballast.
6.2.1932: Register closed.

2. GLENDUN (2) 1931-1940
O.N. 136352   633g 239n   180.5 x 28.6 x 10.8 feet
T. 3-cyl. by Aitchison, Blair Ltd., Glasgow; 852 NHP, 750 IHP, 10 knots.
1915: Launched by Scott and Sons, Bowling (Yard No. 257) for John Kelly Ltd., Belfast as CLAREISLAND.
9.1915: Completed.
7.9.1915: Registered in the ownership of Arthur Guinness, Son and Co. Ltd., Dublin as CLAREISLAND.
10.7.1931: Acquired by the Antrim Iron Ore Co. Ltd., Belfast.
15.9.1931: Renamed GLENDUN.
15.2.1940: Wrecked near Maughold Head, Isle of Man whilst on a voyage from Garston to Belfast with a cargo of coal.
3.5.1940: Register closed.

Glendun [World Ship Photo Library]

RUNCIMAN (LONDON) LTD.
CANATLANTIC LTD.
Roy Fenton

The shipping companies dealt with in this chapter owe their origins to the determination of newspaper owners to maintain their supplies of newsprint, faced with the fall of Norway in the spring of 1940. Compared with the suffering of German-occupied Europe, and the grave danger facing the United Kingdom in the summer of 1940, the plight of the press may not seem a major concern. But newspaper proprietors considered they had a solemn duty to inform the British public about Nazi iniquities, to titillate the people in those dark days, and to maintain their own power and profits.

Paper, pulp and the press

The British paper and printing industry had begun to worry about pulp and paper early in 1940, when war between Finland and Russia as well as German power in the Baltic restricted supplies. The situation became chronic almost overnight with the German invasion of Norway in April, an invasion precipitated by Hitler's conviction that the UK was itself contemplating occupation of Norway, a belief which was correct and which he held to for some time after his own invasion of the country. With the occupation of Denmark as well as Norway, Germany had control of the Skagerrak and Kattegat, leaving no chance of supplies reaching the UK from neutral Sweden.

The paper and printing industries now turned their eyes across the Atlantic. Canada and Newfoundland had expanded pulp and paper production enormously after the First World War, but then experienced embarrassing overcapacity in the depression. However, by the outbreak of the Second World War demand from the United States had almost caught up with supply once again, and Canada's production was rivalling that of the rest of the world. Canada regarded the USA as its natural market, and in 1938 only about 50,000 tons of pulp and paper was sold to the UK, barely one per cent of Canadian production. Despite their membership of the Commonwealth, and they themselves being at war with Germany, Canada and Newfoundland were not falling over themselves to make good the UK's shortages, except at a price. The cost of newsprint therefore rocketed, from £11.5s.0d. per ton in September 1939 to £21.10s.0d. in April 1940, a 91 per cent increase. A secondary problem was shipping as, even when the newsprint could be bought in Canada or Newfoundland, the Ministry of Shipping was not prepared to allocate ships to carry it.

The Newsprint Supply Co. Ltd.

In May 1940, the newspaper industry produced its solution to these problems, a dynamic one as would be expected given the personalities of the proprietors involved, who included Lords Beaverbrook, Camrose, Southwood and Kemsley, plus Esmond Harmsworth and J.J. Astor. These and other members of the newspaper trade organisations came together to set up the Newsprint Supply Co. Ltd., a private company with a nominal capital of just £1,200, but whose 12 directors each gave guarantees of £100,000 to the banks to finance its operations. The company's two objectives were to buy newsprint for resale to its members and to charter or buy ships for its transport. It was stressed that the company was not intended to make a profit, but to purchase newsprint from four Canadian and Newfoundland mills, and share it out amongst the various newspapers, respecting the strict quotas which the Ministry of Supply had instituted. It would seem that the newspaper proprietors had obtained the Ministry of Shipping's agreement to the company chartering ships. The argument that swayed the

Government was, apparently, that 'Canada could not be expected to supply aeroplanes and soldiers if we didn't take its domestic products.' A further difficulty was a chronic shortage of Canadian or US dollars, those available to the UK being spent on war materials. Fortunately, the Canadian-born Lord Beaverbrook had substantial funds in North America, which he generously made available.

The new company was not universally popular. The publishers of periodicals other than newspapers were piqued at being excluded, and approached the Government themselves to obtain permission to import pulp or paper. In addition paper manufacturers, themselves starved of raw materials, bewailed the fact that newsprint, and not pulpwood, was being brought in. They made the point that newsprint needed to be stowed below decks, whilst wood could be carried by ships as deck cargo as well as in the holds.

Ship purchases and charters

Within two months of the formation of the Newsprint Supply Co. Ltd., its principals had registered two shipping companies: the Pachesham Steamship Co. Ltd. on 10th July 1940, and the Barberry's Steamship Co. Ltd. just seven days later. The nominal capital of each was just £100, and just two shares were issued. Despite this lack of capitalisation, funds were available from banks thanks to the guarantees given by directors of the Newsprint Supply Co. Ltd., and this company provided a mortgage for the second ship bought.

Events were moving quickly, and in August the steamship companies each bought a ship, which they named, unsurprisingly, *Pachesham* and *Barberrys*. Both came from United States owners, and were 20-year old survivors of the building programmes begun by the United States Shipping Board during the First World War, one having been completed in Japan and the other in California. The two steamship companies also placed orders for two new ships, although it was mid-1943 before the *Kelmscott* and *Caxton* (1) were delivered.

Management of the ships was placed in the hands of Runciman (London) Ltd., which also had responsibility for the fleet of Anchor Line Ltd., acquired by Runciman in 1935, and managed some ships for the Ministry of War Transport (as the latter ships were not, as far as known, involved in the newsprint business they have not been listed here). One of the younger sons of Newcastle shipowner Walter Runciman, Philip W. Runciman, was a director and took charge of the management of the paper ships. The London operation was distinct from Runciman's Newcastle-on-Tyne activities, which managed the motor tramps of Moor Line Ltd., and crewing was kept separate, which may have been just as well. When Alan Phipps joined the *Baskerville* (2) in dry dock at the Royal Albert Dock, London in 1955, he and others signed on at the nearby Shipping Federation office. Being a unit of a modest fleet, the question of *Baskerville's* ownership was raised, and the answer given 'She's one of Runciman's'. This reply sent one of Alan's erstwhile shipmates on a quick circumnavigation of the dry dock, and seeing no evidence of the word 'Newcastle' on the stern, he came back sufficiently reassured to take the berth. Despite being in his twenties, he was well aware of the pre-war seaman's prayer 'From Ropner, Runciman and Radcliffe, the good Lord preserve us.' His faith in the company was justified, and Alan and his shipmates found that conditions, food and wages were very good, despite the ships being rather basic and dated. *Baskerville*, for instance, still had a solid-fuel galley.

The United States Coast Guard must be thanked for ensuring we have an image of the *Barberrys*, anchored in New York harbour on 1st August 1942, having just arrived from the Clyde. She was to make just one more round voyage, and after leaving New York for the UK on 17th November 1942, was torpedoed with heavy loss of life nine days later. *[Steamship Historical Society of America, courtesy Bill Schell]*

107

Kelmscott unloading into lighters at Convoy's Wharf, Deptford: the usual destination of newsprint bound for London. *[World Ship Photo Library collection]*

War risks

Repeatedly crossing from Canada and the USA, the Runciman paper ships were in the thick of the Battle of the Atlantic. In November 1942 *Barberrys* was torpedoed with heavy loss of life. On 9th February 1944, the six-months old *Kelmscott* was torpedoed by *U 845* whilst off Cape Race, Newfoundland on a voyage from Canada to the UK with paper. Listing, she was towed into St. John's, where her cargo was discharged and she was slowly patched up for the voyage south to Baltimore for permanent repairs. She left St. John's on 14th August, but off Atlantic City on 24th August she collided with the Liberty *William Leavitt* (7,176/1944). Although eventually repaired at Baltimore, as originally intended, she did not load again until December. A relatively new ship had therefore been out of the war for ten months.

Losses were not confined to the owned ships. Speaking after the war, manager of the two companies E.J. Robertson referred to eight other ships being chartered from three companies, and implied that all of these were lost during the war, although this is probably an exaggeration. Nevertheless, a desperate price was paid in seamen's lives and in ships to keep the Fleet Street and regional presses rolling.

Voyage patterns

As intended, the ships initially ran largely between the United Kingdom and Canada and Newfoundland, although some calls were also made during wartime at New York and Philadelphia. Loading ports included Botwood, Corner Brook, Dalhousie, Port Alfred, Port aux Basques, St. John's, Sydney, Three Rivers, and Wabana. Halifax was also a frequent call in wartime, probably in order to assemble to join a convoy. Convoys terminated in Belfast Lough or Loch Ewe, and the ships would sometimes unload at the Clyde Emergency Port. On other occasions they would proceed either to the Mersey, to go up the Ship Canal to Manchester, or make the more hazardous journey round the north of Scotland and down the east coast to London. The hazards were not just enemy aircraft, mines, and E-boats, but also other allied ships: on 5th October 1942, for instance, *Barberrys* was in collision off Cromer. Damage could also be due to heavy weather or, on *Caxton's* maiden voyage, the explosion of depth charges, or to failures of boiler or auxiliary machinery, and these resulted in occasional visits to the Bristol Channel for repairs.

The ships were not particularly efficient in wartime, and indeed it has been estimated that the need to wait for and join convoys reduced the availability of ships by a third during the Second World War. The delays were compounded by loading in several ports, because no one mill could provide a full cargo of newsprint. Crossing the Atlantic, even in convoy, generally took a little over two weeks, but a round trip could be very protracted. *Barberrys* made her first departure from the Mersey on 5th November 1940 but, when lost over two years later, she was on only her seventh round voyage.

After the war, of course, efficiency increased, and voyages became a trifle more varied. In February 1946, *Kelmscott* sailed from the Manchester Ship Canal to Hampton Roads and then proceeded through the Panama Canal and north to load in Vancouver and New Westminster, returning to the Tyne in mid-May. The biggest change, however, was that paper products from the Baltic became available again, and in June 1947 *Pachesham* paid the first visit by one of the ships to Finland, loading at Mantyluoto and Kotka. Occasional visits to the Baltic continued, especially by *Isaac Carter*, but the voyage pattern for the ships generally remained one of loading in Canada for London or Manchester.

Post-war modernisation

Britain's economy did not return to its pre-war state following the end of the war, indeed shortages and rationing continued into the 1950s. Demand for newsprint remained in excess of supply until 1949, and shortages extended to shipping space. Although the formation of the Newsprint Supply Co. Ltd. was a wartime expedient, it was desirable to continue the operation of the company and its ships to import newsprint.

The fleet was gradually modernised, but in a somewhat piecemeal manner. The delivery of the first *Baskerville* in 1946 allowed the sale of the *Pachesham*, which, despite its venerable age, survived until 1961. Arrival of the *Caslon* in 1949 permitted the sale of the war-built *Kelmscott*. But in 1950 the *Baskerville*, only four years old, was sold to the Bristol City Line, who then proceeded to sell an older, war-built steamer back to Barberry's Steamship Co. Ltd. who renamed it *Chepman*. This was only slightly younger than *Kelmscott*, sold two years earlier.

Similarly, design of the new ships seemed to take two steps forward and one back. The first ship ordered

Built under licence in wartime, *Caxton* (1) was essentially a standard Thompson tramp (above). *[Fotoflite incorporating Skyfotos]*

Isaac Carter homeward bound in the Kiel Canal during one of her voyages to the Baltic (right).

Caslon at Convoy's Wharf, Deptford (below). *[World Ship Photo Library]*

Newsprint carriers

At the launch of *Caslon* in February 1948, the chairman of the builders, Fairfield, reminisced that 25 years earlier he had been involved in the first ship built specifically for the carriage of newsprint, the *Geraldine Mary* (7,244/1924). This ship was built by Vickers Ltd. at Barrow for the Anglo-Newfoundland Development Co. Ltd., and managed by Donaldson Line. The Anglo-Newfoundland company was formed by British newspaper companies headed by Lord Northcliffe and Lord Rothermere in the early years of the twentieth century when a shortage of pulp and newsprint from Scandinavian sources had seemed to threaten their newspapers. Mills were established at Grand Falls, Newfoundland, quite close to the port of Botwood. From 1909, when production started, Donaldson Line carried much of its output, but Anglo-Newfoundland became a shipowner in its own right in 1915 when it bought the steamer *Cranley* (4,644/1903). As well as several other secondhand acquisitions, it later had the *Rothermere* (5,356/1938) built, presumably also as a dedicated newsprint carrier. Anglo-Newfoundland were one of the companies with which the Newsprint Supply Co. Ltd. contracted to supply newsprint in 1940.

Soon after *Geraldine Mary* was completed, two other ships were specially built for the paper industry, the *Corner Brook* (5,767/1925) and *Humber Arm* (5,758/1925) for the Newfoundland Power and Paper Co. Ltd., although these carried pulp as well as paper. As related in *Ships in Focus Record* 5, these steamers became the first ships in the Bowater's fleet in 1938.

In post-war years, the Runciman-managed ships detailed in the accompanying chapter were by no means the only newsprint carriers built. In 1953, Denny delivered the *Markland* (6,037/1953) to the Mersey Paper Co. Ltd. of Liverpool, Nova Scotia. Perhaps ignorant of the *Geraldine Mary*, Denny claimed *Markland* to be the first purpose-built newsprint carrier. The *Markland* and some other secondhand vessels owned by Mersey Paper and its subsidiaries passed to Bowaters in 1959. This company did much to develop the newsprint carrier in the 1950s, taking delivery from Denny of three big, well-equipped turbine-engine vessels. In *Sarah Bowater* (6,471/1955), *Margaret Bowater* (6,481/1955) and *Nicolas Bowater* (7,136/1958), this type of ship reached its peak of development under the British flag. Bowater's later ships, six somewhat smaller motor vessels, were designed for carrying pulp from Scandinavia or Canada, although they also carried newsprint on occasion.

Perhaps the most important consideration with newsprint was to avoid damaging the reels when stowed. In Bowater's big newsprint carriers, pillars in the holds were eliminated, and sparring was covered with rubber to help prevent it damaging the rolls of newsprint. All the Bowater ships are described and illustrated in *Ships in Focus Record* 5, and the Anglo-Newfoundland vessels in *Donaldson Line* by P.J. Telford (World Ship Society, Kendal, 1989).

Three of the four Anglo-Newfoundland newsprint carriers shown here were torpedoed in the North Atlantic during the Second World War.
Rothermere, seen in the Manchester Ship Canal (above), was sunk by *U 98* on 20th May 1941. *[World Ship Society Brownell collection]*

Geraldine Mary, seen opposite top on the Thames, was torpedoed by *U 52* on 4th August 1940. *[World Ship Photo Library]*
Cranley, seen in Harris and Dixon's colours (opposite middle), was broken up by Wards at Briton Ferry in 1931. *[RA Snook, courtesy World Ship Photo Library]*

Esmond (4,976/1929, ex-*Traprain Law*) (opposite bottom) was sunk by *U 110* on 9th May 1941 off Cape Farewell. *[World Ship Society Brownell collection]*
Three ships and 25 lives was a very high price to pay for keeping the presses rolling.

after the war, *Caslon* from Fairfields, had steam turbines, but *Isaac Carter* of 1952 and the second *Baskerville* of 1954 reverted to triple-expansion steam engines - generally regarded as obsolescent by the 1950s, although *Baskerville* had an exhaust turbine to make better use of low pressure steam from the main engine. The second *Caxton* of 1958, the company's last newbuilding, was the only motor vessel ordered.

With the sale of the war-built *Caxton* (1) and *Chepman* in 1957, purpose-built newsprint carriers comprised the entire fleet of Barberry's Steamship Co. Ltd.; the Pachesham Steamship Co. Ltd. having disappeared with the sale of *Kelmscott* in 1949. However, the company's ships do not seem to have been very specialised; it made do with several ships which were not designed for its trades, and all its ships happily found employment in general cargo and tramping trades after their sale. Although built to serve ports in Canada which were regularly ice-bound in winter, the ships had some features which were not conducive to their serving in cold weather. In the account of his voyages in the second *Baskerville* (see pages 114-5), Alan Phipps comments on the unsuitability of her winches and that, with the sole exception of the last ship *Aragona* which was second-hand, none of the company's vessels was strengthened for navigation in ice.

New owners

In 1958 it was announced that the four ships owned by Barberry's Steamship Co. Ltd. were to be sold to the British International Paper Ltd. with effect from January 1959. In fact, the new owners turned out to be Transatlantic Carriers Ltd., a London-based company set up on 29th October 1958. Its major shareholders were five Canadian paper companies: Abitibi Power and Paper Co. Ltd., the Canadian International Paper Co., the Consolidated Paper Corporation Ltd., Price Brothers and Co. Ltd., and the St. Lawrence Corporation Ltd. The *Caslon*, *Isaac Carter*, *Baskerville* (2) and *Caxton* (2) were transferred to Transatlantic Carriers Ltd. and the Barberry's Steamship Co. Ltd. was wound up.

Initially, management of the ships remained with

Bought in 1951, *Chepman* was another war standard ship, and in this view is still in wartime rig with stump fore and main masts. *[World Ship Photo Library]*

Runcimans, who were now styled Walter Runciman and Co. Ltd. However, in 1962 Canatlantic Ltd. was established at the same Pall Mall address as Transatlantic Carriers Ltd. to take over the management of the ships. Both changes in ownership and management were signalled by changes to the funnel colours and the houseflag worn (see endpapers).

Companies rarely give reasons why they are selling up, but it can be assumed that the Newsprint Supply Co. Ltd. was no longer needed once supply of newsprint exceeded demand, and possibly because the thrusting spirit of the 1950s meant co-operation gave way to competition, even in buying newsprint. The Canadian paper companies, however, would have wished to see their sales to the UK continue, even if part of the price was to take over a small British shipping company. The establishment of their own management company could be read as dissatisfaction with the way things were run by Runciman, a traditional British shipowner. Perhaps there were grounds for this, with the generous manning which was the custom in the fifties. As an example of doubtfully-economic practices, during 1956 Alan Phipps received a 'cargo bonus' of five shillings per voyage, which resulted from an agreement with the Conference Lines on the North Atlantic, even though the ships carried no cargo westbound. But other and deeper problems were besetting shipping under the British flag.

Run down and sale

Within two years of the change of ownership, the fleet began to be run down. Two steamers, *Caslon* and *Isaac Carter*, were sold, although the fleet was brought up to three with the only further purchase, the ice-strengthened motorship *Aragona* bought from Finnish owners in 1964. The surviving steamer *Baskerville* (2) went in 1967, and the two motorships, *Caxton* (2) and *Aragona*, in 1968. Factors in the sale may well have

The ships' UK destinations were usually London or Manchester, where northern editions of some daily papers were printed. *Baskerville* (2) is seen in the Manchester Ship Canal in her original colours (above). *[Ken Cunnington]*

Caxton (2) in new funnel colours (right).

The handsome *Isaac Carter* had a North Eastern Marine Engineering Co. Ltd. reheat engine rated at 3,000IHP at 84 rpm, giving 12 knots. The ship could carry 4,000 tons of newsprint in four holds served by 10 five-ton derricks. She is seen in her original funnel colours (below).

Baskerville in the ice off Botwood, Newfoundland in February or March 1956. *[Alan Phipps]*

To Botwood in *Baskerville*
Alan Phipps

When I signed on, 29th December 1955, *Baskerville* was quite a happy, comfortable ship under the command of Captain Wilson, a God-fearing Ulsterman of genial disposition. His brother was a surgeon and, not to be outdone, our gallant skipper was ever ready with bandages and plaster, and even cat-gut and needle when an opportunity arose. Our chief steward lost his footing when descending to the storeroom and trapped his upper arm behind the handrail. The skin was quite seriously split, but he survived the Captain's treatment (skill with a needle) in great style.

In the early part of 1956 we made a later than usual visit to Botwood. Our running mate, the old *Caxton*, had just completed loading, and the town mayor had visited us to thank the skipper for keeping unemployment at bay for a little longer. Loading started in the two after holds and quite rapid progress was made. But unfortunately, overnight, the wind went about and the bay began filling with pack ice. Nevertheless, we headed out to sea, preceded by a Government icebreaker and the homeward-bound *Caxton*. With the ship well trimmed down by the stern and our speed restricted by floating ice, progress was slow and erratic. On this occasion I was stuck with the lookout, but it was daylight, and as far as the eye could see the surface was littered with ice of all shapes and sizes. It looked like the floor of a Greek restaurant after a big celebration. On enquiring as to my current purpose in life, I was told 'to report any large pieces of ice'. Seeking further clarification of 'large', I was informed 'anything bigger than a table'. With a mental image of a variety of tables - coffee tables, snooker tables and dining tables - I decided to ignore all sub-Titanic-sized chunks. In any case, with the helmsman unable to steer a tail-heavy ship, and the raised bow sheering wildly from side to side, we simply pushed on amid the deafening racket caused by the empty forepart bashing through the ice field until we finally came clear and headed for our next cargo in Nova Scotia.

Knowing how extremely cold such North Atlantic winter voyages can be, it seemed very strange to fit out a ship for this service with steam winches. When temperatures plummet, all the deck hydrants must be opened to drain the water-mains on deck because the piping can freeze and fracture even though it carries sea-water. Steam winches are worse because the condensed steam is, of course, fresh water and wrecked winches are more costly and crucial than burst pipes. Damage to a steam winch can only be prevented by securing the winch wires (cargo runners) with chain stoppers to stop them unreeling from the winch drum, which is then disengaged from the drive, and the winch run continually. Fortunately, the more modern Clarke Chapman winches were totally enclosed in an oil-bath, but with about 18 of them running there was a fair amount of noise and much vibration.

Strangely enough, the coldest I have ever been was when we tied up for one night at Runcorn, inward-bound on the Manchester Ship Canal, and it was decided to proceed beyond the first bridge. This required the fore topmast to be telescoped, a fairly simple and regularly-practised affair. But that night it was still and bitterly cold when I was up on the mast table. When about three-quarters of the way through the task I could not move my fingers or even feel them and had to descend the mast with my hands just hooked over the rungs of the ladder.

On my second trip we sailed, as was common practice, from Manchester in ballast but without our regular carpenter. His less-than-suitable replacement was accompanied by his lady friend, and she informed us that he had not been very well, but that she had kept him reasonably functional on a diet of rum and milk. She didn't specify whether these ingredients were administered together or separately. In the event they voyaged with us for most of the Canal's length, whereupon he and Miss Macclesfield 1908 disembarked, and we proceeded seawards, possibly illegally, *sans* Chippy.

During this voyage we were treated to the edifying sight of the chief officer, resplendent in full uniform and cap, sawing away manfully at bilge limbers requiring repair, assisted by the ubiquitous apprentices. At least Captain Wilson's medical aspirations relieved the mate of any responsibility in that direction, as would normally be the case. Instead he could concentrate on honing his skills in basic woodwork and the dropping of anchors.

However, the short-lived career of the official carpenter did leave us with one unsavoury problem. The ship was an open-shelter decker and it was possible to enter No. 1 hold and walk aft as far as the poop bulkhead, with just the trunking for funnel uptakes on the centreline. Just before the midpoint she had deeptanks for water ballast, and these were covered by simple rectangular steel covers which rested on a rubber seating. They were secured by captive hinged bolts which entered slots around all four edges, and were normally tightened down by hand. To be precise, by the carpenter's hand. But on this occasion the few bolts that were engaged had not been tightened and, once at sea, vast quantities of ballast water spurted from under the edges and flooded the deck from end to end. All the debris, particularly Kraft paper wrapping from newsprint rolls, wood fragments from cargo battens, and general litter deposited by the dockers, swirled around the deck, with much of the water finding its way into the lower holds. Calling it water was a little euphemistic because these tanks were filled from the Manchester Ship Canal with a semi-viscous liquid which could turn any painted surface to a colour vaguely reminiscent of the Wehrmacht uniform. 'Too thick for swimming, and too thin for ploughing' is one description used by Mancunians and near neighbours. It was a long and noisome task to get most of the cargo space reasonably clean and, above all, dry so that loading could begin.

One final peculiarity on *Baskerville* was a problem with funnel painting, a procedure usually undertaken by climbing a ladder either inside, or up the forward end of the same, to reach a steel decking about knee-high to the inside of the funnel rim. It was possible to rig a bosun's chair with the rope gantline passed through the ring in a long hook, which fitted over the rim. With some agility, you had to swing yourself over the edge into the start position, collect

Caxton and *Baskerville* (right) follow an ice breaker off Botwood (above) and a view of ice from *Baskerville* (below). *[Alan Phipps]*

the paint pot, and then off you went. Unfortunately, like so many steamships which burnt oil sludge or similar, the smoke emission was horrendous. An additional six feet of plating had been added, but no provision had been made to reach the new rim. It was therefore necessary to take all the hooks up in place by ladder, with lines rove through the rings, to hook over the rim and, from the deck, to flick the ropes to space the hooks equally around the funnel. Your only problem then was that the chair and its occupant were still on deck, and could only be elevated by hauling on the gantline. Because the latter passed through a simple metal ring with no sheave, it offered a great deal of frictional resistance. In practice we found the best technique was to take up the slack line, lean well back, and then literally 'walk' up the funnel, almost at right-angles. A method calculated to give today's Health and Safety Executive apoplexy.

No. 55

S.S. "BASKERVILLE" LONDON

ACCOUNT OF WAGES
(Sect. 132, M.S.A. 1894.)

Name of Ship and Official No.

Name of Seaman	Ref. No. in Agreement	Income tax Code	Rating
A. Phipps.	10	8.	A·B.

Date wages Began	Date wages Ceased	Total Period of Employment		Allotment Note given for		
		Months	Days	£	s.	d.
8 2/56	8 3/56	1	1	–	~	–

A. EARNINGS	£	s.	d.
..........Months at £...38...per month	30	0	0
..........Days at...1·0·0...per day	1	0	0
Promotion by £.....p.m. for.......m.....d*			
Overtime....43 hours at...3/6...per hour	7	10	6
CARGO BONUS	3	10	0
TOTAL EARNINGS	42	0	6

B. DEDUCTIONS	Amount
Reduction by £.....p.m. for.......m.....d*	
Advance on Joining	*
Fines	
Forfeitures	
CARGO BONUS	5	0
Current Income Tax	2	0	0
Arrears of Income Tax...O.T.	1	5	0

OTHER DEDUCTIONS
Date

	CARGO BONUS	3	0	0
	Bonus #3	1	1	6
	St Johns #5	1	15	6
	CANTEEN	1	0	0
	UNION 5 @ N	7	6

National Insurance for...5.6/9...weeks	1	13	9
TOTAL DEDUCTIONS, exclusive of Allotments and Cash on leaving Ship ... ... £	12	18	3
TOTAL EARNINGS (A) less		
TOTAL DEDUCTIONS (B)	29	2	3
Allotments		–
Cash on leaving Ship		
Amount Due on day of Discharge £	29	2	3

C.
Leave Due for Voyage.........Days		
Leave Due for Sundays at sea.........Days		
Leave taken during Voyage.........Days		
Total leave due..4..d.at1·0·0.p.d.£....:...	4	0	0
Less Nat. Ins.........weeks £....:...		
Subsistence Allowance ......d. at...... p.d.	–	–	–
FINAL BALANCE DUE £	33	2	3
National Insurance Contributions paid to date wages ceased

*National Insurance Contributions paid on leave to............
* This line to be deleted if it does not apply

The above Account of Earnings and of Deductions exclusive of Allotments is correct.

Signature of Master..............
Signature of Seaman..............

IMPORTANT. This Account of Wages should be retained as a record of National Insurance Contributions.

M.....OFFICE -8 MAR 1956

Alan Phipp's wage slip: £33. 2s. 3d. for one month's work.

included changing patterns of supply in the paper industry, with Scandinavian pulp and newsprint resuming its dominance in the British market. It was also becoming less attractive to own ships, especially under the Red Ensign. With supply of ships again exceeding demand, it made sense for a shipper to rely on chartering ships to meet his needs, and it also meant they could benefit from the newer and more efficient vessels which were making the conventional cargo ships of the paper fleet uneconomic. As the other big British fleet of pulp and newsprint carriers, Bowaters, found, in the 1960s the paper industry had to be leaner and fitter to survive, and there was no place for peripheral activities such as shipowning. After 28 years, this small but interesting fleet was therefore no more.

Derivations of Runciman Names
Names given to the ships were those of large houses, and of British pioneers of printing.

Barberrys   No trace of this name can be found in the Dictionary of National Biography, in encyclopaedias of printing, in gazetteers of the British Isles or in the Oxford Dictionary, although the last named notes it as an alternative spelling of the name *Berberis*, a shrub. By analogy with *Pachesham* (see below), *Barberrys* may be the name of the home of one of the directors of the Newsprint Supply Co. Ltd.

Baskerville   A skilled calligrapher and cutter of monumental inscriptions, John Baskerville (1706-1775) moved from Worcestershire to Birmingham and began type-founding about 1750. His typeface, which he spent many years developing, was greatly admired, and the early books he printed (1757-1763) are regarded as some of the finest ever published. But the work of Baskerville, who also made his own ink and paper, was probably too good to be commercially successful, and he made little profit from his printing business.

Caslon   Another Worcester man, William Caslon (1692-1766) was Baskerville's only peer as a type founder. Originally employed engraving the stocks of guns, he was 'discovered' whilst working in London, and went on to run a type foundry and printing press which achieved both critical acclaim and commercial success.

Caxton   William Caxton (1422?-1491) was the first man to set up a printing press in Britain (1476, in Westminster Abbey) and the first to print a book in English. Born in Tenterden, Kent, he originally had a textile business, and whilst in Cologne learned the art of printing on paper. Fewer than 40 of his printed works survive.

Chepman   A wealthy Edinburgh merchant, Walter Chepman (1473?-1538?) shares the credit for producing the first book printed in Scotland, in 1508. However, his partner Andrew Myllar had learned printing in France, and Chepman was probably the financier rather than the printer.

Isaac Carter This name cannot be found in the *Dictionary of National Biography* or in encyclopaedias of printing.

Kelmscott   A house on the Thames in Oxfordshire most closely associated with William Morris (1834-1896). Amongst his extraordinary range of talents - poet, painter, architect, interior designer, textile designer, and socialist - Morris was also a typographer and printer, and his Kelmscott Press produced a number of fine editions.

Pachesham   A large house on Leatherhead Common, Surrey, and probably Lord Runciman's home: it was used as the emergency offices of Runciman (London) Ltd. during the Second World War.

Fleet list

1. PACHESHAM 1940-1948
O.N. 167625 6,090g 3,862n 402.6 x 53.0 x 32.2 feet
Two-stage steam turbine by W.A. Fletcher Company, Hoboken, New Jersey, USA.
1929: T. 3-cyl. by Allis Chalmers Manufacturing Company, Milwaukee, Wisconsin, USA; 539 NHP, 2,800 IHP.
10.1920: Completed by the Moore Shipbuilding Company, Oakland, California, USA (Yard No. 2236) for the United States Shipping Board, Washington DC, USA as MURSA.
1928: Sold to the Los Angeles Steamship Co. Inc., Los Angeles, USA and renamed GENERAL M.H. SHERMAN.
1935: Sold to the Matson Navigation Company, San Francisco, USA.
1938: Renamed KAINALU.
10.8.1940: Registered in the ownership of the Pachesham Steamship Co. Ltd. (Runciman (London) Ltd., managers), London as PACHESHAM.
7.2.1948: Sold to the Chios Shipping Co. Ltd. (S.G. Embiricos), London.
1948: Sold to Compania de Naviera Las Cruces S.A., Panama (Carras Ltd., London), and renamed FENIX.
1951: Sold to Nippoh Kaiun K.K., Tokyo, Japan and later Kobe, Japan and renamed NISSHU MARU.
12.12.1958: Laid up at Onomichi.
22.2.1961: Breaking up began at Osaka, Japan.

2. BARBERRYS 1940-1942
O.N. 167636 5,170g 3,237n 399.9 x 54.7 x 27.6 feet
T. 3-cyl. by Ishikawajima Shipbuilding and Engineering Co. Ltd., Tokyo, Japan; 513 NHP, 10 knots.
3.1920: Completed by the Uchida Shipbuilding and Engineering Co. Ltd., Yokohama, Japan (Yard No. 6) for the United States Shipping Board, Washington DC, USA as EASTERN GLEN.
1926: Sold to the American South African Line Ltd., New York, USA.

1933: Sold to Steamship Oriole Inc. (American Foreign Steamship Corporation, managers), New York and renamed AMERICAN ORIOLE.
1939: Owners became the American Foreign Steamship Corporation, New York.
28.8.1940: Registered in the ownership of the Barberry's Steamship Co. Ltd. (Runciman (London) Ltd., managers), London as BARBERRYS.
26.11.1942: Sunk by the German submarine U 663 south of Cape Farewell in position 50.36 north by 47.10 west whilst on a voyage from New York to Glasgow with 6,867 tons of general cargo. Of those on board, 22 of the crew of 39, four of the seven gunners, and the Convoy Commodore and his staff of five were lost.
1.9.1943: Register closed.

3. KELMSCOTT 1943-1949
O.N. 168465 7,039g 4,889n 430.9 x 56.2 x 55.2 feet
T. 3-cyl. by John Readhead and Sons Ltd., South Shields; 342 NHP, 2,500 IHP, 11 knots.
7.5.1943: Launched by John Readhead and Sons Ltd., South Shields (Yard No. 534).
24.6.1943: Registered in the ownership of the Pachesham Steamship Co. Ltd. (Runciman (London) Ltd., managers), London as KELMSCOTT.
7.1943: Completed.
2.3.1949: Sold to the Queen Line Ltd. (38/64) and Cadogan Steamship Co. Ltd. (26/64) (Thomas Dunlop and Sons, managers), Glasgow.
7.3.1949: Renamed QUEEN ANNE.
12.1954: Sold to Polish Ocean Lines, Gdynia, Poland and renamed MARIAN BUCZEK.
Prior to 30.3.1968: Arrived at Whampoa, China to be broken up.

Pachesham as *General M.H. Sherman* transiting the Panama Canal. *[National Maritime Museum P10450]*

117

In 1949 *Kelmscott* was sold and spent five years tramping as *Queen Anne* under the management of Thomas Dunlop and Co. (above). *[Ivor Rooke collection]*

Caxton (1) in the Thames, March 1953 (left).

The first *Baskerville* was sold after only four years' service, presumably when the owners received a good offer from the Bristol City Line, in whose colours she is seen at Swansea as *Birmingham City* (below). *[World Ship Photo Library]*

The turbine steamer *Caslon* is seen in the Thames, with the company's green and white houseflag prominent at the main (opposite page). *[World Ship Photo Library]*

4. CAXTON (1) 1943-1957
O.N. 169626 7,242g 4,184n 423.8 x 57.2 x 35.9 feet
T. 3-cyl. by George Clark (1938) Ltd., Sunderland; 509 NHP.
2.6.1943: Launched by J.L. Thompson and Sons Ltd., Sunderland (Yard No. 627) for the Barberry's Steamship Co. Ltd. (Runciman (London) Ltd., managers), London as CAXTON.
10.1943: Completed.
1957: Sold to Buries Markes Ltd., London and renamed LA COSTA.
9.1958: Sold to the North Breeze Navigation Co. Ltd. (John Manners and Co. Ltd., managers), Hong Kong and renamed HONG KONG BREEZE.
8.1960: Owners became the Cambay Prince Steamship Co. Ltd. (John Manners and Co. Ltd., managers), Hong Kong.
1.1965: Owners became the San Roberto Steamship Co. S.A., Panama (China Pacific Navigation Co. Ltd., Hong Kong, managers, although the beneficial owner remained John Manners and Co. Ltd., Hong Kong) and renamed PANAM TRADER.
13.7.1967: Left Wakayama for Keelung to be broken up.
10.1967: Demolition completed.

5. BASKERVILLE (1) 1946-1950
O.N. 180932 5,571g 3,186n 452.0 x 56.7 x 25.4 feet
T. 3-cyl. by John Readhead and Sons Ltd., South Shields, with low pressure turbine by Swan Hunter and Wigham Richardson Ltd., Wallsend-on-Tyne; 339 NHP.
31.5.1946: Launched by John Readhead and Sons Ltd., South Shields (Yard No. 550) for the Barberry's Steamship Co. Ltd. (Runciman (London) Ltd., managers), London as BASKERVILLE.
8.1946: Completed.
1950: Sold to the Bristol City Line of Steamships Ltd. (Charles Hill and Sons, managers), Bristol and renamed BIRMINGHAM CITY.
1963: Sold to Kinabatangan Shipping Co. Ltd. (United China Shipping Co. Ltd., managers), Hong Kong and renamed SEMPORNA BAY.
1965: Renamed VICTORIA BAY.
20.6.1969: Went aground whilst leaving Chittagong for Chalna.
6.7.1969: Refloated, but declared a constructive total loss.
10.8.1969: Arrived at Hong Kong to be broken up by Lee Sing and Co.

6. CASLON 1949-1964
O.N. 183030 5,684g 3,018n 453.0 x 59.2 x 25.3 feet
Two steam turbines DR geared to single shaft by the Fairfield Shipbuilding and Engineering Co. Ltd., Govan; 3,960 SHP, 11.5 knots.
17.2.1949: Launched by the Fairfield Shipbuilding and Engineering Co. Ltd., Govan (Yard No. 744) for the Barberry's Steamship Co. Ltd. (Runciman (London) Ltd., managers), London as CASLON.
6.1949: Completed.
1958: Owners became Transatlantic Carriers Ltd. (Walter Runciman and Co. Ltd., managers), London.
1962: Managers became Canatlantic Ltd., London.
1964: Sold to Astrofelix Compania Naviera S.A., Panama (Phoenix Shipping Co. Ltd. (Platon B. Metaxas), London, managers) and renamed NINA G under the Greek flag.
1966: Owners became Astronato Compania Naviera S.A., Panama (Eagle Ocean Transport Inc. (Nicholas M. Lyras), New York, managers) and renamed ORIENT TRANSPORTER.
1969: Managers became Orient Mid-East (UK) Ltd., London.
7.8.1970: Arrived at Beaumont, Texas, USA after sustaining severe engine damage, which was considered uneconomic to repair.
1970: Sold to Kroman Celik A.S., Turkey for use as a barge, but resold for breaking up.
1.11.1971: Demolition completed at Davica, Turkey by Kroman Kollektif Sirketi.

7. CHEPMAN 1951-1957
O.N. 182018 6,140g 4,150n 422.0 x 53.5 x 32.8 feet
T. 3-cyl. by Hick, Hargreaves and Co. Ltd., Bolton; 338 NHP.
9.3.1944: Launched by John Readhead and Sons Ltd., South Shields (Yard No. 539) for the Ministry of War Shipping (Meldrum and Swinson Ltd., managers), London as EMPIRE GREY.
5.1944: Completed.
1947: Managers became the Eskdale Shipping Co. Ltd.
1947: Sold to the Zinal Steamship Co. Ltd. (Burness Shipping Co. Ltd., managers), London and renamed BURHILL.
1951: Sold to the Golden Cross Line Ltd., Bristol (Turnbull, Scott and Co., London, managers) and chartered to the Bristol City Line of Steamships Ltd., Bristol as LONDON CITY.
1951: Acquired by Barberry's Steamship Co. Ltd. (Runciman (London) Ltd., managers), London and renamed CHEPMAN.
1957: Sold to Great Eastern Shipping Co. Ltd., Bombay, India and renamed JAG JANANI.
15.5.1961: Demolition commenced at Bombay by Abid and Co.

8. ISAAC CARTER 1952-1964

O.N. 184708 5,626g 2,987n 411.3 x 57.2 x 27.8 feet
T. 3-cyl. reheat engine by North Eastern Marine Engineering Co. (1938) Ltd., Sunderland; 3,000 IHP, 12 knots.
8.5.1952: Launched by the Blyth Drydock and Shipbuilding Co. Ltd., Blyth (Yard No. 352) for the Barberry's Steamship Co. Ltd. (Runciman (London) Ltd., managers), London as ISAAC CARTER.
9.1952: Completed.
1958: Owners became Transatlantic Carriers Ltd. (Walter Runciman and Co. Ltd., managers), London.
1962: Managers became Canatlantic Ltd., London.
1964: Sold to Atlantic Marine Enterprises Inc., Panama (Lemuria Shipping Corporation (Spyros Tsilimparis), New York, managers) and renamed NORTH AMERICA under the Liberian flag.
23.6.1968: Abandoned after an engine room explosion and fire about 650 miles east of Hawai in position 17.55 north by 147.30 west whilst on a voyage from the Philippines to Callao with a cargo of chrome ore.
2.7.1968: Arrived in tow at Honolulu and fire extinguished.
23.12.1968: Arrived at Onomichi, Japan to be broken up by Mitsui and Co. Ltd.

9. BASKERVILLE (2) 1954-1967

O.N. 186100 5,805g 2,987n 453.2 x 59.2 x 25.5 feet
T. 3-cyl. with low pressure turbine by John Readhead and Sons Ltd., South Shields; 4,200 SHP, 12.5 knots.
6.4.1954: Launched by John Readhead and Sons Ltd., South Shields (Yard No. 578) for Barberry's Steamship Co. Ltd. (Runciman (London) Ltd., managers), London as BASKERVILLE.
14.7.1954: Completed.
1958: Owners became Transatlantic Carriers Ltd. (Walter Runciman and Co. Ltd., managers), London.
1962: Managers became Canatlantic Ltd., London.
1967: Sold to Achille Lauro, Naples, Italy and renamed IROLLI.
1970: Sold to Ardee Investments Ltd., Gibraltar (Mullion and Co. Ltd., Hong Kong) and renamed GLENEALY under the British flag.
25.6.1974: Arrived at Kaohsiung for breaking up.
23.7.1974: Demolition commenced by Chin Ho Fa Steel and Iron Co. Ltd., Kaohsiung.

10. CAXTON (2) 1958-1968

O.N. 187802 5,729g 2,793n 460.0 x 60.3 x 25.5 feet
Doxford oil engine 4-cyl. 2SCSA by North Eastern Marine Engineering Co. Ltd., Wallsend-on-Tyne; 4,800 BHP, 14 knots.
7.1.1958: Launched by the Blyth Drydock and Shipbuilding Co. Ltd., Blyth (Yard No. 367) for the Barberry's Steamship Co. Ltd. (Runciman (London) Ltd., managers), London as CAXTON.
6.1958: Completed.
1958: Owners became Transatlantic Carriers Ltd. (Walter Runciman and Co. Ltd., managers), London.
1962: Managers became Canatlantic Ltd., London.
1968: Sold to Chryselena Compania Naviera S.A., Panama (Pergamos Shipping Co. Ltd. (A.K. Antoniou), London, managers) and renamed ELENA M under the Greek flag.
1969: Managers became Andros Shipping Agencies Ltd. (M.D. Paleocrassas), London.
1978: Sold to Circolo Shipping Inc., Monrovia, Liberia (Mycali Maritime Corporation S.A., Piraeus, Greece, managers) and renamed VASSILAKIS under the Greek flag.
1981: Sold to Greek Spirit S.A., Panama (Sotirios Panachrantos, Piraeus, Greece, manager) and renamed SILVER SHARK under the Greek flag.
1982: Sold to Silver Ocean Shipping Inc., Monrovia, Liberia (Mighty Management S.A. (G. Doussopoulos and Vas. Maltezos), Piraeus, Greece, managers) and renamed MIGHTY SEA under the Panama flag.
1984: Sold to Zodiac Shipping Co. Ltd., Valletta, Malta (Tricommerce Ltd., London, managers) and renamed JUPITER STAR.
9.1984: Arrived at Gadani Beach to be broken up by MEK Shipbreakers Ltd.

11. ARAGONA 1964-1968

O.N. 306127 5,194g 2,793n 460.0 x 60.3 x 25.5 feet
Oil engine 4-cyl. 2SCSA by Maschinenbau Augsburg-Nürnberg A.G., Augsburg, West Germany; 6,100 BHP, 15 knots.
15.11.1955: Launched by Oskarshamns Varv A/B, Oskarshamn, Sweden (Yard No. 322) for Laivanvarustusyhtiö Re-Be Rederibolaget (Gunnar Damstrom, manager), Helsingfors, Finland as ARAGONA.
4.1956: Completed.
1956: Owners became Rederibolaget Hans von Rettig, Åbo, Finland.
1964: Acquired by Transatlantic Carriers Ltd. (Walter Runciman and Co. Ltd., managers), London.
1962: Managers became Canatlantic Ltd., London
1968: Sold to Victoriana Corporation, Panama (V. Tricoglu, London, manager) and renamed MAUTRIC under the Greek flag.
1973: Renamed VIRA.
1977: Managers became N., V. and T. Tricoglu, Piraeus, Greece.
1981: Sold to Union Mark Ltd., Chittagong, Bangladesh for breaking up.

Isaac Carter after transfer to Transatlantic Carriers Ltd., and the addition of a white band to the funnel which was previously green with a black top (left). *[E. Jackson]*

Caxton, also in Transatlantic Carriers colours (opposite top). *[E. Jackson]*

Caxton after her sale to become *Elena M* (opposite middle). *[Paul Boot]*

The ice-strengthened motor vessel *Aragona* still with the grey hull of her former owners.

JOHN T. RENNIE AND SONS
HARRISON-RENNIE LINE
Peter Newall

John Thomson Rennie was born in Aberdeen in 1824, the son of a seafarer - Captain George Rennie, who later had shares in a number of Aberdeen-registered ships (these are included in the fleet list). Both John and his brother George were groomed for maritime careers: John joined the Aberdeen shipbrokers George Oswald and Company, whilst George went to sea and eventually became a master.

Although tradition has it that John Rennie became a shipping and insurance broker in his own right in 1849, the fact that the ownership of the first ship *Samson* was given as J. Rennie and Company in the 1845 *Lloyd's Register* shows that he must have been a ship operator from at least the mid 1840s. The *Samson* was built in 1836 by the Aberdeen shipyard Alexander Hall and Company and the original list of owners included George Rennie. Alexander Hall also completed a number of sailing ships for the company including the final and most famous one, the *Quathlamba* of 1879.

Madagascar and Natal

Rennie vessels initially traded to India, Australia and the Cape Colony but in 1853 one of the ships, homebound from Australia, was blown off course and arrived at Madagascar. Here she loaded a cargo of Madagascar humpback black cattle which was sold in Mauritius and Reunion at a good profit. John Rennie saw this trade as an opportunity for expansion and ordered his first steamship in 1854 from the Greenock yard of Scott and Company - Scott had recently delivered Rennie's grandly-titled barque *L'Imperatrice Eugenie*. The *Madagascar* was completed in May 1855 but was immediately chartered by the British Government for Crimean War duty as a mule transport. A second steamship, the *Waldensian*, followed in 1856 and she too became a war transport.

Soon after the completion of the new vessels, it became apparent that the intended Madagascar inter-island cattle trade was fraught with difficulties, including the safety of the crew and ships because Europeans were not welcome in many places in Madagascar. Too small for long-distance trades, *Madagascar* was refitted at Aberdeen so that she could operate as a coaster in South Africa and in November 1856 set out for southern Africa with John Rennie on board. The timing was perfect. In 1856 the Natal Colony, which had been annexed to the Cape Colony in 1843, became self-governing with the new Natal Government keen to develop the local economy.

On arrival at Cape Town, Rennie was asked if he wished to bid for the Cape to Natal mail contract and, to impress the Cape colonists, *Madagascar* was immediately readied for her first voyage to Natal via Algoa Bay and East London which began on 14th January 1857. Later that year Rennie was awarded the Natal to Cape mail contract by the Natal Government and, although the mail contract was not worth much, the mailship priority afforded the Rennie ships meant that the cargo could be off-loaded before their rivals which gave the company a tremendous competitive advantage. In November the *Madagascar* was joined on the coastal run by the *Waldensian* after a refit at Glasgow in August.

The Aberdeen Clipper Line

Leaving his brother George in command of the *Madagascar*, John Rennie returned to Britain to set up a Natal sailing ship service which became known as the Aberdeen Clipper Line of Packets. The first sailing of the new London to Natal direct service was taken by the *L'Imperatrice Eugenie* in November 1858.

Unfortunately, the treacherous coast of southern Africa soon claimed both Rennie's steamships. The *Madagascar* was wrecked in December 1858 south of East London and the *Waldensian* four years later in October 1862 near Cape Agulhas. Although no lives were lost, Rennie abandoned the coastal service and it was twenty years before the company owned another steamship. The Union Steamship Company took over the route in 1864. George Rennie died in 1862 and the Cape Town office was closed, the agency taken over by Thomson, Watson and Company which, interestingly, became part of the Rennie Group in 1966.

The year 1862 also saw the arrival of the first South African-named Rennie sailing ship, the *Natal Star.* Five new ships were built later that decade as the London to Natal direct service grew. All these sailing vessels were less than 500 tons gross with shallow drafts because of the sand bar at the entrance to Durban Bay. In 1869 Rennie started a joint service with Bullard, King and Company under the banner of the Aberdeen Clipper Line of Packets London to Natal Direct with all the vessels flying the Rennie house flag. The London company was known as John T. Rennie, Son and Company.

In 1874 Rennie decided to take control of the Natal end of the business and John Rennie's son George Hall Rennie opened the John T. Rennie and Sons' office in

Madagascar
[Mrs Anne
Rennie Collection]

Natal Star to the left. The other ship in frame is the *Coulnakyle* (above). *[Aberdeen Maritime Museum]*
Matabele (right). *[Martin Leendertz Collection, SA Library]*

Durban. This marked the start of a long association between the Rennie family and Durban. Four years later, John Rennie died and his three younger sons John (known as Jack), Alexander and David later joined their brother George in the business.

Hall, Russell steamers

When Bullard, King introduced their first steamship, the *Pongola*, in 1879, it was inevitable that Rennies would have to move from sail to steam and in 1882 the 1,537 gross tons *Dabulamanzi* was completed by the Aberdeen shipyard Hall, Russell and Company which, over the next 28 years, built all the company's ships except one. In 1885 the second ship, *Matabele*, was delivered as the first South African trader built with triple expansion engines.

By 1890 Rennies had a fleet of six handsome steamers of under 2,000 gross. With French-grey hulls and yellow funnels they also carried a small number of passengers. Most of the ships had Zulu *In* or *I-* names to distinguish them from the *Um-* names of the Bullard, King vessels with which they operated alternate fortnightly sailings from London. The following year a new Durban to East Africa coastal service started with the purpose-built *Induna* and the *Matabele*. The company also continued to own sailing vessels until 1895 when the *Quathlamba* was sold.

Although still small, the size of the ships gradually increased and in 1904 the first over 4,000 gross, *Inanda* (2), joined the fleet. She had a passenger capacity of over 100. By now the sandbar at Durban had been reduced significantly and the *Armadale Castle* (12,973/1903) became the first mailship to cross the bar on 26th June 1904. The following year the *Inkosi* (1) was the first ship on the South African run to be fitted with wireless telegraphy.

The Harrison-Rennie Line

The final and largest ship built for John T. Rennie and Sons was *Intaba*, which was completed towards the end of 1910 and was the last Aberdeen-built Rennie ship. In 1911 the Liverpool-based Thos. and Jas. Harrison bought the ships and goodwill of the company and a new company was established, Harrison-Rennie Line. As part of the deal, the London company John T. Rennie, Son and Company became Harrison's loading broker in Britain whilst John T. Rennie and Sons was appointed Harrison's agent in South Africa. George and John Rennie retired whilst Alexander and David continued to run the Rennie operations in South Africa which have grown into a major South African conglomerate still with the Rennie name. The Rennie name also surfaced as a South African shipowner in the 1960s with the formation of Rennie Coasters. This company merged with the Green 'R' Line in 1975.

The first vessel built for Harrison-Rennie was the cargo ship *Intombi* in 1912 and she was followed in 1913 by the only passenger ship ordered for the Harrison-Rennie South African service, the 114-capacity *Ingoma*. After the First World War *Intaba* and *Ingoma* were the sole Harrison-Rennie passenger ships operating to South Africa and in May 1921 the passenger service was abandoned, although Harrisons continued to be heavily involved in the South African cargo trade. The Rennie name was dropped and both ships were transferred to Harrison's London to West Indies passenger service. Two further passenger ships with Rennie names were built for the West Indies service in 1925 and 1937, the *Inanda* (3) and *Inkosi* (2), and their damage in a 1940 air raid marked the end of passenger ships for the company and the end of Harrison ships bearing *In-* names. When the only survivor was returned to Harrisons after the war, it was renamed *Planter*.

Intaba [Peter Newall collection]

Derivations of Rennie names

Rennies used a variety of names in their early years, but later standardised on Zulu and other names from the south of Africa, mostly beginning *In-* to distuinguish them from Bullard, King vessels. Many thanks to Phyllis Connerty and Sarala Majudith at the Don Africana Library, Durban for providing the following derivations of these names.

Dabulamanzi The divider of water: the name of one of the Zulu King Cetswayo's brothers.

Ifafa River in Natal which flows with a sound like 'fa-fa'.

Illovo River in Natal, said to derive its name from the Mlovu trees (*Cordia caffra*) which grew on its banks.

Inanda The place of plentiful grazing for stock.

Inchanga A narrow serrated ridge on the main line to Pietermaritzburg.

Induna Governor, captain, ministry, supervisor, commander.

Ingane Infant or small child.

Ingeli A serrated, precipitous place, at the base of which stands Harding.

Ingoma A ballad, hymn or sacred song. A dance performed at festivals, especially that of the first fruits, royal song.

Inkonka The male bushbuck.

Inkosi King.

Insizwa Means fully developed, clear or bright, or cloudless. It also means young person approaching manhood; a vigorous young man who has not yet assumed the head ring.

Intaba Mountain.

Intombi Daughter or girlfriend.

Inyati Nyathi - buffalo, a very strong person.

Inyoni Bird.

Maritzburg A town in Natal, known in Zulu as Umgungundlovu - the enclosure of the royal elephant.

Matabele Ndebele tribe.

Quathlamba The crashing mountain barrier. The Drakensberg range. Also known as Ulundi. It is also the name of the Zulu King Cetswayo's capital kraal on the white Umfolozi.

Tugela River in Natal. A river that acts with frightening suddenness.

Umgeni River in Natal. The river that flows through thorn trees.

Umkomanzi River in Natal. The great whale river. There used to be a great number of whales frequenting its mouth.

Umvoti River in Natal - a slow flowing river.

Fleet list

1. SAMSON 1836-1868 Wooden hermaphrodite brig
O.N. 6877   120b 68.7 x 18.0 x 11.9
1844: 136b 79.4 x 18.0 x 11.9 feet
1859: 129g 83.5 x 20.7 x 11.8 feet
1836: Launched by Alexander Hall and Co., Aberdeen (Yard No. 76).
12.7.1836: Registered in the ownership of R. Spring, George Rennie and others, Aberdeen as SAMSON.
10.2.1844: Owners became R. Spring, R. Youngson, George Rennie and others, Aberdeen.
20.8.1859: Owners became R. Youngson, J.T. Rennie, George Rennie and others, Aberdeen.
27.8.1868: Sold to George Smith, Aberdeen and William Harty, Sunderland.
22.4.1869: Owner became William Harty, Sunderland and George Smith, Aberdeen.
9.3.1884: Stranded in Keiss Bay, Caithness during a force 10 gale whilst on a voyage from Sunderland to Aberdeen with a cargo of lime. The crew of five was lost.

2. ELIZA HALL 1843-1854 Wooden brig
O.N. 24485   199g 87 x 19.7 x 14 feet
1843: Launched by Walter Hood and Co., Aberdeen.
20.6.1843: Registered in the ownership of George Rennie and others, Aberdeen as ELIZA HALL.
5.1854: Sold to W. Nicol, Liverpool.
1855: Sold to E. Turner, Whitby.
22.10.1864: Wrecked outside Granton breakwater.

3. LORD HADDO 1847-1867 Wooden barque
O.N. 5821   291g   117.6 x 23 x 16.5 feet
1847: Completed by Lunan and Robertson, Peterhead.
21.1.1847: Registered in the ownership of George Rennie and others, Aberdeen as LORD HADDO (owners in *Lloyd's Register* J. Rennie and Co.).
27.1.1867: Scuttled and stranded on Newcome Sands at the approaches to Lowestoft whilst on a voyage from Newcastle-on-Tyne to Cartagena with a cargo of coal. Later refloated.
2.1867: Sold to T. Small, Lowestoft.
6.1869: Sold to John Birnie Adam, Aberdeen.
4.1871: Sold to French owners.

4. CONQUEROR 1850-1855 Wooden ship
O.N. 6874   458g   134.8 x 25 x 18 feet
1850: Completed by Alexander Hall and Co., Aberdeen (Yard No. 173).
25.5.1850: Registered in the ownership of J. Rennie and Co., Aberdeen as CONQUEROR.
7.1855: Registered in the ownership of John and James Richardson, Swansea.
13.2.1867: Wrecked on north west side of Long Cay, Bahamas whilst on a voyage from Santiago de Cuba to Swansea with a cargo of copper ore.

5. CONTENT 1852-1853 Wooden ship
O.N. 31774   147g   78.5 x 18 x 12.3 feet
14.7.1842: Launched by William Johnston, Greenock.
7.9.1842: Registered in the ownership of James and John Hamilton, Irvine as CONTENT, having been bought from the bankrupt estate of the builder.
12.1846: Sold to T. Muir, Glasgow.
23.12.1852: Registered in the ownerhip of J. T. Rennie, Aberdeen.
11.1853: Sold to Alfred Hooker, Melbourne, Australia.
4.1854: Sold to Horton, Thompson and Co., Melbourne.
8.1856: Sold to James Macandrew, Dunedin, New Zealand.
1859: Sold to Melbourne owners.
10.1860: Sold to Joseph Darwent, Adelaide, Australia.
1861: Sold to J. Wimro and C. W. Gallois, Melbourne.
7.1862: Sold to the Provincial Government of Southland, Invercargill, New Zealand.

1875: Sold to John Munro and another, Melbourne.
1877: Reported missing.

6. CATHCART 1854-1867 Wooden ship
O.N. 3259   422g   122.1 x 23.9 x 17.4 feet
1852: Completed at Miramichi, New Brunswick.
15.5.1854: Registered in the ownership of J. T. Rennie, Aberdeen and others as CATHCART.
1867: Sold to A. Robinson, Aberdeen.
12.1867: Sold foreign and renamed PHILIPP MELANCHTHON
10.1869: Sold to George Hermann Wulff and Benjamin Sydney Smith, London and renamed CHINA.
1872: Sold to T. P. Wiibe and others, Porsgrunn, Norway.
1885: Last listing in Norske Veritas register.

7. L'IMPERATRICE EUGENIE 1854-1867 Iron barque
O.N. 3192   251g   127 x 22.5 x 12.8 feet
31.5.1854: Launched by Scott and Co., Greenock (Yard No. 17).
26.6.1854: Registered in the ownership of J. Rennie and Co., Aberdeen as L'IMPERATRICE EUGENIE.
1856: Chartered by the British Government for use as Crimean War Transport Ship No. 220.
6.2.1867: Wrecked on Thunderbolt Reef off Cape Recife near Port Elizabeth, South Africa whilst on a voyage from Algoa Bay to London with a cargo of wool. No lives were lost.

8. MADAGASCAR 1855-1858 Iron screw steamer
O.N. 3274   321g   165.2 x 23.5 x 13.9 feet
2-cyl. simple by Jas. Abernethy, Aberdeen; 60 HP.
5.4.1855: Launched by Scott and Co., Greenock (Yard No. 25).
25.5.1855: Registered in the ownership of J. Rennie and Co., Aberdeen as MADAGASCAR.
Chartered by British Government for Crimean War service as Transport Ship No. 240.
3.12.1858: Struck Madagascar Reef, forty miles south of East London, South Africa whilst on a voyage to Algoa Bay. Beached at the Bira River mouth and later declared a constructive total loss. No lives were lost.

9. WALDENSIAN 1856-1862 Iron screw steamer
O.N. 13547   369g 251n   164.6 x 24.5 x 14.1 feet
11.1857: 403g 285n
2-cyl. simple by A. and J. Inglis, Glasgow; 60HP.
7.3.1856: Launched by Scott and Co., Greenock (Yard No. 35).
19.3.1856: Registered in the ownership of J. Rennie and Co., Aberdeen as WALDENSIAN.
Chartered by British Government for Crimean War service as a transport.
13.10.1862: Wrecked on Bulldog Reef, Struis Point near Cape Agulhas, South Africa. No lives were lost.

10. HUGUENOT 1858-1862 Wooden ship
O.N. 21647   472g   155.4 x 28.2 x 18 feet
1858: Completed by William Duthie Junior and Co., Aberdeen.
17.7.1858: Registered in the ownership of J. Rennie and Co., Aberdeen as HUGUENOT.
31.1.1862: Stranded at Merlemont, north west France whilst on a voyage fom Colombo to London with a cargo of coffee. Later became a constructive total loss.

11. EARL OF SOUTHESK 1860-1874 Wooden barque
O.N. 25179   336g   127.3 x 25 x 16.2 feet
1858: Completed at Arbroath.
12.11.1858: Registered in the ownership of William Carnegie, London as EARL OF SOUTHWARK.
4.1860: Acquired by J.T. Rennie, Aberdeen.
1874: Sold to Anderson and Marshall, Melbourne, Australia.
28.5.1874: Wrecked on the south end of Barrett's Reef, Wellington, New Zealand whilst on a voyage from Newcastle, New South Wales to Wellington with a cargo of coal. The crew was saved.

Prince Alfred [Aberdeen Maritime Museum]

Illovo [John Naylon Collection]

12. NATAL STAR 1862-1874 Wooden ship
O.N. 45203 366g 137.1 x 25.7 x 14.9 feet
12.1862: Launched by Alexander Hall and Co., Aberdeen (Yard No. 230).
15.12.1862: Registered in the ownership of J. Rennie and Co., Aberdeen as NATAL STAR.
1871: Rerigged as a barque.
19.7.1874: Wrecked during a gale one and a half miles east of Buffalo River, East London, South Africa whilst on voyage from London to East London with general cargo.

13. PRINCE ALFRED 1862-1878 Wooden barque
O.N. 44431 258g 130.6 x 23.9 x 12.8 feet
1862: Completed by John Duthie, Aberdeen.
13.2.1862: Registered in the ownership of J.T. Rennie and Co., Aberdeen as PRINCE ALFRED.
3.1878: Sold to S. Wiborg, Krageroe, Norway and renamed DIANA.
1885: Last listing in Norske Veritas register. Lost on a voyage to Scotland

14. TUGELA 1864-1868 Wooden ship
O.N. 45219 475g 148 x 26.9 x 16.2 feet
1864: Completed by Alexander Hall and Co., Aberdeen (Yard No. 236).
21.1.1864: Registered in the ownership of J. Rennie and Co., Aberdeen as TUGELA.
3.2.1868: Drifted ashore on Back Beach, Durban when anchor chain broke in a heavy swell. Later declared a constructive total loss.

15. UMGENI 1864-1882 Wooden ship
O.N. 48860 365g 136.6 x 26.1 x 15.5 feet
10.1864: Launched by Smith, Aberdeen.
4.11.1864: Registered in the ownership of J. Rennie and Co., Aberdeen as UMGENI.
1875: Rerigged as a barque.
1882: Converted into a coal hulk at Durban.

16. ILLOVO (1) 1867-1887 Wooden ship
O.N. 56610 398g 138.9 x 27 x 15.9 feet
12.1867: Launched by Alexander Hall and Co., Aberdeen (Yard No. 254).
17.12.1867: Registered in the ownership of J. Rennie and Co., Aberdeen as ILLOVO.
1875: Rerigged as a barque.
3.1887: Sold to Captain C.A.R. Hoare, London and renamed MERCURY.
1901: Converted into a static training ship for young boys who planned to enter the merchant marine or Royal Navy and based in the River Hamble, Southampton.
12.1916: Lost off Dungeness whilst under tow from Southampton to Longhope.

17. UMVOTI 1869-1891 Iron ship
O.N. 60697 465g 158.9 x 28.7 x 15.9 feet
19.10.1869: Launched by Hall, Russell and Co., Aberdeen (Yard No. 167).
25.10.1869: Registered in the ownership of J. Rennie and Co., Aberdeen as UMVOTI.
1872: Rerigged as a barque.
1891: Sold to William B. Hay, Adelaide, South Australia.
10.1912: Sold to Ireland, Fraser and Co., Port Louis, Mauritius.
1928: Broken up

18. ASSYRIAN 1872-1877 Wooden ship
O.N. 12956 605g 152.7 x 25.9 x 18 feet
1854: Completed by Walter Hood and Co., Aberdeen.
1.1.1855: Registered in the ownership of Alexander Nicol and Co., Aberdeen as ASSYRIAN.
1872: Acquired by J. Rennie, Aberdeen.
7.10.1877: Arrived at Port Elizabeth, South Africa in a leaky condition and condemned. She was on a voyage from Lacepe Islands, north west Australia, to London with a cargo of guano.
12.12.1877: Remains sold locally.

19. UMKOMANZI 1874-1894 Wooden barque
O.N. 65103 334g 135 x 27 x 12.9 feet
12.1873: Launched by John Crown, Sunderland.
4.2.1874: Registered in the ownership of J.T. Rennie and Co., Aberdeen as UMKOMANZI.
1894: Sold to C. M. Bache, Drammen, Norway.
11.12.1897: Towed into Flekkefjord, Norway after capsizing on a voyage from Fredrikshald to Sunderland with a cargo of sleepers. Later condemned and sold.

20. TRANSVAAL 1874 Wooden barque
O.N. 65110 384g 140.4 x 27 x 13.7 feet
1874: Built by John Crown, Sunderland.
5.8.1874: Registered in the ownership of J.T. Rennie and Co., Aberdeen as TRANSVAAL.
8.12.1874: Dragged anchor and driven ashore whilst sheltering from a gale one and a half miles south of the Umgeni River, Durban whilst on her maiden voyage from London with general cargo. Twelve lives were lost.

21. IFAFA (1) 1875-1888 Wooden barque
O.N. 70439 365g 142.5 x 27.2 x 13.9 feet
2.1875: Completed by John Crown, Sunderland.
29.3.1875: Registered in the ownership of J.T. Rennie and Co., Aberdeen as IFAFA.
11.1888: Sold to Larchevêque, St. Valery, France and renamed UNION.
19.11.1893: Abandoned in the North Atlantic after losing her rudder whilst on a voyage from Newfoundland to Bordeaux with a cargo of fish.

22. MARITZBURG 1876-1890 Iron barque
O.N. 70447 456g 157.1 x 27.3 x 13.6 feet
1.1876: Launched by Alexander Hall and Co., Aberdeen (Yard No. 288).
9.2.1876: Registered in the ownership of J.T. Rennie and Co., Aberdeen as MARITZBURG.
11.1890: Sold to J. H. Wollner, Arendal, Norway.
11.1893: Abandoned.
1894: Sold to Otto Banck, Helsingborg, Sweden and renamed HILDUR.
1900: Sold to J. Labayle et Compagnie, Bordeaux, France and renamed MADELEINE.
16.8.1901: Caught fire whilst loading for Bordeaux at St. Pierre, Martinique and abandoned. Her cargo included 800 casks of rum and 125 barrels of sugar.

23. NATAL 1876-1888 Iron barque
O.N. 70458 459g 155.6 x 27 x 13.6 feet
12.1876: Launched by Alexander Hall and Co., Aberdeen (Yard No. 290).
12.12.1876: Registered in the ownership of J.T. Rennie and Co., Aberdeen as NATAL.
16.11.1888: Left Calcutta for Port Natal with cargo of rice, 13 crew and 23 passengers and disappeared.

24. QUATHLAMBA 1879-1895 Iron barque
O.N. 77453 495g 167.9 x 29.1 x 13.6 feet
6.2.1879: Launched by Alexander Hall and Co., Aberdeen (Yard No. 300).
7.3.1879: Registered in the ownership of J. Rennie and Co., Aberdeen as QUATHLAMBA.
11.1895: Sold to Edward Shuckburg, Bristol and Captain Peter Lawry Francis, London.
3.1899: Sold to Joseph James Craig, Auckland, New Zealand.
10.1905: Renamed HAZEL CRAIG.
1906: Sold to the Joseph Kennedy, Gisborne, New Zealand.
3.1908: Sold to The Ship Hazel Craig Company Ltd., Gismore.
4.1908: Sold to George Turnbull Niccol, Auckland and renamed WHITEPINE.
4.1912: Sold to Peter John McGennan, Warrnambool, Victoria.

Quathlamba [Rick Hogben Collection]

Dabulamanzi [Rennies' Collection]

9.1915: Sold to Captain Thomas Proctor (H. Bleakley and Co., managers), Sydney, New South Wales. Owner later became the Whitepine Ship Co. Ltd., Sydney.
5.1922: Sold to James Paterson and Co. Pty. Ltd., Melbourne, Victoria for use as a coal hulk.
1927: Sold to the Commissioners of the Melbourne Harbour Trust, Melbourne.
14.7.1947: Towed out and scuttled off Melbourne.

25. DABULAMANZI 1882-1900 Iron steamer
O.N. 84359 1,537g 980n 260.6 x 35.5 x 21.2 feet
C. 2-cyl. by Hall, Russell and Co., Aberdeen; 200 NHP, 10 knots.
1888: Engines tripled by Hall, Russell and Co., Aberdeen.
12.5.1882: Launched by Hall, Russell and Co., Aberdeen (Yard No. 227).
6.10.1882: Registered in the ownership of J.T. Rennie and Co., Aberdeen as DABULAMANZI.
1900: Sold to Compagnie Franco-Tunisienne de Navigation, Marseilles, France and renamed VILLE DE

SFAX. Passengers: 15.
10.1906: Sold to Compagnie Générale Transatlantique, Paris, France.
1913: Sold to S.A. Unione Austriaco di Navigazione, Trieste, Austria-Hungary and renamed ANNA.
8.1914: Laid up in Havana.
6.4.1917: Seized at New Orleans by the United States Government and operated by the United States Shipping Board Emergency Fleet Corporation, New York, USA.
1920: Sold to Indies Navigation Co., Valparaiso, Chile and renamed CALERA.
1923: Owners became Compañia de Vapor Calera, Valparaiso.
1924: Sold to Central Power and Light Company, Valparaiso.
1927: Sold to S.A. Comercial Braun and Blanchard, Valparaiso and renamed MAULE.
8.9.1928: Ran aground at Columbine Point, Farquhar Pass, Magellan Strait whilst on a voyage from Magallanes to Lota. Later declared a constructive total loss.

Matabele [Martin Leendertz Collection, SA Library]

26. MATABELE 1885-1905 Iron screw steamer

O.N. 88868 1,556g 1,005n 250.3 x 35.2 x 22.2 feet
T. 3-cyl. by Hall, Russell and Co., Aberdeen; 170 NHP, 8 knots.
10.11.1885: Launched by Hall, Russell and Co., Aberdeen (Yard No. 241).
21.12.1885: Registered in the ownership of J.T. Rennie and Co., Aberdeen as MATABELE.
9.1905: Sold to the Khedivial Mail Steamship and Graving Dock Co. Ltd., London and renamed KENEH. Passengers: 36 first, 16 second, 200 deck.
1930: Broken up at Savona.
5.1930: Register closed.

27. INANDA (1) 1888-1903 Steel screw steamer

O.N. 94523 1,758g 1,128n 270.4 x 35.2 x 23 feet
T. 3-cyl. by Hall, Russell and Co., Aberdeen; 220 NHP, 3,500 IHP, 10 knots.
9.5.1888: Launched by Hall, Russell and Co., Aberdeen (Yard No. 247).
1.6.1888: Registered in the ownership of J. Rennie and Co., Aberdeen as INANDA.
2.1903: Sold to the Khedive of Egypt, Egypt and renamed ABD-EL-MONEM.
1905: Sold to the Khedivial Mail Steamship and Graving Dock Co. Ltd., London and renamed MENZALEH.
6.6.1918: Torpedoed and sunk by the German submarine UB 105 230 miles east south east of Malta whilst on voyage from Alexandria to Bristol with a cargo of cotton seed. Ten lives were lost and the master was taken prisoner.

28. IFAFA (2) 1889-1906 Iron steamer

O.N. 94534 1,788 g 1,162n 270.2 x 35.2 x 23.5 feet
T. 3-cyl. by Hall, Russell and Co., Aberdeen; 230 NHP, 12 knots.
7.9.1889: Launched by Hall, Russell and Co., Aberdeen

(Yard No. 252).
27.9.1889: Registered in the ownership of J.T. Rennie and Co., Aberdeen as IFAFA.
12.1906: Sold to the Khedivial Mail Steamship and Graving Dock Co. Ltd., London and renamed TANTAH. Passengers: 20 first, 26 second, 141 deck.
8.1923: Sold to Italian owners and renamed JEAN.
1.1924: Renamed JEAN M.
1.1925: Sold to William John Hutchison, Piraeus but registered at London.
12.1925: Sold to Joseph Gasan, Malta and renamed MALTANA, registered in London.
8.1928: Sold to Oscar Daring, Kalchis, Greece and renamed ANNA.
1934: Sold to L. Teryazos, Piraeus, Greece.
1937: Sold to Christos Peppas and partners, Piraeus and renamed EKATERINI PEPPA.
7.2.1938: Sank in collision with the Dutch steamer PLUTO (1,156/1905) half a mile north west of the Adlergrund Light Vessel whilst on a voyage from Danzig to Oran with a cargo of coal.

29. ILLOVO (2) 1890-1910 Steel screw steamer

O.N. 94543 1,930g 1,242n 275.3 x 36.2 x 24.7 feet
Passengers: 20 first.
T. 3-cyl. by Hall, Russell and Co., Aberdeen; 250 NHP, 1,500 IHP, 11½ knots.
21.1.1890: Launched by Hall, Russell and Co., Aberdeen (Yard No. 255).
12.2.1890: Registered in the ownership of J.T. Rennie and Son, Aberdeen as ILLOVO.
11.1910: Sold to Società di Navigazione a Vapore Puglia, Bari, Italy and renamed CALABRO.
4.1.1917: Captured, shelled and sunk by the German submarine U 82 about 80 miles west of Ouessant whilst on a voyage from Cartagena to Middlesbrough.

Illovo [A. Andrews Collection]

129

Inyoni (top). *[Martin Leendertz Collection, SA Library]*

Induna, probably when running on the Australian coast (middle). *[Ian Farquhar collection]*

Inyati (bottom). *[Mrs Anne Rennie Collection]*

Inchanga. [Mrs Anne Rennie Collection]

30. INYONI 1890-1911 Steel screw steamer
O.N. 98544 1,945g 1,250n 275.6 x 36.3 x 24.5 feet
Passengers: 24 first.
T. 3-cyl. by Hall, Russell and Co., Aberdeen; 250 NHP, 1,500 IHP, 11½ knots.
16.9.1890: Launched by Hall, Russell and Co., Aberdeen (Yard No. 257).
14.10.1890: Registered in the ownership of J.T. Rennie and Co., Aberdeen as INYONI.
6.1911: Sold to Administration de Navigation à Vapeur Ottomane, Istanbul, Turkey and renamed KIZILIRMAK.
13.9.1915: Shelled and sunk by Russian warships near Sakarya.

31. INDUNA 1891-1904 Steel screw steamer
O.N. 98564 699g 428n 190.6 x 28.5 x 11.2 feet
T. 3-cyl. by Hall, Russell and Co., Aberdeen; 98 NHP, 600 IHP, 10 knots.
4.7.1891: Launched by Hall, Russell and Co., Aberdeen (Yard No. 266).
1891: Registered in the ownership of J. T. Rennie and Son, Aberdeen as INDUNA.
9.1904: Sold to Henry Edwin Campbell, London.
12.1904: Sold to Burns, Philp and Co. Ltd., Sydney, New South Wales.
8.1914: Detained by Germans in the Marshall Islands. Subsequently released by a Japanese warship.
5.1920: Sold to the Patrick Steamship Co. Ltd., Sydney.
7.1923: The Patrick Steamship Co. Ltd. went into voluntary liquidation and assets were taken over by the newly formed Patrick Steamships Ltd.
6.1925: Sold to the Railway Commissioners for New South Wales, Sydney and converted into a train ferry for use at Grafton.
5.1932: Laid up and sold for use as a wharf at Grafton.
1934: Dismantled during first quarter after lying derelict and flooded.
1957: Broken up.

32. INCHANGA 1895-1911 Steel screw steamer
O.N. 104507 2,197g 1,403n 288.2 x 39.2 x 24.7 feet
Passengers: 15 first; 6 second (later 26 first).
T. 3-cyl. by Hall, Russell and Co., Aberdeen, 310 NHP, 2,000 IHP, 12 knots.
14.12.1894: Launched by Hall, Russell and Co., Aberdeen (Yard No. 283).
7.1.1895: Registered in the ownership of J. Rennie and Co., Aberdeen as INCHANGA.

11.1911: Sold to Arab Steamers Ltd., Bombay, India and renamed BAHREIN as a pilgrim ship.
1915: Taken over as a transport by the Indian Government.
11.1922: Sold by liquidators of Arab Steamers Ltd. to Bombay and Persia Steam Navigation Co. (The Mogul Line), Bombay.
11.1923: Sold to Victor Schemeil, Alexandria, Egypt, but registered in Bombay.
4.1926: Laid up on the Thames.
7.1927: Sold to Mehanna Kouri Haddad, Alexandria.
1933: Broken up at Alexandria.

33. INYATI 1896-1912 Steel screw steamer
O.N. 106542 2,516g 1,600n 310.7 x 40.2 x 24.7 feet
Passengers: 28 first.
T. 3-cyl. by Hall, Russell and Co., Aberdeen; 398 NHP, 2,350 IHP, 13 knots.
6.10.1896: Launched by Hall, Russell and Co., Aberdeen (Yard No. 301).
27.10.1896: Registered in the ownership of J.T. Rennie and Co., Aberdeen as INYATI.
10.1911: Sold to the Charente Steamship Co. Ltd. (T. and J. Harrison, managers), Liverpool.
1912: Sold to Compañia Valenciana de Vapores Correos de Afrıca, Valencia, Spain and renamed M. BENLLIURE.
25.12.1915: Left Glasgow for Genoa.
27.12.1915: Distress signals heard when 40 miles north west of the Scilly Islands but not heard of again, and believed to have foundered in gale.

34. INGELI 1897-1914 Steel screw steamer
O.N. 108651 2,928g 1,868n 330.1 x 41.2 x 28.1 feet
Passengers: 36 first.
T. 3-cyl. by Hall, Russell and Co., Aberdeen; 428 NHP, 2,500 IHP, 12 knots.
20.8.1897: Launched by Hall, Russell and Co., Aberdeen (Yard No. 303).
26.10.1897: Registered in the ownership of J.T. Rennie and Co., Aberdeen as INGELI.
10.1911: Sold to the Charente Steamship Co. Ltd. (T. and J. Harrison, managers), Liverpool.
2.1914: Sold to Vaccaro Brothers and Co., Ceiba, Honduras and renamed TEGUCIGALPA.
1924: Owners became Standard Fruit and Steamship Co., Ceiba.
1933: Owners became Standard Navigation Corporation (Standard Fruit and Steamship Co., managers), Ceiba.
1936: Passenger capacity reduced to 12.

3.1941: Sold to the Swiss War Transport Office (Honegger and Ascott, managers), Basle, Switzerland and renamed CHASSERAL.

1947: Sold to Nautilus S.A., Basle.

1951: Sold to Franco Maresca, Genoa, Italy and renamed MAR CORRUSCO.

10.1953: Broken up by ARDEM at Savona, Italy.

35. INSIZWA 1899-1913 Steel screw steamer
O.N. 108673 2,984g 1,915n 330.2 x 41.1 x 18.6 feet
Passengers: 40 first; 20 second.
T. 3-cyl. by Hall, Russell and Co. Ltd., Aberdeen; 428 NHP, 2,500 IHP, 12¼ knots.

23.8.1899: Launched by Hall, Russell and Co. Ltd., Aberdeen (Yard No. 317).

20.10.1899: Registered in the ownership of J.T. Rennie and Co., Aberdeen as INSIZWA.

9.1911: Sold to the Charente Steamship Co. Ltd. (T. and J. Harrison, managers), Liverpool.

12.1913: Sold to S.A. di Navigazione Sicilia, Palermo, Italy and renamed TOLEMAIDE.

1923: Owners becames Società di Navigazione Italia, Rome, Italy.

10.1924: Owners went into liquidation.

1925: Owners became Compania Italiana Transatlantica (CITRA), Genoa, Italy.

8.1929: Laid up at Genoa.

6.4.1931: Arrived at Savona for demolition.

36. INKONKA 1902-1919 Steel screw steamer
O.N. 109650 3,430g 2,206n 368 x 45.1 x 24.2 feet
Passengers: 14 first.
T. 3-cyl. by Central Marine Engine Works, West Hartlepool; 450 NHP, 3,000 IHP, 11 knots.

11.10.1900: Launched by William Gray and Co. Ltd., West Hartlepool (Yard No. 620).

11.1900: Registered in the ownership of the Anglo-Arabian and Persian Steamship Co. Ltd. (F.C. Strick and Co. Ltd., managers), London as TABARISTAN.

1902: Acquired by J. T. Rennie and Son, Aberdeen and renamed INKONKA.

1911: Sold to the Charente Steamship Co. Ltd. (T. and J. Harrison, managers), Liverpool.

1915: Served from March to April as a support ship during the Gallipoli landings.

1919: Sold to David MacIver and Co. Ltd., Liverpool and renamed TUSCANY.

1929: Sold to the West of Scotland Shipbreaking Co. Ltd.

19.6.1929: Arrived at Troon to be broken up.

37. INGANE 1902-1906 Steel and iron twin screw tug
O.N. 101572 216g 18n 110.1 x 23.1 x 11 feet
C. 2-cyl. by Hall, Russell and Co. Ltd., Aberdeen; 74 NHP, 430 IHP, 10½ knots.

25.3.1902: Launched by Hall, Russell and Co. Ltd., Aberdeen (Yard No. 360).

6.8.1902: Registered in the ownership of Chiazzario and Co., Durban (Chiazzario and J. T. Rennie, joint owners) as INGANE.

4.1906: Sold to Portuguese Government and renamed JOÃO COUTINHO. Based at Lourenço Marques.

1923: Owners became Capitano do Porto, Lourenço Marques, Mozambique and renamed POLANA.

1986: Deleted from *Lloyd's Register.*

38. INKOSI (1) 1902-1918 Steel screw steamer
O.N. 115582 3,575g 2,261n 350.2 x 43.3 x 28 feet
Passengers: 50 first; 36 second.
T. 3-cyl. by Hall, Russell and Co. Ltd., Aberdeen; 484 NHP, 3,000 IHP, 12½ knots.

2.10.1902: Launched by Hall, Russell and Co. Ltd., Aberdeen (Yard No. 361).

22.11.1902: Registered in the ownership of J.T. Rennie and Co., Aberdeen as INKOSI.

1911: Sold to the Charente Steamship. Co. Ltd. (T. and J. Harrison, managers), Liverpool.

28.3.1918: Torpedoed and sunk by German submarine U 96 ten miles south of Burrow Head, Luce Bay whilst on a voyage from Liverpool to Pernambuco with general cargo and coal. Three lives were lost.

Ingeli (opposite top). *[World Ship Photo Library]*
Insizwa (opposite middle). *[Martin Leendertz Collection, SA Library]*
Inkonka (opposite bottom). *[Ambrose Greenway Collection]*
An earlier view of *Ingeli* with yard arms (this page top). *[Peter Newall collection]*
Two views of *Inkosi* (this page bottom). *[Upper: National Maritime Museum; lower: Peter Newall Collection]*

Inanda (2) (opposite). *[Glasgow University Archives DC 101/0303]*
Intaba in Rennie's (above) and Harrisons' liveries (below). *[Top: A. Duncan; below: Ambrose Greenway collection]*

39. INANDA (2) 1904-1920 Steel screw steamer
O.N. 118187 4,090g 2,607n 370 x 46.2 x 26.5 feet
Passengers: 62 first, 50 second.
T. 3-cyl. by Hall, Russell and Co. Ltd., Aberdeen; 525 NHP, 3,000 IHP, 13½ knots.
15.6.1904: Launched by Hall, Russell and Co. Ltd., Aberdeen (Yard No. 379).
8.1904: Completed.
20.9.1904: Registered in the ownership of J. Rennie and Co., Aberdeen as INANDA.
9.1911: Sold to the Charente Steamship Co. Ltd. (T. and J. Harrison, managers), Liverpool.
4.6.1920: Sold to Ellerman's Wilson Line Ltd., Hull and renamed ORLANDO. Passengers now 76 first, 534 third.
21.12.1928: Laid up at Hull.
4.7.1932: Sold to T. W. Ward Ltd., Sheffield.
11.7.1932: Left Hull in tow for demolition at Briton Ferry.
20.7.1932: Work began.

40. INTABA 1910-1927 Steel screw steamer
O.N. 129345 4,832g 3,062n 386.1 x 48.2 x 27.1 feet

Passengers: 64 first, 58 second.
T. 3-cyl. by Hall, Russell and Co. Ltd., Aberdeen; 572 HP, 3,000 IHP, 13 knots.
6.9.1910: Launched by Hall, Russell and Co. Ltd., Aberdeen (Yard No. 476).
28.10.1910: Registered in the ownership of J. Rennie and Co., Aberdeen as INTABA.
8.1911: Sold to the Charente Steamship Co. Ltd. (T. and J. Harrison, managers), Liverpool.
7.1915: Requisitioned as a transport.
1916-1917: Served as Q-Ship Q.4 under the name WAITOMO.
5.1927: Sold to Hajee Mohamed Hassan Nemazee, Hong Kong and renamed ENGLESTAN.
8.1929: Sold to the Bengal Burma Steam Navigation Co. Ltd., Rangoon, Burma.
5.1951: Owners became Scindia Steam Navigation Co. Ltd., Bombay, the beneficial owners since 5.1933.
31.10.1952: Left Calcutta under tow for Ghent.
21.1.1953: Arrived at Ghent for demolition by Van Heyghen Frères.

Intombi in Rennie livery (opposite). *[Peter Newall Collection]*
Intombi arriving at Preston to lay up (top) and (bottom) in Greek ownership as *Maliakos.*

41. INTOMBI   1912-1932   Steel screw steamer
O.N. 131443   3,884g   2,304n   365 x 47 x 27 feet
T. 3-cyl. by William Hamilton and Co. Ltd., Port Glasgow;
371 NHP, 2,100 IHP, 11½ knots.
30.5.1912: Launched by William Hamilton and Co. Ltd.,
Port Glasgow (Yard No. 237).
2.7.1912: Registered in the ownership of the Charente
Steamship Co. Ltd. (T. and J. Harrison, managers),
Liverpool as INTOMBI. She had been laid down as
ACTOR.
8.1914-3.1915: Chartered as a store ship by the Admiralty.
1924: Transferred to Gulf of Mexico service.

5.1930: Laid up at Preston.
1.1932: Sold to M. A. Embiricos, Andros, Greece and
renamed MALIAKOS.
1949: Sold to Ibrahim Kalkavan, Istanbul, Turkey and
renamed SARAYKÖY.
1954: Sold to Sevket Manioglu and Naci Ucler, Istanbul.
1955: Owners became Sapanca Vapur Isletmesi (Manioglu
and Ucler, managers), Istanbul and renamed SAPANCA.
28.2.1956: Sunk in collision with the Dutch steamer
BLOMMERSDYK (6,855/1920) at Schaar Van de Noord,
off Bats, River Scheldt whilst on a voyage from Antwerp
to Istanbul with a cargo of fertiliser and chalk.

Ingoma in Rennies' colours, but note that the steel bands for Harrison's funnel colours are visible (opposite). *[Peter Newall Collection]*

Ingoma as *San Giovanni Battista* at Montevideo (right). *[Raul Maya/William Schell]*

Inanda (3) (below).

42. INGOMA   1913-1937   Steel screw steamer
O.N. 135475   5,686g   3,566n   400.6 x 52.2 x 28.3 feet
Passengers: 114 first.
T. 3-cyl. by D. and W. Henderson and Co. Ltd., Glasgow; 616 NHP, 4,000 IHP, 14 knots.
22.4.1913: Launched by D. and W. Henderson and Co. Ltd., Glasgow (Yard No. 483).
28.6.1913: Registered in the ownership of the Charente Steamship Co. Ltd. (T. and J. Harrison, managers), Liverpool.
1914: Chartered as a troopship.
1919: Returned to owners.
1921: Transferred to the West Indies service.
10.1937: Sold to Compagnia Ligure di Navigazione, Genoa, Italy and renamed SAN GIOVANNI BATTISTA.
31.1.1942: Torpedoed by British aircraft in position 33.47 north by 12.17 east whilst on a voyage from Italy to Tripoli.
2.2.1942: Stranded two miles west of Tagiura after towline broke. Subsequently refloated and towed to Tripoli.
19.1.1943: Scuttled in the harbour entrance. Later salved by the British and scrapped.

43. INANDA (3)   1925-1941   Steel screw steamer
O.N. 147310   5,985g   3,746n   407 x 52.2 x 28.5 feet
Passengers: 91 first.
Q. 4-cyl. by Wallsend Slipway and Engineering Co. Ltd., Wallsend-on-Tyne; 605 NHP, 4,100 IHP, 14 knots.
24.2.1925: Launched by Swan, Hunter and Wigham Richardson Ltd., Newcastle-on-Tyne (Yard No. 1259).
27.4.1925: Registered in the ownership of the Charente Steamship Co. Ltd. (T. and J. Harrison, managers), Liverpool.
5.1925: Completed.
7-9.9.1940: Bombed and sunk during air attacks on the London Docks. Raised and repaired without passenger accommodation. She had been hired by the Royal Navy and was fitting out as an Ocean Boarding Vessel.
11.1941: Owners became the Ministry of War Transport, London (T. and J. Harrison, Liverpool, managers) and renamed EMPIRE EXPLORER.
9.7.1942: Torpedoed and sunk by the German submarine U 575 off Trinidad in position 11.40 north by 60.55 west whilst on voyage from Demerara to Barbados with a cargo of pitch, sugar and mail bags. The crew were later picked up by a motor torpedo boat and landed at Tobago. Three lives were lost.

Inkosi (2) (above). [Peter Newall Collection]
Empire Chivalry as Inkosi became between 1941 and 1946 (below). [National Maritime Museum P22250]
Planter (opposite). [Fotoflite incorporating Skyfotos]

44. INKOSI (2) 1937-1941
O.N. 164323 6,618g 4,055n 414.8 x 56 x 28.5 feet.
Passengers: 82 first.
Q.4-cyl. by Wallsend Slipway and Engineering Co. Ltd., Wallsend-on-Tyne; 835 NHP, 14 knots.
25.2.1937: Launched by Swan, Hunter and Wigham Richardson Ltd., Newcastle-on-Tyne (Yard No. 1525) for the Charente Steamship Co. Ltd. (T. and J. Harrison, managers), Liverpool as INKOSI.
6.1937: Completed.

7.9.1940: Bombed and sunk during an air attack on the London Docks. She had been hired by the Royal Navy and was fitting out as an Ocean Boarding Vessel. Raised and repaired without passenger accommodation.
1941: Owners became the Ministry of War Transport, London (T. and J. Harrison, Liverpool, managers) and renamed EMPIRE CHIVALRY.
1946: Returned to owners and renamed PLANTER.
22.9.1958: Arrived at Ghent, Belgium under tow for demolition by Van Heyghen Frères.

CARDIFF HALL LINE
David Burrell

During the short life of the Cardiff Hall Line, its founder Edward Nicholl was arguably one of Cardiff's most successful shipowners; innovating in ship design, promoting new companies with ease, reporting very healthy voyage profits, and selling out in a way that guaranteed him maximum profit. Yet Nicholl remains something of an enigma. His profit figures did not tell the whole story of his enormous indebtedness to shipbuilders, and his shareholders did not get as good a deal as he did during the sell off. On the other hand, he fought publicly for probity in marine insurance, and gave very generously of his time and money to both public and professional causes.

The rise of Cardiff shipowners

Deposits of iron ore, coal and limestone in South Wales led to the establishment of iron works at Merthyr Tydfil, Dowlais and elsewhere. The ironworks required phosphorus-free ore, which had to be imported from elsewhere in Britain or abroad (mainly from Spain) due to the high phosphorus content of local ore. Cardiff, originally a modest market town, was the natural gateway for the valleys and the import of ore and export of iron formed its major traffic when the West Dock, the first to be built, opened in 1839.

The second half of the nineteenth century saw spectacular growth of heavy industry in South Wales and of mining in the valleys to satisfy the demand for Welsh steam coal, and Cardiff boomed.

Edward Nicholl [National Museums and Galleries of Wales 83.763]

Until late in the nineteenth century Britain was the largest producer and exporter of coal, the primary source of power for ships, railways and utilities. The growing band of Cardiff shipowners carried coal and manufactured iron and tinplate products from Cardiff and brought back iron ore, copper ore and pitwood to meet local demand. To this was added the Black Sea grain trade which provided return cargo, mainly to North European ports from where ships ballasted back to Cardiff to load another outward cargo of coal. Opportunities in Cardiff drew people from all over Wales, England and abroad. From the West Country came Anning, Cory, Seager, Smith and Cornishman Edward Nicholl, the last-named a member of the small band of marine engineers who aspired to ownership in their own right.

Nicholl the engineer

Edward Nicholl was born on 17th June 1862 at Pool, a small village between Redruth and Camborne. The son of a draughtsman, Nicholl commenced work aged ten as a telegraph messenger boy and letter stamper at Redruth Post Office. In 1876 he began an engineering apprenticeship at the Carn Brea Railway Works, later moving to the Swindon works of the GWR under Chief Mechanical Engineer Sir Daniel Gooch. Breaking his indentures he went to West Hartlepool from where, after

three months in the engine works of Thomas Richardson and Sons Ltd., he went to sea in 1882 as third engineer on Ropner's *Wave* (957/1871). The following year he was second engineer on Morel Brothers' Cardiff-registered *Portugalette* (1,510/1882) before becoming foreman at Richards and Hopkins' Newport ship repair yard in 1883. Three months later he was back at sea, the youngest chief engineer to sail out of Cardiff on John Cory and Sons' *Ross* (1,356/1881). Two longer-term relationship commenced in 1884. On 17th April he married Frances Garby from Redruth (they were to have a son and three daughters), and signed on as chief engineer on the *Gwenllian Thomas* (1,082/1882), the first ship of Evan Thomas, Radcliffe and Co. He remained with this company until 1894.

Nicholl came ashore in 1893, having been promised the job of Radcliffe's Superintendent Engineer. However, this was given to another, and Nicholl became Assistant Superintendent and Consulting Engineer. Piqued at not getting the promised top job, Nicholl left in January 1894 to become Superintendent with W. and C.T. Jones. By 1904 he had supervised the construction of nine ships, giving him an excellent grounding in the design and building of tramp steamers.

Nicholl the shipowner

In the summer of 1903 a chance meeting with Lord de Blaquiere on a train between Bath and London led to Nicholl entering shipowning. Lord de Blaquiere and others gave encouragement, including his employers W. and C.T. Jones (who pledged £1,000 for each vessel acquired) and Frederick Knight, who was associated with Jones. His employers requested that for five years he continue in a dual role as their consultant engineer and have his offices within their premises.

In October 1903 Nicholl placed orders with William Doxford and Sons for two turret deck steamers, the first to be owned in Cardiff. To a standard Doxford design, they were to load 6,350 tons deadweight. Two boilers set at 160 psi and a triple expansion engine were to give 1,350 IHP and a speed between 9 and 11 knots. The price was £34,000 each.

Nicholl's first ship, *Whateley Hall* was launched on 16th June 1904 by the daughter of Frederick Knight, Nicholl's largest backer, after whose residence the ship was named. The maiden voyage of *Whateley Hall* was from Cardiff, where she loaded coal, to Port Said. She then ballasted to Nicholaieff in the Black Sea to load maize, wheat and barley for Rotterdam. Voyage profits were £754 on a total earning of £3,428 and an interim dividend of £1 was paid on each £50 share (equivalent to 10% per annum). Nicholl's second ship, *Eaton Hall*, launched on 12th July 1904, undertook exactly the same voyage and showed a voyage profit of £1,133 (allowing a 14% annual dividend). For her third voyage, *Whateley Hall* introduced the Nicholl flag to the River Plate.

The launch of Nicholl's first ship, *Whateley Hall*, at Sunderland on 16th June 1904. *[National Museums and Galleries of Wales 86407 and 86408]*

The turret ship

Edward Nicholl was, in 1904, the first Cardiff shipowner to commission a turret ship, even though the design had been trading since 1892. It was inspired by the arrival at Liverpool on 21st July 1891 of the American whaleback *Charles W. Wetmore* with 72,000 bushels of grain loaded at Duluth. She sailed on 29th July for New York, before proceeding to the North Pacific where she was wrecked near Coos Bay, Oregon on 8th September 1892.

The whaleback was designed to allow waves to wash over the hull, and to permit this watertight hatches were fitted. It was claimed the design would ride better in bad weather and not be the obstacle to waves that caused damage in other ships. However, in practice it proved difficult to maintain the watertight seals, and ingress of water caused damage to cargo. William Doxford and Sons, Sunderland took a long look and their design office developed the turret. Both turret and whaleback plans were shown to customers including Norddeutscher Lloyd, Lane and Macandrew, McIlwraith McEachern, Jones Price and Co, Percy Jackson, Temperley, and John Carlisle. William Johnston and Co., Liverpool ordered a whaleback, the *Sagamore* of 1893. Both Walter Runciman and Co., Newcastle, and Gastaldi and Co., Genoa, signed preliminary agreements for whalebacks, but these were not confirmed.

The form of the turret hull with its continuous trunk had several advantages. Under the tonnage regulations, the hull had a net tonnage up to 10% lower than a similar-sized conventional hull, thereby reducing port charges. The turret gave greater longitudinal strength, whilst lack of sheer made for easier construction. It was self trimming with a bulk cargo like grain and coal, and threw off green seas, protecting the hatches. Being better sea boats, turrets were claimed to make quicker passages in bad weather. The lack of well decks removed the risk of flooding. Freeboard was substantially increased - a Nicholl prospectus had it doubled to 11 feet, and this was said to make deck damage virtually nil.

Owners were reluctant to order the untried turret design. Doxfords had to prove their confidence, which they did after the first turret, named *Turret*, was launched on 19th November 1892. She was owned by the Turret Steam Shipping Co. Ltd., jointly controlled by Doxford and Captain William Petersen, with management by Petersen, Tate and Co. of Newcastle. Having proved the turret, in July 1897 Doxfords sold their interest in the *Turret* to the managers, who ordered a further seven turrets for their Canadian Great Lakes operations. Similarly, Doxfords took a 50% holding in the Belgian-American Maritime Co. Ltd., Antwerp in partnership with William Johnston and Co., Liverpool, to own the whaleback *Sagamore* and the turrets *Ashmore, Noranmore,* and *Beechmore*. Doxford sold their interest to Johnston in June 1900, making a profit of £10,000.

A total of 183 turret ships were built, all but seven by Doxfords in their Sunderland yard. Swan and Hunter built three as joint ventures or as sub-contracts from Doxford, as was one by Hawthorn, Leslie and Co. Three were built under licence, two by Vickers, Sons and Maxim and the other by Krupp at Kiel. *Whateley Hall* was the 100th turret to be delivered when handed over to Edward Nicholl in 1904.

Changes in tonnage, load line and freeboard regulations after 1907 impacted on the practical advantages of the turret, affecting tonnage calculations, hence operating costs, and deadweight. The regulations now favoured the shelter decker, which became the popular design for the next fifty years. Few turrets were built after this change, only nine in the period from 1908 till the last, *Orangemoor*, was delivered in 1911.

The First World War saw many turrets lost by enemy action. Advancing age and the adverse freight market during the depression sent many more to the breakers. But it was to be January 1963 before the last, the Spanish *Diciembre* of 1895, ended her career when wrecked off Vallcarca as *Nuestra Senora Del Carmen*.

The Plate trade

Late in the nineteenth century Argentina became one of the major suppliers of meat and grain to Britain and a large employer of both liner and tramp shipping. This was made possible, in part, by suppression of hostile Indians in the ruthless extermination campaign started in 1879.

Since the arrival of European settlers distance had been the limiting factor, restricting trade to non-perishables. Frigorificos were established as the infant refrigeration industry made it possible to transport perishable commodities through the tropics. The meat trade grew from early shipments in 1883 by the steamers *Meath* and *Loch Ard*.

Until the railways developed, grain production was limited by the cost of transport over dirt roads to ports. Before they were nationalised in 1948, some two-thirds of the Argentinean railways were British owned. Argentineans preferred to invest in land rather than railways or industry. Land value appreciated fabulously thanks to the railways, and gave a 10-15% annual income at no risk, compared with zero appreciation, similar annual income and some risk from investing in railways and utilities. The Argentineans left European investors to finance and build railways and utilities but then complained that they were being exploited. The rail network extended to just 1,000 miles in 1875, but grew to 5,000 miles in 1889, 10,000 in 1899, and 22,000 in 1914.

Before 1890 wheat exports had exceeded 100,000 tons in only three years. The last decade of the century saw rapid growth, with exports exceeding one million tons in 1893 and two million in 1904, by which time some 44% was destined for Britain. In 1934 grain exports were over 12 million tons.

The Plate grain trade eclipsed the Russian Black Sea trade after the First World War. The carriage of over a million tons of Welsh coal to fuel the railways and utilities provided outward cargoes, some owners finding full employment for their ships as dedicated Plate traders.

The Ottawa Conference in 1932 replaced free trade with protectionism ('Buy from those who buy from us'), offering the Commonwealth preferential tariffs. Relations with Argentina were strained as Britain was its largest export market. However, meetings, such as Roca-Runciman Pact of 1933 and the Miranda-Eady Agreement in 1946, gave Argentina favoured nation status and protected the trade.

The first *Grindon Hall* was commissioned in 1905, *Tredegar Hall* in 1906, and the second *Grindon Hall* in 1908 to replace the first which had been lost. These were all turrets to the same design as the *Whateley Hall* and *Eaton Hall*. In 1905 Nicholl agreed to take Doxford's yard number 360, but this was cancelled, probably by mutual agreement, and completed for Bowring as *Gafsa*. It was replaced by number 382 which entered service in 1907 as the *Silksworth Hall*, costing £45,500. A sister, *Haigh Hall*, followed in 1908.

By the time Nicholl's seventh and last turret, the *Grindon Hall*, was delivered in 1908 the design was losing popularity. Changes in tonnage and load line regulations removed the quirks which gave financial advantages to the design, and self trimming could be built into other designs. A series of single deckers started with the delivery of the 6,400 deadweight *Windsor Hall* in 1910. She was followed in 1912 by the larger 7,150 deadweight *Standish Hall* and *Cardiff Hall* (2), and by the Readhead-built *Westoe Hall* of 1914 which cost £52,600. Three Doxford deliveries in 1914 - *Welbeck Hall* (2), *Bland Hall* and *Albert Hall* - were shelter deckers and the largest ships in the fleet, loading 8,250 deadweight, and priced between £56,500 and £57,500 - significant increases in cost since *Whateley Hall* of 1904, and reflecting the end of the shipping recession.

Nicholl also diversified, buying second-hand ships. In May 1907 the Newcastle-owned and built two-decker *Lady Palmer* was acquired by a company in which, initially at least, Nicholl and one other were the only investors, subscribing a total of £11,500. Two years later, Nicholl was boasting that *Welbeck Hall*, as she had become, had proved an exceptionally good bargain, returning dividends of 28%, despite the worst depression shipping had ever known. He invited investment in a new company, the Cardiff Hall Steam Ship Co. Ltd., which was attempting to secure a secondhand ship on similar terms. This was the awning decker *Duchess of York* from Whitby, which he renamed *Cardiff Hall*.

Nicholl was not only running his own ships, but was continuing to help superintend those of W. and C.T. Jones. To help manage his own fleet, which had come to be called the Cardiff Hall Line, in 1906 he and his son-in-law Ivor D. Griffin formed a partnership known as Edward Nicholl and Co. Griffin initially described himself as a shipping clerk but quickly promoted himself to the status of shipowner as he took modest holdings in the single-ship companies. Much later, Nicholl was to introduce his son Albert as a partner, and the company was also to include Ernest Griffin.

Nicholl the promoter

How did Nicholl, with modest financial resources of his own, finance his fleet? Firstly, and most significantly, he negotiated low prices and obtained excellent credit terms from Doxfords the builders. The contract for *Whateley Hall* called for a £1,000 down payment, followed by £9,000 on delivery and the balance over five years with interest at 4.5%. This meant considerable, long-term indebtedness to the builders. By May 1905, with two ships trading, Doxford's held post-dated bills for £34,500.

Secondly, Nicholl called on his business friends to back his venture. The Whateley Hall company was capitalised at £20,000 (the ship cost £34,000) with 400 shares at £50 each. Frederick Knight, who was already an investor in the Jones fleet and hence known to Nicholl, took £3,000 worth of shares in the Whateley Hall Steam Ship Co. Ltd., and W. and C.T. Jones took a more modest £550. Nicholl himself took £1,550.

Nicholl's third step was to do some artful promotion of the new single-ship company to potential investors. The prospectus of the Whateley Hall company stressed the quality of the new ship, the advantages of its turret design in reducing Suez Canal tolls and other dues, and its exceedingly low cost. He then went on to discuss how advantageous it was to buy shipping at low prices: 'Several Cardiff firms have demonstrated by the amount of money paid in dividends that shipping purchased at such a low figure and well managed affords an excellent investment.' But Nicholl had no track record as a shipping manager, so he had to cite his 20 years' experience of superintendence, building and working steamers with Evan Thomas, Radcliffe and with W. and C.T. Jones.

Nicholl's prospectus worked spectacularly well. The Whateley Hall Steam Ship Company Ltd. was registered on 14th August 1903, but by 7th September - just over three weeks - its full £20,000 capital had been subscribed. This was particularly impressive, as it was to be July 1904 before the *Whateley Hall* was due to start trading and earning dividends. Apart from Knight, Nicholl and W. and C.T. Jones, most of the 89 individual investors had very modest holdings, and were widely scattered geographically. Nicholl's success was especially striking as shipping was going through a depressed period, as evidenced by the low prices he was getting from Doxfords. Although we know the arguments Nicholl used, we do not know how he spread the word to the many potential investors who were clearly not known to him personally. There is more research to be done into the promotion of steamship companies, in which Cardiff owners seem to have been masters.

The management agreements with the owning companies gave Edward Nicholl and Co. 2.5% of gross earnings or 5% on time charters. These terms were not the most advantageous for shareholders as the percentages were earned irrespective of whether the ships were operating at a profit. It would have been better to pay a percentage of the profit, as this was an incentive for the manager to ensure that vessels operated profitably.

The success of the Whateley Hall company flotation was cited in Nicholl's subsequent prospectuses for his single-ship companies (it was to be 1912 before any Nicholl company owned more than one ship). For his third company, the Grindon Hall Steam Ship Co. Ltd., the *Grindon Hall* (1) was described as 'a duplicate of the *Whateley Hall* and *Eaton Hall* . . . the capital of these companies was considerable over-applied for.' Nicholl also stressed its low cost: *Grindon Hall* was priced at £34,000 but only four years before similar ships were worth £46,000, he noted. Again, the Grindon Hall company was capitalised at £20,000. Perhaps because investors were becoming more cautious, or because Frederick Knight reduced his investment to just twenty £50 shares, the Grindon Hall company shares were slow to sell. Registered on 13th October 1904, five months later only 294 of its 400 shares had been taken up by 65 individuals.

With Nicholl's success at both financing ships and paying good dividends, he grew in confidence, and the single-ship companies set up in 1906 and 1907 to own *Silksworth Hall* and her sister *Haigh Hall* were capitalised at £30,000, the cost of turrets now having risen to £45,500 each. Nevertheless, the prospectuses still reminded investors that 'when shipping is at its lowest is the time to buy'. The additional cost of the ships was justified by their being 'larger and having more numerous winches, and more powerful engines to perform the guaranteed speed'. Nicholl's bigger backers had deserted him, and with forty shares of £50 each he was by far the largest shareholder. Nevertheless, within a few months of these flotations, most of the shares had been taken up by small investors.

By 1909, the costs of ships had fallen very low, and *Windsor Hall* was ordered for just £31,500. This allowed Nicholl to claim in the prospectus of the Windsor Hall Steam Ship Co. Ltd. that 'unquestionably, no steamers have been purchased on more favourable terms than those comprising the fleet of Edward Nicholl and Co., believed to be the cheapest and best equipped cargo steamers in the country'. According to Nicholl the opportunity for shareholders was made even more attractive because there were indications of an all-round improvement in trade. The accompanying graph of profits per £1,000 invested is from the prospectus of the Windsor Hall company.

Three of the 1914 newbuildings - *Bland Hall*, *Westoe Hall*, and *Albert Hall* - were registered under the ownership of a new company with a capital of £150,000, Nicholl Steamships Ltd. This was the only time Nicholl moved away from single-ship companies. The latter had the advantage that, if a ship was involved in an accident, the financial liability of its owning company could not exceed its capital value. But the disadvantages included a much larger amount of administration, as prospectuses had to be issued individually, records of shareholdings had to be kept, and accounts had to be made up, audited and filed for each company every year. A larger company owning more ships reduced the administrative burden at the expense of extra risk.

As the prices Nicholl negotiated show, the years following the founding of his fleet were a period of recession with many owners failing. Despite this, Nicholl

Eaton Hall (above), and *Grindon Hall* (1) (right). The latter has a letter N added to her funnel. It is said that Nicholl's wife, having seen one of Anning Brothers' ships with a large letter A on the funnel, suggested that Nicholl's ships were identified with a letter N. *[Ivor Rooke collection and George Scott collection]*

EDWD. NICHOLL & Co., CARDIFF.

CARDIFF "HALL" LINE.

	TONS D.W.			
S.S. "CARDIFF HALL"	4100		due in October to complete first Voyage Account.	
„ "WELBECK HALL"	4300	Cost £11,500.	From May 8, 1907, to July 19, 1909.	PROFIT £4,161 15s. 5d.
„ "WHATELEY HALL"	6350	„ £34,000.	From July 9, 1904, to July 12, 1909.	PROFIT £16,692 3s. 6d.
„ "EATON HALL"	6350	„ £34,000.	From August 5, 1904, to September 15, 1909.	PROFIT £18,840 3s. 1d.
„ "GRINDON HALL"	6350	„ £34,000.	From September 26, 1905, to August 18, 1909.	PROFIT £13,934 4s. 11d.
„ "TREDEGAR HALL"	6350	„ £34,000.	From August 22, 1906, to August 28, 1909.	PROFIT £8,380 11s. 2d.
„ "SILKSWORTH HALL"	8250	„ £45,500.	From July 8, 1907, to August 6, 1909.	PROFIT £6,456 17s. 7d.
„ "HAIGH HALL"	8250	„ £45,500.	From July 22, 1908, to July 4, 1909.	PROFIT £3,782 15s. 9d.

BUTE DOCKS, CARDIFF,
5th October, 1909.

Dear Sir or Madam,

We have every confidence in asking for more capital because our past and present contracts cover some of the cheapest and best equipped steamers afloat, and we believe that no other firm possess such modern and well equipped steamers, **at the same cost.**

The following results of the working of our Steamers, not selected from isolated voyages, **but in each case from the steamers' first to the last completed voyage,** will show the success that has attended our efforts.

Mr. Nicholl is the largest individual shareholder in our fleet of Steamers, the firm's interests are consequently identical with those of the shareholders.

Should this steamer at any time become a total loss, the money received from the Underwriters will not be used in the purchase of another Steamer without the concurrence of a majority of the Shareholders. We were the first shipping company to introduce this much needed reform in shipping investments, and have already put this into practice.

Capital previously asked for by us has, on each occasion, been considerably over applied for and as much as six months before the steamer has been delivered by the builders.

We trust you will help us to maintain this record and send us your early application conformably with the accompanying prospectus.

The results of the working of our Fleet are as follows :—

S.S. "WHATELEY HALL."
Capital, £20,000.   **PROFIT £16,692 3s. 6d.**   **Original Amount of Debentures, £14,500.**
From July 9, 1904, to July 12, 1909.
After payment of Debenture interest and all other expenses, profits amounting to £8,100 have been distributed amongst the shareholders in dividends, representing 40½% on their invested capital, and £5,117 16s. 10d. has been applied in reduction of Debentures and the creation of a Reserve Fund.

S.S. "EATON HALL."
Capital, £20,000.   **PROFIT £18,840 3s. 1d.**   **Original amount of Debentures, £14,500.**
From August 5, 1904, to September 15, 1909.
After payment of Debenture interest and all other expenses, profits amounting to £8,000 have been distributed amongst the shareholders in dividends, representing 40% on their invested capital, and £7,393 5s. 2d. has been applied in reduction of Debentures and the creation of a Reserve Fund.

S.S. "GRINDON HALL."
Capital, £20,000.   **PROFIT £13,934 4s. 11d.**   **Original amount of Debentures, £14,500.**
From September 26, 1905, to August 18, 1909.
After payment of Debenture interest and all other expenses, profits amounting to £11,165 have been distributed amongst the shareholders in dividends, representing 55¾% on their invested capital, and £115 15s. 6d. has been applied in reduction of Debentures and the creation of a Reserve Fund.

S.S. "TREDEGAR HALL."
Capital, £20,000.   **PROFIT £8,380 11s. 2d.**   **Original amount of Debentures, £14,500**
From August 22, 1906, to August 28, 1909.
After payment of Debenture interest and all other expenses, profits amounting to £3,800 have been distributed amongst the shareholders in dividends, representing 19% on their invested capital, and £2,355 15s. 8d. has been applied in reduction of Debentures and the creation of a Reserve Fund.

S.S. "SILKSWORTH HALL."
Capital, £30,000.   **PROFIT £6,456 17s. 7d.**   **Original amount of Debentures, £16,000.**
From July 22, 1907, to August 6, 1909.
After payment of Debenture interest and all other expenses, profits amounting to £2,700 have been distributed amongst the shareholders in dividends, representing 9% on their invested capital, and £1,726 4s. 6d. has been applied in reduction of Debentures and the creation of a Reserve Fund.

S.S. "HAIGH HALL."
Capital, £30,000.   **PROFIT £3,782 15s. 9d.**   **Original amount of Debentures, £16,000.**
From July 22, 1908, to July 4, 1909.
After payment of Debenture interest and all other expenses, profits amounting to £1,800 have been distributed amongst the shareholders in dividends, representing 6% on their invested capital, and £1,053 5s. 1d. has been applied in reduction of Debentures and the creation of a Reserve Fund.

S.S. "WELBECK HALL."
Capital, £11,500.   **No Debenture issue.**   **PROFIT £4,161 15s. 5d.**
From May 8 1907 to July 19, 1909.
A Profit of 16¾ per cent. per annum on the Capital, out of which has been paid Dividends, £3,622 10s. and placed to Reserve, £341 15s. 5d.

You will notice that we do not single out any particular Steamer, **we show the results of each, and they have all done well.** The earnings of our Fleet show an average **net profit of 11% per annum.**

Yours faithfully,

EDWD. NICHOLL & Co.

THE MARITIME REVIEW, LTD., DOCKS, CARDIFF.

Shipbuilding Statistics for a Period of 50 Years.

THE subjoined Diagram constructed from the official figures published by LLOYDS demonstrates the appropriateness of the present time for replenishing Shipping Tonnage. The prolongation of the black line indicates the actual Tonnage built in each of the past 50 years, whilst the red line shows the normal requirements in those years to meet the gradual expansion in the carrying trade of the world.

A glance at this diagram shows the enormous decrease in ship-building last year, and the new Tonnage that is now required to restore the market to a normal condition.

In 1908 the increase of new Tonnage was 1,000,000 tons less than the average output of the four preceding years.

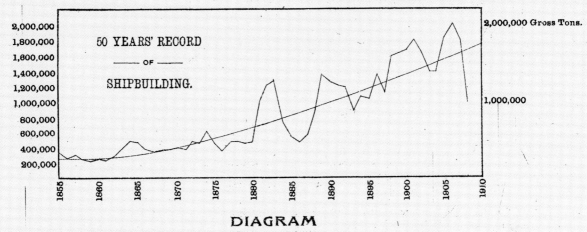

DIAGRAM

shewing the profits earned per £1,000 capital invested in each steamship of

THE CARDIFF "HALL" LINE,

after payment of debenture interest, management expenses, and all other incidental charges.

Pages from the prospectuses for Nicholl's companies stressed in words and graphs the profits made by existing steamers.

maintained his balance sheets in the black and paid dividends to investors. However, he advertised voyage profits rather than balance sheets, which avoided making reference to the liability of bills drawn in favour of the builders for, on average, half the building costs. Table 1 shows the voyage profits he quoted for his fleet in 1909.

In January 1913 Nicholl reported that, for the fleet of nine steamers, dividends totalling £25,500 (an average of 12.5%) had been paid and £35,762 placed in reserve. But the nine steamers had cost £333,500 to build and the capital of the owning companies was £210,000. He did not say what was the purpose of the reserves, but to allow for a reasonable depreciation of 5% would have required a figure in excess of £76,000 for these nine vessels. In addition, *Welbeck Hall* (1), bought secondhand in May 1907 at a cost of £11,000, had earned voyage profits of £16,573 and in December 1912 was sold very profitably for £13,500. Six months later, in the summer of 1913, a further statement gave details of ten vessels and compared the gross voyage profits (£293,833) with the capital of the owning companies (£221,500). This gave very satisfactory percentage figures, but concealed the existence of outstanding debt in the form of post-dated bills of exchange held by Doxford, which in September 1908 had totalled £90,500.

Profit came not only from trading ships but also from selling them. Two ordered by Nicholl were sold on the stocks and two other orders were cancelled at the request of Norwegian buyers, for which Nicholl received £4,000.

Nicholl's experience at sea and ashore doubtless aided him in running his fleet. Although the *Maritime Review* spoke of him as '... one of Cardiff's youngest and certainly the most phenomenally successful steamer managers', the profit levels he declared leave the suspicion that full allowance for depreciation might not have been shown in the accounts. The outbreak of war in 1914 may well have saved Nicholl from having to explain to his shareholders how ships retained in the balance sheet at cost price were sold at depreciated market values.

insure marine risks in which the insurer had no direct pecuniary interest. This meant the insurer took out a policy with some confidence that the ship insured would become a casualty, probably because they were aware of plans to scuttle her. In *Shipowners of Cardiff: a Class by Themselves*, David Jenkins cites the case of the *Albion* (3,650/1892), following the loss of which in 1908 it was discovered that a number of individuals who had no interest in the ship had taken out insurances totalling over £12,000. He also refers to a retired shipmaster who successfully 'gambled' on the loss of three vessels inside a year. Nicholl was one of the most outspoken critics of this practice of 'gambling' on the loss of ships, and after a number of speeches in 1908 he was chosen as the representative of the Cardiff Shipowners' Association at a conference on the issue called by the Board of Trade. Following this, the President of the Board of Trade, Winston Churchill, introduced the Marine Insurance (Gambling Policies) Act of 1909, which made it a criminal offence for persons not having a financial interest in a ship to take out a speculative policy on its loss.

However, although the act stopped outsiders profiting from the loss of ships, it did nothing to stop owners deliberately sinking their ships. Although not confined to Cardiff, this practice seemed particularly rife in this port, particularly once the recession which set in prior to 1905 resulted in a fall in prices of ships, leaving many owners with ships whose insured value was above their market value. Nicholl himself may have been under suspicion of such practice when his *Grindon Hall* (1) went missing in 1907, and this could have fuelled his anger. Ships registered in Cardiff were beginning to gain such a bad reputation that a number of the port's most prominent owners re-registered their ships elsewhere. Nicholl moved the registries of his entire fleet to London in 1912, as did Evan Thomas, Radcliffe and Co. In an even more celebrated move, William Reardon Smith transferred his ships to Bideford registry in 1913.

In 1910, shortly after resigning from the Cardiff City Council, Nicholl formed the Cardiff Naval Brigade, to

Table 1: Voyage profits declared by Nicholl in 1909

Ship	Profit declared	Dates
Whateley Hall	£15,380	9.6.1904-13.2.1909
Eaton Hall	£17,987	5.8.1904-22.1.1909
Grindon Hall	£12,978	26.9.1905-27.11.1908
Tredegar Hall	£5,734	26.8.1906-24.10.1908
Silksworth Hall	£4,461	22.7.1907-11.9.1908
Haigh Hall	£1,834	22.7.1907-13.2.1909
Welbeck Hall	£2,872	18.5.1907-30.8.1908

Nicholl the officer, councillor and campaigner

Unusual for tramp owners, Cardiff Hall Line endeavoured to carry all British crews. This may have stemmed from Nicholl's long association with the Royal Navy, where he had been commissioned Engineer, RNR on 31st December 1889. When his work made it difficult to meet the training requirements he moved to the retired list on 17th October 1901.

In the November of 1907, the year that he moved out of the offices of W. and C.T. Jones and set up his own, Nicholl became a member of the Cardiff City Council. Serving until July 1910, Nicholl followed an enlightened policy on social problems when probing the unsanitary conditions of seamen's boarding houses. He also tackled the problem of the Bute leases. The centre of Cardiff and the docks were largely built on the Bute Estate and the short run left on the leases discouraged much-needed property developments.

Perhaps Nicholl's biggest campaign was directed against abuses of insurance. At the time it was possible to

provide for the needs of youths too old for the Scouts and too young to join the Territorial Army. His other interests included the Presidency of the Cardiff Shipowner's Association in 1912, membership of the London Committee of Bureau Veritas, with which society his ships were classed, and directorships of the West of England Protection and Indemnity Association, the Taff Vale Railway Co. Ltd., and the Penarth Pontoon, Slipway and Ship Repairing Co. Ltd.

Losses in the grain trade

On 4th December 1907 *Grindon Hall* (1) sailed from Sulina with maize and barley valued at £46,000. Bound for Campbeltown and Glasgow she never even reached the Bosphorus, a 28-hour passage. Wreckage and a lifeboat found near Varna led to the conclusion that she had foundered soon after sailing. The Court of Inquiry concluded that the stowage of the cargo had resulted in a lack of stability, as weather conditions had not been extreme at the time. Her loss, coupled with other incidents, raised questions about the safety of turrets. Loading and stowage recommendations were issued, but the inquiry failed to identify any design shortcomings, their loss ratio being no worse than any other design.

Cardiff Hall Line's other peacetime loss was also in the Black Sea. On 19th March 1911 *Cardiff Hall* (1) went ashore near the entrance to Novorossisk Bay, after sailing less than ten miles from Novorossisk with grain for Antwerp. Vincent Grech attempted salvage and 2,000 tons of sound cargo was recovered. However, the damage was so extensive that despite the efforts of four salvage vessels the leaks could not be controlled and *Cardiff Hall* became a total loss.

These two losses hint at the extent to which the Black Sea grain trade, coupled with Welsh coal exports, featured in Nicholl's trade. When *Grindon Hall* (1) was loading her last cargo at Sulina, *Eaton Hall* was also loading for Antwerp. *Eaton Hall* sailed ten hours before her sister and her master was able to give the inquiry detail of weather on the run across to the Bosphorus. Since completion in 1905 *Grindon Hall* had completed nine voyages, eight carrying grain homeward. Richard Burt had been master for all except one and had sailed on the last, fatal, voyage on 16th October 1907 with coal from Cardiff to Kustendje, from whence she ballasted to Sulina to load her last cargo. The varied trades in which the fleet found employment can also be appreciated from their positions in May 1912, as shown in Table 2.

Cardiff Hall Line at war

The declaration of war early in August 1914 found Nicholl's ships mainly in the Plate trade. At greatest risk was *Tredegar Hall*, on passage from Ramallo for Hamburg and Emden. Arriving off Portland on 11th August 1914, she was detained and her cargo of maize later condemned by the Prize Court. *Eaton Hall* and *Whateley Hall* were in port in South Wales. *Windsor Hall* had sailed for the Plate, following *Cardiff Hall* (2) and *Welbeck Hall* (2) which were well down in the South Atlantic. *Silksworth Hall* and *Grindon Hall* (2) had arrived in the Plate. *Haigh Hall* was on passage from Montevideo for Montreal and *Standish Hall* had passed Gibraltar the previous day, en route from Baltimore to Alexandria. In addition, three new ships were nearing completion.

Of the ten ships trading and three building, eight were to be victims of enemy action; two whilst owned by Nicholl, the others after transfer of management. Demands of war, the transport of military forces and their supply, were to see all but *Bland Hall* and *Silksworth Hall* taken on Government charter. First taken were the two in port in South Wales. Two days after the declaration of war *Eaton Hall* became Collier 1636, and a day later *Whateley Hall* became Collier 1020. They remained on Government

service until 1919.

Whilst most of Nicholl's ships were used as colliers, other employment was wide and varied. They served as Expeditionary Force transports, *Windsor Hall* carried part of the Indian Expeditionary Force to Europe, and time was spent in French and Italian Government service. Cargoes included grain from India, the Plate, North America and South Africa; sugar from the USA, Java and Cuba; flax, timber, steel, and minerals. *Tredegar Hall* came off hire on 25th October 1916, having been ashore as Collier 1067.

Prior to his decision to sell and withdraw from shipowning, Nicholl only suffered one loss from enemy action, *Silksworth Hall*, torpedoed without warning by the 140-ton displacement coastal *UB 12* with the loss of three lives. Although transfer to new management had been agreed, *Haigh Hall* was lost before handover could take place. Nearing Malta in a convoy of two merchant ships with three escorts, she was torpedoed by the Austro-Hungarian *U 28* (built to German BII class) and sank one hour later without loss of life. *Whateley Hall* almost became a third loss when, on 18th June 1917, she sighted a U-boat west of Gibraltar and a gunnery duel ensued. An unusual though less disastrous accident befell *Eaton Hall* during the war. On the night of 16-17th August 1915 she was lying at Texas City, USA when a hurricane and the flooding that followed carried her two miles inland where she remained, until refloated and returned to service four months later.

Edward Nicholl also found himself on active service in August 1914. Resigning as chairman of the Cardiff and Bristol Channel Incorporated Shipowners' Association, he was commissioned Acting Lieutenant-Commander RNVR on 1st February 1915. There was no precedent for an engineer RNR being given an executive appointment, hence he was commissioned in the RNVR to cover his wartime duties, initially as Deputy-Chief Examining Officer for Cardiff, Penarth and Barry. Within months he was promoted to be Chief Examining Officer of the Bristol Channel Examination Service, which by September 1917 had carried out 55,388 checks on vessels. In the Birthday Honours List of June 1916 Nicholl was created a Knight Batchelor for his services, and to mark this occasion he gave £16,000 to build the Sir Edward Nicholl Wing of the King Edward VII Hospital, Cardiff. The same year he was appointed High Sheriff of Glamorgan. He resigned as Chief Examining Officer in September 1917, and acted as Area Economy Officer for South Wales and Monmouthshire on behalf of the Petroleum Executive from December 1917 to July 1918.

Cardiff Hall Line sold

Late in 1915 *Grindon Hall* (2) was sold to London owners,

Table 2: Position of Cardiff Hall Line ships in May 1912
(from *Lloyd's Weekly Shipping Index*)

Vessel	From	For	Position
Cardiff Hall (2)	building at Sunderland, launched July 26		
Eaton Hall	Kurrachee 14 May	Port Said	Pd Perim 25 May
Grindon Hall (2)	Rosario 1 May	Las Palmas	
Haigh Hall	Bahia Blanca 1 Apr	Rotterdam Arr 23 May	
Silksworth Hall	Port Said 11 May	Kurrachee Arr 23 May	
Standish Hall	Barry 24 May	Rio Janeiro	Pd Barry Island 24 May
Tredegar Hall	Barry 28 Apr	Buenos Ayres	Pd St Vincent CV 10 May
Welbeck Hall (2)	Sulina 20 Apr	Hull	Pd Zea 21 May
Whateley Hall	Taranto 28 May	Port Said	
Windsor Hall	Bremen 24 Apr	Bahia Blanca Arr 22 May	

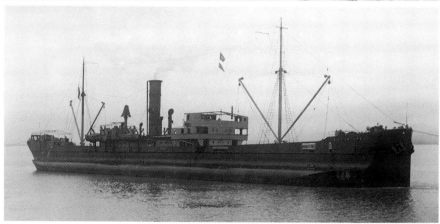

Haigh Hall (above) and *Eaton Hall* (right). The shot of *Eaton Hall* probably dates from after the Cardif Hall Line ships had been sold to Sven Hansen in 1917. Note the name painted on the bridge front and the designation CO862 – presumably an Admiralty collier number, although early in the war she was Collier 1636. [Above: Ivor Rooke collection]

whilst in 1916 all three ships owned by Nicholl Steamships Ltd passed to companies controlled by Furness, Withy and Co. Ltd. The price received for the three was £460,000, which compares with £167,600 paid for them in 1914 and well illustrates the impact of the war on prices. In May 1917 it was announced that the management contract for the remaining eight ships had been sold to Hansen Brothers, although as mentioned *Haigh Hall* was sunk before transfer. Nicholl claimed he had to sell because of pressure of war duties and the depletion of staff: Ivor Griffin had been called up for military service, Nicholl's son Albert was abroad on military service, and Ernest Griffin was ill. Only one member of the pre-war office staff, an accountant, remained and he was likely to receive call-up papers at any time. At this same time the partnership of Edward Nicholl and Co. was dissolved. After further losses, in October 1918 the three remaining ships were transferred from their owning companies to the Hansen Shipping Co. Ltd. Sven Hansen (1876-1958), the Cardiff-born son of Norwegian immigrant Carl Hansen, commenced in business in 1905 and, in partnership with Vyvyan Robinson, acquired a fleet which totalled 56,000 tons deadweight. Hansen also had interests in shipbuilding, ship repairing and coal mining, and was created a baronet in 1921, but saw his business empire crash in 1924.

When given details of the deal with Hansen, Hope Robinson, editor of *Fairplay,* was critical of the action taken by Nicholl without shareholders' knowledge or agreement, a situation which would not have been permitted in the days when most ships were owned as 64th shares rather than through limited liability companies. Nicholl sold his management contracts to Hansen for £250,000 and his personal shares, face value £45,000, at £2.50 each, i.e. £112,500. The eight companies had issued shares of £201,500, had cash reserves of £100,000, and ships which Hope Robinson valued at £900,000 on the enhanced wartime market. The offer to shareholders was twice the face value of the shares and was later increased to 2.5 times, the price Nicholl was himself getting. However, selling the ships individually and winding up the companies would release assets of £5 per £1 share. Under the deal with Hansen, Nicholl benefited by £362,500, whereas he would have received only £225,000 from a sale and winding up, whilst his shareholders would have received double the figure offered to them. Hope Robinson's valuation of the fleet can only be viewed as conservative in the light of prices realised the previous summer, the changed climate due to unrestricted submarine warfare and the consequent demand for tonnage, and a valuation of at least £1.2 million would have been closer to the mark. The break-up value then approaches £6.50 per £1 share and worsens the deal given to shareholders.

After Cardiff Hall Line

On 31st January 1917 Germany declared that unrestricted submarine warfare would commence the following day. Between then and the Armistice horrendous losses were sustained, threatening the survival of Britain. Amongst these losses would be a further four ships of the Cardiff Hall Line, now under Hansen's management. On 12th July 1917 *Tredegar Hall* was attacked by U 48 off Ushant. Two torpedoes missed and a three-and-a-half hour gunnery duel ensued. Robert Smith, the wireless operator, transmitted distress calls and repaired his aerials under fire. For the action in saving the ship Captain George was appointed a DSO, whilst he and Robert Smith each received Lloyd's Silver Medal for Meritorious Services.

Tredegar Hall, possibly on her first visit to her home port: she flies a name pennant and a stem jack which is a pennant version of Nicholl's houseflag. *[Ivor Rooke collection]*

But *Tredegar Hall* was not long to survive and, as the fleet list shows, three others were sunk in the early months of 1918: *Windsor Hall, Standish Hall*, and *Welbeck Hall* (2).

After the war the five ships still afloat passed through various hands and flags. One still carried the name *Cardiff Hall* (2) when lost in January 1925. The most notorious was *Grindon Hall* (2), sold in 1915 and becoming the Greek *Gregorios* in 1920. With the collapse of the freight market in the summer of 1920 many owners were unable to operate at a profit and repay or service loans taken to buy at inflated war prices. Underwriters became aware of an increase in suspicious losses. Between December 1920 and July 1921 eight of ten ships reportedly lost to mines were Greek owned. Investigation gave reason to suspect they were scuttled, and these suspicions were upheld in court when owners refused to accept the underwriters' rejection of their claims.

The owner of *Gregorios*, Denis Anghelatos, reported the loss of three of his four ships in this period. The fourth, *Achilles* (4,239/1900), was repossessed by bank mortgagees in May 1921. On 25th December 1920 *Photios* (1,467/1890) foundered in the Mediterranean. On 26th February 1921 *Gregorios* reported hitting a mine, and on 16th June 1921 *Olympia* (4,654/1896) was wrecked. *Gregorios* was on passage from Philippeville for the Tyne with iron ore when abandoned in fine weather off Sabinal Point. Ships which went to her aid, the Italian *Savona* (3,427/1895) and British *Penmorvah* (4,336/1913), reported nothing to confirm mine damage. The underwriters declined to settle and the matter went to court. In 1924 the case reached the House of Lords, where the Law Lords upheld the verdict of scuttling.

Although no longer a shipowner Sir Edward Nicholl was still busy. He sold his home at Roath Park, Cardiff and moved to London, becoming the Lord of the Manor of Littleton when he purchased it in 1918. During the railway strike in 1919 he recalled his early railway days, driving trains between Swindon and London. Amongst civil and technical positions, he was returned as a Coalition Unionist MP for Penryn and Falmouth in December 1918, a seat from which he retired in October 1922; elected the first honorary member of the Society of Consulting Marine Engineers and Ship Surveyors, becoming President in 1934; and became a member of both the Institution of Naval Architects and the Institute of Marine Engineers. In the 1928 Birthday Honours Nicholl was appointed KBE for political and public services. The largest of a number of his charitable donations was £50,000 to build the Edward Nicholl Home, Cardiff, to care for unmarried mothers and illegitimate children. The site was donated by Lord Tredegar.

Shipowning again

Shipowners were familiar with the cyclical nature of trade. Many anticipated that the recession after the 1920 collapse would be followed by a boom in the latter years of the decade. They prepared by buying and building in readiness. Sir Edward Nicholl returned briefly to owning in 1929 paying £40,000 for the *Harpalyce*, which he renamed *Littleton*: she had been built for one of Nicholl's former employers, Evan Thomas, Radcliffe and Co. The Edward Nicholl Steam Ship Co. Ltd., capitalised at £45,000, was formed to own *Littleton*, with Sir Edward holding £44,000. Nicholl had severed connections with Cardiff, and the new company had an address in London. Sadly, hopes of an economic recovery were dashed as the Wall Street collapse of 1929 heralded even greater depression. *Littleton* was sold to Greece in 1932 for £14,500 and Nicholl, now aged about 70, retired. Despite the losses which must have been sustained with *Littleton*, he left an estate valued at £392,567 gross when he died on 30th March 1939, aged 76 years.

Nicholl's erstwhile partners, the Griffin Brothers, also returned to shipowning in 1920, operating four coasters: *Spurnpoint* (235/1908), *Stertpoint* (312/1920), *Torpoint* (214/1905), and *Castlerock* (259/1904). However, the collapse in freight rates in post-war years affected coasters as badly as it did deep-sea ships, and the Griffins also withdrew from shipowning in 1927 with their fingers burnt.

Postwar developments confirmed that Nicholl's withdrawal from shipowning in 1917 had been a wise move. Although the war years left owners with healthy balance sheets, those who continued trading saw them evaporate in the 1920s. The Government had introduced an Excess Profits Tax on all businesses to help pay for the war. The last years of peace were taken as 'normal' years, and profits above those for these years were taxed. Shipowners objected as these had been poor years in the shipping industry. Nicholl was at one with his fellow shipowners in criticising and opposing Excess Profits Tax, which normally exceeded sums paid as dividends. A reduced level of Excess Profits Tax would have allowed more owners to survive the difficult inter-war years, but instead many collapsed into bankruptcy, and only those who had retired by 1920 truly benefited. For instance, the Hansen Shipping Co. Ltd. which had bought most of Nicholl's fleet, and which was capitalised at £100,000 in 1917, went bankrupt and was dissolved in 1928. In the light of this, Nicholl's criticism and opposition to the Excess Profits Duty may have been justified.

Derivations of Cardiff Hall Line names

Albert Hall   The famous concert hall in South Kensington, London, named after Prince Albert, the prince consort to Queen Victoria.

Bland Hall   Origin not known.

Cardiff Hall   Possibly from Cardiff's City Hall, built 1901-1906. The City Hall was the first building to be completed on the site of today's Civic Centre, and on its official opening in 1905 Cardiff was elevated to the status of a city.

Eaton Hall   The seat of the Grosvenors, the Dukes of Westminster, and lies on the River Dee between Eccleston and Aldford, Cheshire.

Grindon Hall   At Grindon on the outskirts of Sunderland was, in 1905, the home of Sir William Theodore Doxford, MP, one of the famous shipbuilding family. Later the home of Harry Short of the shipbuilders, Short Brothers, it was subsequently used as a hospital.

Haigh Hall   Situated two miles north of Wigan, was once the home of the Earls of Crawford and Balcarres. It was later acquired by Wigan Corporation and is now part of Haigh Hall Country Park.

Silksworth Hall   At Silksworth in Sunderland, was the home of Robert Pile Doxford, another member of the shipbuilding family. It later became a public house.

Standish Hall   Between Standish and Shevington, 2.5 miles north north west of Wigan.

Tredegar Hall   Once the home of Lord Tredegar, and more generally known as Tredegar House, in the grounds of Tredegar Park on the western outskirts of Newport, Monmouthshire.

Welbeck Hall   Also known as Welbeck Abbey, a seventeenth-century house in the Dukeries area of Nottinghamshire near Worksop.

Westoe Hall   Home of the Readhead shipbuilding family at Westoe in South Shields.

Whateley Hall   The home of Frederick Knight, an early supporter of the Nicholl shipping venture, at Whateley, about six miles north east of Sutton Coldfield.

Windsor Hall   Possibly from a home of the Windsor family, who were connected with the Earls of Plymouth and owned estates and land in South Wales. However, there was a Windsor Hall in the Grangetown area of Cardiff, which was the home of Solomon Andrews, a local businessman and pioneer of public transport in the area.

Fleet List

1. WHATELEY HALL   1904-1917   Turret
ON 119946   3,712g 2,380n   342.3 x 46.6 x 24.7 feet.
T. 3-cyl. by William Doxford and Sons Ltd., Sunderland; 313 NHP, 1,350 IHP, 9½ knots.
16.6.1904: Launched by William Doxford and Sons Ltd., Sunderland (Yard No. 321).
7.1904: Completed.
6.7.1904: Registered in the ownership of the Whateley Hall Steam Ship Co. Ltd. (Edward Nicholl and Co., managers), Cardiff as WHATELEY HALL.
2.7.1917: Manager became Sven Wohlford Hansen.
22.6.1917: Managers became Hansen Brothers Ltd.
25.10.1918: Owners became the Hansen Shipping Co. Ltd.

(Hansen Brothers Ltd., managers), Cardiff.
4.11.1924: Sold by National Provincial Bank Ltd., mortgagees, to Monument Steam Navigation Co. Ltd. (Richards, Longstaff and Co. Ltd., managers), London.
17.12.1924: Renamed YORKRIVER.
1.1926: Sold to S.A. Parodi and Corrado, Genoa, Italy and renamed RONCHI.
1929: Owners became S.A. E.V. Parodi, Genoa.
1934: Sold to Matteo Scuderi, Catania, Italy and renamed SAN MATTEO.
28.1.1937: Wrecked 17 miles north of Stolpmünde whilst on a voyage from Gdynia to Italy with a cargo of coal.

Whateley Hall dressed overall when new. She carries funnel colours that were seemingly soon abandoned: a yellow basic funnel with a red band and a white N. *[Ivor Rooke collection]*

Eaton Hall

2. EATON HALL   1904-1917   Turret

ON 119951   3,711g   2,380n   342.1 x 46.6 x 24.7 feet.
T. 3-cyl. by William Doxford and Sons Ltd., Sunderland;
313 NHP, 1,350 IHP, 9½ knots.
12.7.1904: Launched by William Doxford and Sons Ltd.,
Sunderland (Yard 322).
30.7.1904: Registered in the ownership of the Eaton Hall
Steam Ship Co. Ltd. (Edward Nicholl and Co., managers),
Cardiff as EATON HALL.
8.1904: Completed.
22.6.1917: Managers became Hansen Brothers Ltd.,
Cardiff.
25.10.1918: Owners became the Hansen Shipping Co. Ltd.
(Hansen Brothers Ltd. managers), Cardiff.
13.10.1924: Sold by the National Provincial Bank,
mortgagees, to the Monument Steam Navigation Co. Ltd.
(Richards, Longstaff and Co. Ltd., managers), London.
16.1.1925: Renamed YORKBROOK.
2.1926: Sold to Compagnia del Tirreno S.A. di
Navigazione, Genoa, Italy and renamed PRIMIERO.
1927: Sold to G.M. Chapira (United Chartering and
Steamship Co. S.A., managers), Genoa and renamed
MARIA TERESA.
1932: Broken up in Italy.

3. GRINDON HALL (1) 1905-1907   Turret

ON 119978   3,721g   2,380n   342.2 x 46.6 x 24.7 feet.
T. 3-cyl. by William Doxford and Sons Ltd., Sunderland;
313 NHP, 1,350 IHP, 9½ knots.
31.8.1905: Launched by William Doxford and Sons Ltd.,
Sunderland (Yard No. 346), having been laid down for the
Red Line Ltd.
9.1905: Completed.
21.9.1905: Registered in the ownership of the Grindon
Hall Steam Ship Co. Ltd. (Edward Nicholl and Co.,
managers), Cardiff as GRINDON HALL.
4.12.1907: Left Sulina for Glasgow with a cargo of maize
and barley with a crew of 26 under Captain Richard Burt
and disappeared.
1.1908: Posted missing.
16.3.1908: Register closed.

4. TREDEGAR HALL   1906-1917   Turret

ON 123167   3,764g   2,408n   342.1 x 46.6 x 24.8 feet.
T. 3-cyl. by William Doxford and Sons Ltd., Sunderland;
313 NHP, 1,350 IHP, 9½ knots.
26.7.1906: Launched by William Doxford and Sons Ltd.,
Sunderland (Yard No. 364).
8.1906: Completed.
21.8.1906: Registered in the ownership of the Tredegar
Hall Steam Ship Co. Ltd. (Edward Nicholl and Co.
managers), Cardiff as TREDEGAR HALL.
22.6.1917: Managers became Hansen Brothers Ltd.,
Cardiff.
8.1914: Detained at Passage West.
5.7.1915: Part cargo condemned by Prize Court in London.
12.7.1917: Attacked by the German submarine U 48 off
Ushant but the torpedo missed and gun action followed.
23.10.1917: Torpedoed and sunk by the German submarine
UB 57, 4.5 miles east south east of Flamborough Head
whilst on a voyage from Melilla to Middlesbrough with a
cargo of iron ore. Three lives were lost.
12.11.1917: Register closed.

5. SILKSWORTH HALL   1907-1916   Turret

ON 123183   4,777g   3,042n   360.4 x 53.1 x 26.1 feet.
T. 3-cyl. by William Doxford and Sons Ltd., Sunderland;
342 NHP, 1,550 IHP, 9½ knots.
11.6.1907: Launched by William Doxford and Sons Ltd.,
Sunderland (Yard No. 382).
7.1907: Completed.
10.7.1907: Registered in the ownership of the Silksworth
Hall Steam Ship Co. Ltd. (Edward Nicholl and Co.
managers), Cardiff as SILKSWORTH HALL.
10.4.1916: Torpedoed by the German submarine UB 12,
1.25 miles north east of Corton Lightship whilst on a
voyage from Hull to Philadelphia in ballast. Three lives
were lost.
5.6.1916: Register closed.

Grindon Hall (1) (this page top). *[Ivor Rooke collection]*
A superb view of *Tredegar Hall* which shows her turret deck to perfection (this page middle). *[World Ship Photo Library]*
Silksworth Hall (this page bottom). *[Ivor Rooke collection]*
Welbeck Hall (1) (opposite page upper)
Haigh Hall (opposite page lower).

154

6. WELBECK HALL (1)   1907-1913

ON 96159   2,760g   1,782n   322.0 x 40.3 x 24.8 feet.
T. 3-cyl. by Palmers Shipbuilding and Iron Co. Ltd.,
Newcastle-on-Tyne; 244 NHP, 1,500 IHP, 10½ knots.
14.8.1889: Launched by Palmers Shipbuilding and Iron
Co. Ltd., Jarrow, Newcastle-on-Tyne (Yard No. 624).
10.1889: Completed
29.10.1889: Registered in the ownership of John Hall,
trading as Hall Brothers, Newcastle-on-Tyne as LADY
PALMER.
8.5.1907: Acquired by the Lady Palmer Steamship Co. Ltd.
(Edward Nicholl and Co., managers), Cardiff.
23.11.1907: Owners become the Welbeck Hall Steamship
Co. Ltd. (Edward Nicholl and Co., managers), Cardiff.
14.10.1907: Renamed WELBECK HALL.
1.1913: Sold to A/S Ellavore (Lundegaard and Stray,
managers), Farsund, Norway and renamed ELLAVORE.
6.2.1917: Torpedoed by the German submarine UC 24 off
Cape Finisterre (60 miles north by east of Corunna and 35

miles from Cape Vilano) whilst on a voyage from Genoa,
Naples and Valencia to London with a cargo of fruit and wine.

7. HAIGH HALL   1908-1917   Turret

ON 128481   4,809g   3,069n   360.1 x 53.1 x 26.1 feet.
T. 3-cyl. by William Doxford and Sons Ltd., Sunderland;
342 NHP, 1,550 IHP, 9½ knots.
16.6.1908: Launched by William Doxford and Sons Ltd.,
Sunderland (Yard No. 397).
20.7.1908: Registered in the ownership of the Haigh Hall
Steamship Co. Ltd. (Edward Nicholl and Co., managers),
Cardiff as HAIGH HALL.
8.1908: Completed.
22.6.1917: Managers became Hansen Brothers Ltd.,
Cardiff.
30.6.1917: Torpedoed by the Austro-Hungarian submarine
U 28 forty miles east of Malta whilst on a voyage from
Bombay to Naples with a cargo of wheat.
13.8.1917: Register closed.

8. GRINDON HALL (2) 1908-1915 Turret
ON 128482 3,712g 2,365n 342.2 x 46.6 x 24.7 feet.
T. 3-cyl. by William Doxford and Sons Ltd., Sunderland;
313 NHP, 1,350 IHP, 9½ knots.
29.7.1908: Launched by William Doxford and Sons Ltd.,
Sunderland (Yard No. 398).
8.1908: Completed.
18.8.1908: Registered in the ownership of the Grindon
Hall Steamship Co. Ltd. (Edward Nicholl and Co.,
managers), Cardiff as GRINDON HALL.
4.11.1915: Sold to the Leadenhall Steam Ship Co. Ltd.
(William McAllum of McAllum, Soulidi and Co.,
managers), London.
20.8.1920: Sold to Denis Anghelatos, Argostoli, Greece
and renamed GREGORIOS.
26.2.1921: Sank off Sabinal Point having reportedly struck
a mine whilst on a voyage from Cephalonia and
Philippeville to Tyne, with a cargo of iron ore. It was later
ruled by the House of Lords that she had been scuttled.

9. CARDIFF HALL (1) 1909-1911
ON 99150 2,605g 1,649n 300.0 x 41.0 x 18.5 feet.
T. 3-cyl. by Blair and Co. Ltd., Stockton; 200 NHP, 1,120
IHP, 9 knots.
25.6.1895: Launched by John Blumer and Co., Sunderland
(Yard No. 131).
30.7.1895: Registered in the ownership of Welburn G.
Robinson, Whitby as DUCHESS OF YORK.
8.1895: Completed.
6.1907: Owners became the Robinson Brothers Steamship
Co. Ltd. (Robinson Brothers, managers), Whitby.
5.1909: Acquired by the Cardiff Hall Steam Ship Co. Ltd.
(Edward Nicholl and Co., managers), Cardiff.
30.7.1909: Renamed CARDIFF HALL.
19.3.1911: Wrecked at Miskhak Point, near the entrance to
Novorossisk Bay, whilst on a voyage from Novorossisk to
Antwerp with a cargo of grain.
3.6.1911: Register closed.

This is believed to be the second *Grindon Hall.* Comparison with the photograph on page 154 shows very few differences, notably the lack of topmasts and differences in paint scheme.

Duchess of York, later to become the first *Cardiff Hall.*

Windsor Hall on trials (above) and the second *Cardiff Hall* (below). *[George Scott collection and Ivor Rooke collection].*

10. WINDSOR HALL   1910-1917
ON 128516   3,693g   2,339n   345.0 x 48.2 x 24.6 feet.
T. 3-cyl. by William Doxford and Sons Ltd., Sunderland;
315 NHP, 1,450 IHP, 9½ knots.
21.7.1910: Launched by William Doxford and Sons Ltd.,
Sunderland (Yard 414).
8.1910: Completed.
16.8.1910: Registered in the ownership of the Windsor
Hall Steamship Co. Ltd. (Edward Nicholl and Co.,
managers), Cardiff as WINDSOR HALL.
22.6.1917: Managers became Hansen Brothers Ltd.,
Cardiff.
17.1.1918: Torpedoed by the German submarine UB 66, 45
miles north west of Alexandria whilst on a voyage from
Karachi to Marseilles with a cargo of grain. Twenty seven
lives were lost and the master was taken prisoner.
16.3.1918: Register closed.

11. STANDISH HALL   1912-1917
ON 132716   3,996g   2,544n   349.9 x 50.9 x 28.0 feet.
T. 3-cyl. by William Doxford and Sons Ltd., Sunderland;
291 NHP, 1,400 IHP, 10 knots.
19.4.1912: Launched by William Doxford and Sons Ltd.,
Sunderland (Yard No. 438).
5.1912: Completed.
14.5.1912: Registered in the ownership of the Standish
Hall Steamship Co. Ltd. (Edward Nicholl and Co.,
managers), Cardiff as STANDISH HALL.

22.6.1917: Managers became Hansen Brothers Ltd., Cardiff.
4.2.1918: Torpedoed by the German submarine U 33, 38
miles west by north of Alexandria whilst on a voyage from
Bizerta to Alexandria serving as an Admiralty Collier.
6.8.1918: Register closed.

12. CARDIFF HALL (2) 1912-1917
ON 135131   3,994g   2,541n   350.0 x 50.8 x 25.6 feet.
T. 3-cyl. by William Doxford and Sons Ltd., Sunderland;
291 NHP, 1,400 IHP, 10 knots.
26.7.1912: Launched by William Doxford and Sons Ltd.,
Sunderland (Yard No. 444).
8.1912: Completed.
24.8.1912: Registered in the ownership of the Standish
Hall Steamship Co. Ltd. (Edward Nicholl and Co.,
managers), Cardiff as CARDIFF HALL.
22.6.1917: Managers became Hansen Brothers Ltd., Cardiff.
25.10.1918: Owners became the Hansen Shipping Co. Ltd.
(Hansen Brothers Ltd. managers), Cardiff.
15.12.1924: Sold by the National Provincial Bank,
mortgagees, to the Wyn Shipping Co. Ltd. (William A.
Young and Co., managers), London.
13.1.1925: Wrecked on South Point, Seven Heads near the
Old Head of Kinsale whilst on a voyage from Rosario to
Cork with a cargo of maize. Although registered in the
ownership of the Wyn Shipping Co.Ltd., she had not yet
been delivered to her new owners.
6.2.1925: Register closed.

13. WELBECK HALL (2)   1914-1917

ON 136651   4,258g 2,737n   390.0 x 52.0 x 23.5 feet.
T. 3-cyl. by William Doxford and Sons Ltd., Sunderland;
421 NHP, 2,000 IHP.
10.2.1914: Launched by William Doxford and Sons Ltd.,
Sunderland (Yard No. 463).
3.1914: Completed.
14.3.1914: Registered in the ownership of the Welbeck
Hall Steam Ship Co. Ltd. (Edward Nicholl and Co.,
managers), Cardiff as WELBECK HALL.
22.6.1917: Managers became Hansen Brothers Ltd.,
Cardiff.
22.4.1918: Torpedoed by the German submarine UB 53, 75
miles north east by north of Port Said whilst on a voyage
from Piraeus for Port Said whilst in ballast. Four lives
were lost.
24.5.1918: Register closed.

14. BLAND HALL   1914-1916

ON 136709   4,259g 2,738n   390.0 x 52.0 x 23.5 feet.
T. 3-cyl. by William Doxford and Sons Ltd., Sunderland;
421 NHP, 2,000 IHP, 10 knots.
8.8.1914: Launched by William Doxford and Sons Ltd.,
Sunderland (Yard No. 468).
10.1914: Completed.
29.9.1914: Registered in the ownership of Nicholl
Steamships Ltd. (Edward Nicholl and Co., managers),
Cardiff as BLAND HALL.
30.5.1916: Sold to the Norfolk and North American Steam
Ship Co. Ltd. (Furness, Withy and Co. Ltd. managers),
London.
25.7.1916: Renamed CORNISH POINT.
9.1926: Sold to Reederei A.G. Unterweser, Bremen,
Germany and renamed GONZENHEIM.
28.7.1933: Sold to Atlantic Tank-Rhederei G.m.b.H. (John
T. Essberger G.m.b.H., managers), Hamburg, Germany.
2.10.1933: Renamed LISA.
31.7.1936: Sold to H. Vogemann, Hamburg and renamed
WALKÜRE.
22.12.1942: Wrecked at Hjelmbodan west of Hafstenssund

whilst on a voyage from Danzig for Christiansand with a
cargo of coal and coke.

15. WESTOE HALL   1914-1916

ON 136714   4,241g 2,702n   369.5 x 51.0 x 26.0 feet.
T. 3-cyl. by John Readhead and Sons Ltd., South Shields;
386 NHP, 2,000 IHP, 9 knots.
5.9.1914: Launched by John Readhead and Sons Ltd.,
South Shields (Yard No. 444).
10.1914: Completed.
15.10.1914: Registered in the ownership of Nicholl
Steamships Ltd. (Edward Nicholl and Co., managers),
Cardiff as WESTOE HALL.
27.6.1916: Sold to the Gulf Line Ltd. (Furness, Withy and
Co. Ltd., managers), London.
1.7.1916: Renamed TURINO.
4.2.1917: Torpedoed by the German submarine U 43, 174
miles west of the Fastnet in position 50.25 north by 13.50
west whilst on a voyage from Norfolk to Liverpool with
general cargo. Four lives were lost.
17.3.1917: Register closed.

16. ALBERT HALL   1914-1916

ON 136722   4,258g 2,737n   390.0 x 52.0 x 23.5 feet.
T. 3-cyl. by William Doxford and Sons Ltd., Sunderland;
421 NHP, 2,000 IHP, 10 knots.
6.10.1914: Launched by William Doxford and Sons Ltd.,
Sunderland (Yard No. 469).
11.1914: Completed.
12.11.1914: Registered in the ownership of Nicholl
Steamships Ltd. (Edward Nicholl and Co., managers),
Cardiff as ALBERT HALL.
30.5.1916: Sold to the Norfolk and North American Steam
Ship Co. Ltd. (Furness, Withy and Co. Ltd., managers),
London.
24.5.1916: Renamed SOUTH POINT.
11.6.1917: Torpedoed by the German submarine UB 32, 30
miles south west by half south of Bishop Rock whilst on a
voyage from London to Newport News in ballast.
14.8.1917: Register closed.

Welbeck Hall

Nicholl's last ship, *Littleton,* earlier in life as *Shannonmede* (above) and later as *Leonidas Z. Cambanis* (below). *[Upper: Ivor Rooke collection]*

17. LITTLETON   1929-1932

ON 140294   4,274g   2,671n   390.0 x 53.3 x 23.5 feet.
T. 3-cyl. by Richardsons, Westgarth and Co. Ltd., Hartlepool; 475 NHP, 2,150 IHP, 10¼ knots.
7.2.1917: Launched by William Pickersgill and Sons Ltd., Sunderland (Yard No. 193).
5.1917: Completed.
2.5.1917: Registered in the ownership of the Llanover Steamship Co. Ltd. (Evan Thomas, Radcliffe and Co., managers), Cardiff as LLANOVER.
5.6.1917: Sold to the Johnston Line Ltd., Liverpool (Furness, Withy and Co. Ltd., London, managers) and renamed LINMORE.
9.8.1920: Sold to the Canute Steam Ship Co. Ltd. (David and Thomas G. Adams, managers), Newcastle-on-Tyne.
9.8.1920: Renamed SHANNONMEDE.
2.4.1925: Sold to the Willis Steam Ship Co. Ltd. (J. and C. Harrison (1920) Ltd., managers), London.
27.7.1926: Renamed HARPALYCE.
30.1.1929: Acquired by the Edward Nicholl Steam Ship Co. Ltd. (Sir Edward Nicholl, KBE, manager), Cardiff.
2.2.1929: Renamed LITTLETON.
1932: Sold to Mina L. Cambani (L.Z. Cambanis, manager), Athens, Greece and renamed LEONIDAS Z. CAMBANIS.
3.4.1941: Torpedoed by the German submarine U 74 south east of Cape Farewell in position 58.12 north by 27.40 west

whilst on a voyage from Halifax to Swansea with a cargo of 6,500 tons wheat. Two lives were lost.

Vessels ordered by Edward Nicholl and Co. but not completed for their account.

1. (NEWBRIDGE)   Turret

ON 123648   3,737g   2,397n   342.1 x 46.6 x 24.8 feet.
T. 3-cyl. by William Doxford and Sons Ltd., Sunderland; 313 NHP, 1,350 IHP, 9½ knots.
2.10.1905: Ordered by Edward Nicholl and Co., Cardiff for £34,000 from William Doxford and Sons Ltd., Sunderland.
5.2.1906: Taken back
7.5.1906: Sold to John Temperley and Co. for £38,000, subject to underwriters agreeing a total loss on WEYBRIDGE.
27.4.1906: Launched by William Doxford and Sons Ltd., Sunderland (Yard No. 358).
6.1906: Completed.
21.5.1906: Registered in the ownership of the Temperley Steam Shipping Co. Ltd. (John Temperley and Co., managers), London as NEWBRIDGE.
15.11.1914: Scuttled in the Rufiji delta to prevent escape of the German cruiser SMS KONIGSBERG.
12.11.1917: Register closed.

2. (GAFSA) Turret

ON 113664   3,922g 2,501n   349.8 x 50.2 x 23.4 feet.
T. 3-cyl. by William Doxford and Sons Ltd., Sunderland;
332 NHP, 1,500 IHP, 9½ knots.

2.10.1905: Ordered by Edward Nicholl and Co., Cardiff for
£34,000 from William Doxford and Sons Ltd., Sunderland.
6.11.1905: Order transferred to C.T. Bowring and Co.,
London for £38,750 and replaced by Yard No. 382 (see
SILKSWORTH HALL).
28.5.1906: Launched by William Doxford and Sons Ltd.,
Sunderland (Yard No. 360).
6.1906: Completed.
26.6.1906: Registered in the ownership of the English and
American Shipping Co. Ltd. (C.T. Bowring and Co. Ltd.,
managers), London as GAFSA.
16.6.1916: Captured and sunk by gunfire from the German
submarine U 35, 80 miles south west by west of Genoa
whilst on a voyage from Swansea to Genoa with a cargo of
coal and patent fuel.
4.7.1916: Register closed.

3. (HILDA)

(O.N. 168625)   3,544g 2,261n   360.0 x 50.3 x 21.5 feet.

T. 3-cyl. by William Doxford and Sons Ltd., Sunderland;
259 NHP, 8 knots.

3.9.1906: Ordered by Edward Nicholl and Co., Cardiff for
£45,500.
26.1.1910: Launched by William Doxford and Sons Ltd.,
Sunderland (Yard No. 405) for Mark Whitwill and Son,
Bristol as HILDA.
1910: Completed for Navigazione Libera Giovanni Racich
and Co., Ragusa/Dubrovnik, Austria as ISTINA.
1919: Owners became Atlanska Plovidba Ivo Racic A.D.,
Split, Yugoslavia.
1935: Sold to Oceania Brodarsko A.D., Susak, Yugoslavia
and renamed VID.
18.8.1941: Registered in the ownership of the Ministry of
War Transport, London (E.R. Management Co. Ltd.,
Cardiff, managers) as RADCHURCH.
8.8.1942: Abandoned during an attack on convoy SC94
whilst on a voyage from Wabana and St John's
Newfoundland to Belfast Lough and Barry with a cargo of
iron ore.
9.8.1942: After drifting for 17 hours, found abandoned by
the German submarine U 176 and sunk in position 56.15
north by 32 west.
23.9.1942: Register closed.

Newbridge at Manchester (upper) and after being scuttled in the Rufiji River to help capture SMS *Konigsberg*. [Both: George Scott collection]

160

Gafsa in Bowring's colours (top) and at the
moment of sinking by gunfire from *U 35* in
June 1916 (middle). *[Ivor Rooke collection
and T. Siersdorfer, courtesy George Scott]*

Launched as *Hilda*, but sold on completion,
this raised quarter deck steamer ordered
by Nicholl is seen as the Yugoslavian *Vid*
(bottom). *[World Ship Photo Library]*

THE CARRON COMPANY
Graeme Somner

Carronades to cast iron baths

When the Carron Company was set up in 1759 as iron founders in the Stirlingshire town of Carron on the north bank of the river of the same name the country was at war and a major portion of their production was cast-iron naval and military ordnance. Their famed carronade gun was so reliable that the Duke of Wellington would have no other. Carronades were used at the Battle of Trafalgar in 1805 and at Waterloo in 1815. But there was still a good market for cast-iron in peacetime and, as well as producing cannon balls and small arms, Carron's range included cast-iron ploughs, cookers and baths. In addition, the company owned and worked large fields of coal, iron ore and limestone in the surrounding area, which not only supplied all the basic materials for its iron foundry, but also provided a surplus of coal for sale.

It was vital for the company to transport their cast-iron goods to the important centres of population, which included those in southern England but, with roads poor and slow, the only means of transport was by sea. Carron acquired its first vessel in 1760, a flat (a barge or lighter) which was used to move goods from the factory down the River Carron to larger vessels moored in deeper water at Greenbrae Reach. These larger vessels could not sail up the River Carron and had previously been pulled by between 12 and 20 men walking along the banks. But sea transportation had its problems: sailings were infrequent and uncertain because of the weather, and ships were liable to seizure by privateers. Clearly, to ensure a reasonable service Carron needed its own ships.

From 1763 Carron's shipping business was handled by Samuel Garbett and Company, which placed first *Glasgow* (1)(1763), *Paisley* (1764), *Stirling* (1767), and *Forth* (1)(1768), and later *Kingston* on sailings to London. This arrangement continued until 1772 when Samuel Garbett and Company was wound-up with debts of over £193,000 and the ships were sold to the Carron Shipping Company. The majority shareholder in the latter company was the Honourable William Elphinstone, who was later to become chairman of the East India Company. It is said that in 1782 this adventurous gentleman decided to go privateering, and his interests in the Carron Shipping Company were taken over by the Carron Company.

In the meantime the Carron Company had built its first ship, named *Carron* (1), in 1765. In February 1770, under Captain Porteous, *Carron* (1) sailed from the River Carron bound for London with plates, sugar pans, ovens and stoves, and ten guns. In 1777 the frigate *King of Spain* was bought to deliver guns to the King of Spain. She was renamed *Earl of Dunmore* in 1782 in recognition of the part played by the Earl of Dunmore in persuading the King of Spain to order carronade trials. The sloops *Lady Charlotte, Falkirk* (1), *Roebuck, Eagle,* and *Furnace* are known to have been in the fleet in the early 1770s, and were employed to carry goods to the larger port of Leith, lower down the Forth.

Further landmarks for Carron Company were receiving a Royal Charter of Incorporation in recognition of its services to the Crown in 1773, and then in 1785 buying the 170-ton sailing vessel *Empress of the Russias* with the intention of opening trade with Russia. However, she was soon sold following an incident with a Captain Strathearn, who clandestinely attempted to take Carron employees to work in Russia and produce carronades there.

In 1779 all Carron's ships were fitted with fourteen 12-pounder carronades to protect themselves from attack. This meant that they were able to sail independently instead of in convoy. The *Edinburgh Evening Courant* of 26th May 1779 reported the engagement, some four days earlier, of *Paisley* with a French frigate and a privateer when the Carron sloop, on passage from London to Carron, was some five miles off the Tyne. Two broadsides from the *Paisley* made the attackers sheer off and look elsewhere for a trophy. A special fare of 10s.6d. (52p today) was offered to mariners, soldiers and others accustomed to the use of fire arms who took passage on Carron's ships, if they would undertake to defend the ship if she was attacked. At that time a basic wage for a skilled tradesman was 12s.0d. (60p) per week, whilst a labourer's weekly wage was just 5s.0d. (25p).

Early connection with steam engines

When steam engines first appeared, the Carron Company was in the forefront. James Watt, the inventor of the steam engine, was a friend of Dr Roebuck, one of the founders of Carron, and the first set of castings for Watt's steam engine was made at the Carron works in 1789. This engine, which cost £363.10s.2d. (£363.51p), was erected at Dr Roebuck's home, Kinneil House, near Bo'ness and subsequently fitted to a vessel (believed to have been unnamed) constructed by William Symington on the River Carron. In the early years horses were used on the canal to tow passage boats. Mechanically propelled boats were not allowed until 1828 because it was feared that their wash might erode the sides of the canal. The early steamboat, *Charlotte Dundas*, was employed on the canal between January 1801 and April 1803, but her services were discontinued because of this concern.

Towards the end of the eighteenth century replacements for the older vessels were put in hand and 11 sloops were built for the trade between 1790 and 1800. Three of these, *Jamie and Jennie* (1785), *Apollo* (1795) and *Banton Packet* (1799), were to serve the company for 90, 87 and 95 years respectively. This was remarkable for wooden vessels of that era; and the *Banton Packet* finally serving still longer as a coal hulk until 1894. The threat of attack by sea receded after the Battle of Trafalgar and, with trade increasing, Carron's fleet had reached around 17 vessels by 1806.

By the time the Forth and Clyde Canal was completed in 1790, the company had six vessels available for carrying goods through to Glasgow: *Carron* (2), *Glasgow* (2), *Leith* (1), *Banton Packet, Falkirk* (2), and *Prince of Wales*. But the opening of this canal also brought problems to the company as a proportion of the water that had until then flowed down the River Carron was now diverted to fill the canal. Proposals were made about the possibility of routing the canal close to the works on the River Carron but no agreement was reached. Although a cut was made to connect the canal with the river, it was disused by 1810. In 1812 a basin was dug out on the north bank of the canal near Bainsford Bridge, Falkirk to provide better berthing and loading facilities. Manufactured goods were conveyed from the works to the basin by rail, and it was from this basin that the Carron's vessels sailed to London, and later to Liverpool and Glasgow.

A further batch of nine sloops was built between 1802 and 1810, and allowed the company to expand sailings to Liverpool and Glasgow. Another eight new vessels followed between 1812 and 1825. All these vessels were armed with carronades as they still had to protect themselves from French privateers. There is a report of one such attack in October 1810 when the sloop *Fame* was captured by a privateer off the coast of Northumberland and the crew taken prisoners. All were transferred to the attacking vessel, except for an old man and a boy. Six Frenchmen boarded *Fame* with instructions to sail her to a French port but, shortly after the two vessels parted, a severe storm blew up. *Fame* was driven north instead of southwards, eventually reaching the mouth of the Firth of Forth during the hours of darkness. The Frenchmen were unfamiliar with the area, as was the old man, so allowed the ship to go before the wind. However, the boy had made one or two voyages along that coast before and recognised the beacons burning on the island of Inchkeith. Knowing that a warship was normally stationed in St Margaret's Hope, near North Queensferry, on the Fife coast, he took over the abandoned helm and set course up the Firth. He sailed up to the warship and called on her to send over a party, as he had six prisoners to hand over. Fortune, indeed in this case, favoured the brave!

After these two programmes of building, only three more sailing ships joined the fleet: *Juno* (2) in 1832; the second-hand *Lily* (1792) purchased in 1836 but sold the next year; and *Vulcan* in 1840. However, by 1840 some of the older vessels had been broken up, with four going to their last berth in 1838. Others were sold. By 1845 the fleet numbered 15, and ranged in age from the 60-year old *Jamie and Jennie* to the five-year old *Vulcan*.

Expansion of Grangemouth

Grangemouth, a small town in the angle formed by the canal and River Carron where the two entered the Firth of Forth, had not existed in the middle of the eighteenth century. Before the canal was built, the harbour at the mouth of the River Carron was originally known as Greenbrae. With the additional trade that the canal had brought, the town began to flourish and expand. By 1814 it already had a small tidal dock at the entrance to the canal (known then as Sealock), and a Custom House that had opened in 1810. Before this, clearance for ships and cargoes had to be obtained from the Custom House at Bo'ness, some eight miles away, which involved crossing the River Avon. Now that the landing of iron ore had reached some 2,000 to 2,500 tons annually, proposals were in hand to expand the dock system. As well as the ore, increased quantities of timber were arriving from Norway, Sweden and North America, and more coal was being exported. The first enclosed dock, the Old Dock, was finally opened in 1843, with entry to it from the River Carron being made some distance down river to that from the canal.

By the early 1850s competition from the railways was being felt and the reliability of steam ships had been established. Responding to these changes, Carron gradually withdrew its sailings to Liverpool and Glasgow, and concentrated on sailings to London and the introduction of steam to that route. Between June 1852 and September 1853 the Carron Company sold eight of its sailing ships, retaining just seven.

Two families were the mainstays of the company - the Staintons and the Dawsons. Joseph Stainton came from Keswick and was originally a watchmaker. In 1780, at the age of 25, he joined the company as a clerk, but he became manager by 1786, and a partner in 1795. It was Stainton's business acumen and forward thinking that made the company what it became. On his death in 1825 he was succeeded by his nephew, William Dawson, who remained in charge until he retired in 1873. William Dawson died in the following year, and was succeeded by his brother Thomas, then 66 years old. But Thomas died after only a few months and his position was taken by Andrew Gordon, the first non-partner to be manager since 1786. It was the drive and management of the Stainton and Dawson families that guaranteed Carron's future. They created a dynasty that lasted through the 19th century and well into the next. Wars and the Carron Company always went hand

in hand: Carron was there - with its divers products - to help the country in turbulent times.

The introduction of steam

Carron ordered two iron screw passenger steamers (the passenger service on the sailing vessels had been suspended some years earlier) from the Clyde shipbuilders Smith and Rodgers. The sisters, *Carron* (3) and *Clyde*, were three-masters with the funnel abaft the mainmast and had fiddle bows. They came into service within eight days of each other, sailed for London, and made their maiden voyages from London to Grangemouth on 2nd and 10th January 1852, respectively. Grangemouth was the last of the major east Scottish ports to be connected to London by steamers. Leith, the port for Edinburgh, had had a paddle steamer connection with London since 1821, Aberdeen from 1827, and Dundee from 1834. Initially, the Carron Company had been cautious about adopting steam, but with screw propulsion beyond the experimental stage and much more reliable, they ordered screw steamers from the beginning, unlike most of their competitors who were only now changing to screw propulsion. In fact, Aberdeen did not change to screw propulsion until 1865.

With just two exceptions, Carron was to use the names of rivers for all their future steamers. Their third, *Thames* (2), was built in 1853, by Barclay, Curle and Company of Glasgow, and this permitted the company to offer three sailings a week to London. Two more, *Forth* (1) and *Grange* (1), were delivered in 1855-6 by J and G. Thomson of Glasgow, bringing the number of steamers in the fleet to five.

During the Crimean War from 1854 to 1856, some of the company's sailing vessels were despatched to the Black Sea loaded with military ordnance. Lying off shore they would hoist a cannon ball to the mast to show that munitions of war were being carried. This emblem was subsequently incorporated into the main mast of steamers built for Carron. However, the cannonball device may well be much older, and is reputed to have acted as a sign of recognition of a Carron vessel as opposed to a privateer during the war with France. Their original house flag was white with a red border but later it was redesigned and became red with a white oval incorporating the company's crest. Steamers had black hulls, the boot-topping was red, and boats and upperworks were brown.

One evening in December 1856 *Thames* (2) was in collision in the Firth of Forth. Coming up the river she struck the wooden paddle tug *Harvest Home* (50/1837) of Alloa when off the Kinneil Iron Works, Bo'ness. The tug was showing only a masthead light and no side lights, and she cut across the bows of *Thames* whilst she was changing course to enter harbour. The tug was badly damaged and her helmsman lost. She had to be beached, but was subsequently raised and repaired.

In July 1859, the company lost its first steamer, *Carron* (3), when she sank after a collision off Lowestoft. She was replaced in April 1860 by *Carron* (4), built by Barclay, Curle, which had a straight stem although still retaining three masts. She reduced the journey time between Grangemouth and London to just over 38 hours. In the same year the seven-year-old *Thames* (2) was sold and replaced in November 1860 by *Thames* (3), which was also from the Barclay, Curle yard. A similar new-for-old exchange took place in October 1862, when *Forth* (2) replaced *Forth* (1), but in this case the older vessel was sold to Barclay, Curle, presumably as part payment for the new one.

Growth of the fleet

In 1866 the Carron Company launched what was to become one of its most famous products, the cast-iron bath, at a time when the demand for such a domestic fitting was slowly increasing. The early baths had a painted or japanned finish and were nothing like the enamelled baths which arrived at around the end of the nineteenth century. Baths meant increased trade and between 1864 and 1867 a further three vessels joined the Carron fleet, *Clutha* (1864), *Avon* (1)(1865), and *Greata* (1867). However, in 1863 and 1867 respectively *Clyde* and *Grange* (1) were sold, so in 1868 the fleet numbered six. All three new vessels were built by Barclay, Curle, and were originally fitted with simple two-cylinder engines, but in 1871 *Greata* was given a new compound engine to improve her efficiency, and *Avon* (1) was similarly re-engined the following year. *Clutha* ran ashore in the River Thames in December 1873 but was subsequently refloated none the worse for her experience; whilst *Avon* (1) inward bound to Grangemouth in July 1874 actually struck Bass Rock, the large and very prominent 350-foot high landmark at the entrance to the Firth of Forth. Luckily the damage was such that she was able to continue her voyage.

In 1867, in its quest to develop the export traffic of coal to northern Europe, the Caledonian Railway purchased both Grangemouth Docks and the Forth and Clyde Canal. Grangemouth had a commanding position close to the Lanarkshire coalfield, and the canal provided the means for transferring coal direct from the pits to the port. The Old Dock had been opened in 1836, and the adjacent Junction Dock followed in 1859. But the increasing trade demanded additional facilities: in 1867 some 464,000 tons of cargo was handled, but by 1874 this had nearly doubled to 920,000 tons. Thus in 1876 the Railway Company sought authority to expand the docks and dredge the River Carron so that larger vessels could use the port. As a direct result Grangemouth boomed and was promoted to the status of a burgh in recognition of its growing importance to the industrial heartland of Scotland.

On 2nd January 1878 the sale of 17-year-old *Thames* (3) to owners in Sunderland was completed '...with the receipt of the second half of Bank of England notes for £2,500' from the new Sunderland owners. (This quote from the letter of acknowledgement suggests that the Bank notes were received physically in two halves, but this sounds a shade too dramatic!). *Thames* (3) sailed from Grangemouth on 16th January 1878.

Between 1874 and 1878 a further four steamers entered service: *Derwent* (1874), *Tay* (1875), *Margaret* (1878) and *Caroline* (1878). All were fitted with compound engines and with the exception of *Margaret*, which was just 160 feet, the other three were 190 feet long. *Margaret*, which was equipped with three Carron-built deck cranes that were originally fitted to *Thames* (3), and had been bought back from her Sunderland owners for £130, had been below specification when handed over by her builders, and was sold after 11 years. *Tay* was to be the last of eight ships built for Carron by Barclay, Curle over a period of 15 years. Since 1851 all the Carron ships had been named after rivers, but this practice was broken when the names *Margaret* and *Caroline* were given. The story goes that these two ships were named after William Dawson's wife Margaret (1790-1867), and Joseph Stainton's daughter Caroline (born 1821), who married James MacLaren, junior, a partner in Carron since 1795, and at one time the company's agent in Liverpool. Both vessels were completed in the summer of 1878 - *Margaret* at Barrow and *Caroline* at Liverpool. They took over the London sailings of *Forth* (3) and *Clutha*, and were also frequently employed on the Hull and King's Lynn sailings, a service that was inaugurated in 1874 by *Carron* (4).

In July 1878 *Forth* (3) and *Clutha* were laid up at Grangemouth, but in December 1878 agreement was reached on chartering *Clutha* to Robertson and Company of Grangemouth for £100 per calendar month to carry coal to northern French ports. Robertsons were given the option to purchase her for £4,000, but their request to have the 'tween decks removed was refused on the grounds that, whilst removal was relatively cheap, re-instatement - should this be necessary - would have been costly.

Tay proceeding down the River Thames. *[National Maritime Museum 7373]*

Robertson and Company bought her in 1881.

Tay, *Caroline* and *Margaret* were not exactly fortunate ships. On 12th December 1878 *Tay* collided with and sank the Grangemouth Coal Company's lighter, *Tender*. Then, on 9th February 1879 off Flamborough Head, she was involved in another collision, this time with the steamer *Echo* (556/1873) of Rotterdam. The Dutch vessel towed *Tay* up the Humber to Grimsby, where repairs costing £500 were undertaken, and kept her out of service for one month. Just three months later *Tay* collided with a lighter in the Thames, but this was less serious. In July 1880, *Caroline* was nearly lost when she ran ashore in fog on the island of Fidra, two miles west of North Berwick, at the entrance to the Firth of Forth, whilst heading south with a cargo of castings and whisky. She became submerged at high water, but six days later after her cargo was discharged she was refloated and towed to the Prince of Wales Dry Dock at Leith for repairs. On 8th March 1883 *Margaret*, the smallest vessel in the fleet and normally operating the Hull and King's Lynn sailings, sank after a collision with the *Clan Sinclair* (2,933/1882) off Blackwall Point in the River Thames. The enquiry blamed the master of *Margaret* for 'reckless navigation' in trying to squeeze past the larger ship. The total cost of this mishap to the company was a massive £12,000. The next mishap occurred in February 1891 when *Caroline* was sunk for a second time. On this occasion she was in collision with the collier *Lambeth* (923/1879), whilst in the Thames. *Caroline* was lifted, beached and repaired, but not before the Leith steamer *Malvina* (1,182/1879) struck the submerged hull and slightly damaged herself.

Before Grangemouth had a dock, the small port of Bo'ness experienced a rapid rise in prosperity. From being a small town of just a few houses at the end of the sixteenth century, Bo'ness developed to become the second busiest port on Scotland's east coast by 1750. All Carron Company vessels were registered there until about 1810. Bo'ness continued to flourish until the opening of the Forth and Clyde Canal in 1790, but after this time its activities declined slowly in favour of Grangemouth, some five miles to the west. A proposal in 1768 to built a branch canal to connect with the Forth and Clyde Canal came to nothing when the money ran out in 1789, although a large section including a viaduct over the River Avon had already been completed. However, in 1878, with a loan from the North British Railway Company, the Bo'ness Harbour Commissioners started work on a small dock and the extension of the tidal dock. Large quantities of pit props were to be imported through this dock for use in the many coal mines in the area, and coal and pig iron were to be exported. The dual control of the port proved difficult and in 1895 the Harbour Commissioners transferred their liabilities to the Railway Company.

As well as its steamers, the Carron Company owned a number of barges and steam lighters for service to other ports on the Firth of Forth such as Alloa, and to convey goods to Glasgow on the Forth and Clyde Canal. A seven-year-old paddle tug, *Rob Roy*, and a

lighter, *James*, were purchased in 1854 to transport goods and coal in the dock and on the River Carron. Between 1858 and 1860 four dumb steel barges (*Nos. 1,2,3* and *4*) were delivered from the Clyde yard of J and G. Thomson, followed in 1861 by two locally-built wooden barges. In 1865/6 two further lighters, *Nos. 5* and *6*, were built, and in 1866 the company brought into service its first steam lighter, *No. 7*. Details of the service of these barges and lighters is incomplete as many were not registered. It must be assumed that they were confined to the docks or operated only along the River Carron or on the Forth and Clyde Canal. Two steam lighters joined the fleet in 1871 (*No. 9* and *No.10*) when the tug *Rob Roy* was broken up. Two further steam lighters, *Number Twelve* and *No. 13* and costing £1,280 each, were delivered in July 1878 by H. Murray and Company, Port Glasgow.

No. 9 towing a barge on the Forth and Clyde Canal. Astern can be seen a pleasure boat, probably either *May Queen* of 1903 or *Gipsy Queen* of 1905. [Glasgow University Archives ALB179]

In 1880 the fleet stood at nine steamers, together with various steam and dumb lighters. In 1881 *Forth* (3) and *Clutha* were sold to Robertson and Company of Grangemouth for £2,380. Two years later it transpired that the registered owners of *Clutha* had not been changed at the time due to an administrative error. This only came to light when a claim was received from a third party: Carron was not amused! For the next seven years *Forth* (3) and *Clutha* carried coal to Rouen. Carron turned down an offer of £5,000 for *Avon* (1) from Liverpool ship owners.

With only two small docks, of about eight acres in extent, and a restricted entrance from the River Carron, it was still not possible for Carron to increase the size of their vessels to much more than 190 feet. However, this situation changed when the much larger (20 acre) Carron Dock opened in 1882. With a new entrance to the River Carron, a channel depth of 25 feet dredged below high water mark, together with the erection of new storage sheds at a total cost of some £2,000,000, Carron Company were able to use larger vessels. Just a year earlier a new berth had opened on the Thames, the London and Continental Wharf. Built on the site of Downe's Wharf, the new berth was adjacent to the Carron Wharf. This meant that the Carron Company now had improved facilities at both ends of their principal route. After moving their berth to the Carron Dock, their new steamer, *Carron* (5), was placed on the Grangemouth to London sailings in 1884. She took the place of *Carron* (4) which was sold in 1884, prior to the delivery of the new vessel. For the three months when neither *Carron* was available, the company chartered the steamer *Glasgow* (471/1869) from James Rankine and Company, Grangemouth for £390 per month.

The first month of 1887 saw the stranding of *Greata* on the Beamer Rock near North Queensferry in the Firth of Forth. Whilst proceeding down river from Grangemouth bound for London on 24th January she ran onto the isolated islet and staved in her bottom. Her cargo was discharged into lighters but it was not until 15th February that she was eventually pulled off by two tugs and taken to Leith for repair.

Passenger services re-introduced

Passenger traffic, which had been discontinued for some years, was re-introduced on 3rd May 1887 when the new *Forth* (4), and later her sister ship *Thames* (4), came into service and offered a thrice-weekly service. Their service speed of 14 knots reduced the normal running time to London to 30 hours, and in 1889 *Forth* (4) reduced it further to 27 hours. These two steamers were equipped to meet the growing demand for passenger travel, being nearly 40 feet longer than any previous vessels in the fleet, and having accommodation for 65 first-class and 30 second-class passengers. Once these new passenger steamers had settled into service, *Greata* and *Avon* (1) were sold in January and May 1888 respectively. In 1892 the two passenger steamers were joined by the even larger *Grange* (2), built by Wigham, Richardson at Newcastle-on-Tyne, and with a speed of 17 knots. Five years later the even larger twin-funnelled *Avon* (2) joined the fleet but unfortunately she only achieved a speed of 16.46 knots on her trials, not the 17 knots guaranteed. After arbitration, her cost of building was reduced from £52,750 to £49,000.

In the late 1870s Carron had introduced a once weekly cargo-only sailing from Bo'ness to London, but in May 1897, following the introduction of *Avon* (2), *Forth* (4) and *Thames* (4) were transferred to this route to provide a secondary, twice-weekly passenger service. However, facilities for passengers on board these latter vessels were withdrawn at the end of the season due to lack of support for this service.

Margaret was sold in March 1889 to Scottish west coast owners but, as she was involved in a minor collision in Larne Harbour, Northern Ireland in January 1889, it is apparent that she was being tried out by her new owners before the sale was completed. *Margaret* was replaced by *Derwent* on the Hull to King's Lynn service.

On 4th June 1889 there was a national strike of seamen and firemen. The crews of most of Carron's ships were not involved but they needed protection from strike pickets. *Forth* (4) was lying in Grangemouth at the time, and it is said that the shipping manager stood on her bridge with a pistol in his pocket to prevent pickets boarding. At Bo'ness *Tay* was also under threat from pickets, and the captain had his crew arrested for desertion and placed in nearby Linlithgow jail for their own protection. As there was no strike pay from the newly formed National Union of Seamen, some crew men drifted back to work, and non-union labour was also recruited from London. The strike ended after 14 days.

Forth (4) off Dumbarton in the Firth of Clyde after running her trials in 1886. *[Glasgow University Archives DC101/1159]*

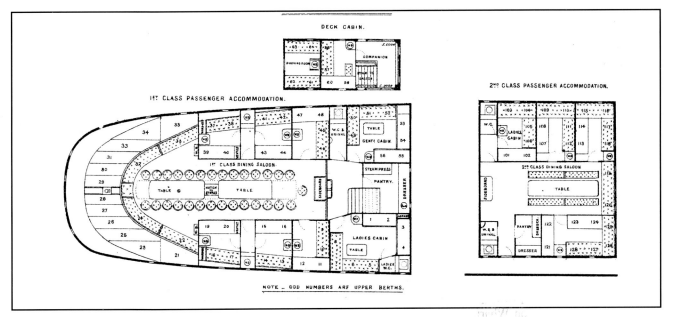

Saloon and cabin plans of *Forth* (4) and *Thames* (4).

During the 1889 season the company maintained a twice-weekly passenger service from Grangemouth to London on Wednesday and Saturday with return sailings from London on Tuesday and Saturday. Fares for a first-class cabin were 22 shillings (£1.10) single, 34 shillings (£1.70) return; and 16 shillings (80p) single, 24 shillings (£1.20) for second class accommodation. If you were a soldier or sailor and did not mind being a deck passenger, the single fare was just 10 shillings (50p). The Grangemouth to Hull sailings ran on Tuesdays. They returned from Hull on a Thursday, going via King's Lynn and departing from the latter on a Saturday.

It was not until 1894 that the last of the sailing vessels and barges went. Although most had been sold in 1853, some were retained together with two dumb barges. *Latona* and *Nestor* were sold in May 1865, and *Melampus* in December 1865; *Jamie and Jennie* was sold in May 1875; and *Apollo* in August 1882. In May 1877 *Argo* was reduced to a crane barge, and *Banton Packet* to a coal hulk in February 1894. The two dumb barges, *Leith* (2) and *Number One*, remained in service until February 1894 and June 1887 respectively, after which they were confined to harbour work.

By 1894 traffic was on the increase and during the first six months of that year a total of 84,206 tons of cargo was carried: 54,472 tons to London and 29,734 tons to Grangemouth. The imbalance of traffic resulted in northbound ships sailing light. At the beginning of 1895 Carron was operating three passenger steamers, *Forth* (4), *Thames* (4) and *Grange* (2); four cargo-only ships, *Derwent*, *Tay*, *Caroline*, and *Carron* (5); five steam lighters, *No. 7*, *No. 9*, *No. 10* (sold later that year), *Number Twelve*, and *No. 13*; plus a number of dumb lighters.

Just before the turn of the century the *Avon* (2), the only twin-funnelled, twin-screwed vessel in the fleet and larger than *Grange* (2), was introduced on the London sailings. Built by the Newcastle-on-Tyne yard which built *Grange* (2), *Avon* (2) had berths for 94 first-class, 52 second-class, and 214 third- or deck-class passengers. It was the first time that the berths and saloon were located amidships. Her maiden voyage on 22nd May 1897 marked a milestone in Carron's history: they now had four passenger vessels available to operate a twice or thrice weekly service (depending on the season) with a voyage time of just 30 hours when the tides at both ends were favourable.

Avon (2) on passage at speed. *[Graeme Somner collection]*

The opening of the Carron Dock in 1882 proved a great success, and a total of 6,310 and 4,805 passengers were carried in the first half of 1895 and 1896 respectively. The cargo uplifted in the six months to June 1896 was 68,277 tons southwards and 35,662 northwards. The total tonnage for 1896 was 240,000 tons, nearly six times the amount moving through the port some 30 years earlier. However, there was so much silt coming down the River Carron that the Railway Company had great difficulty in keeping the channel to the port adequately dredged, and in 1898 work commenced to build a series of new docks. When completed in 1906 the new system provided a dock of 30 acres (Grange Dock); a canting basin of 10 acres; a channel connecting the new system with the old and known as Western and Eastern Channels; and a sea lock at the northern end opening directly into the Firth of Forth.

At the beginning of the twentieth century, the fleet comprised four 15/16-knot passenger ships, the twin-screw *Avon* (2), the single-screw *Grange* (2), *Thames* (4), and *Forth* (4) together with two cargo-only ships, *Carron* (5) and *Caroline*. *Derwent* and *Tay* had been sold in September 1896 and November 1899 respectively.

When replaced by *Carron* (5) on the Hull to King's Lynn sailings, *Derwent* was sold to the Venezuelan Government for service as an armed cruiser, and passed to the Grangemouth Dockyard Company for conversion. At this time Britain and Venezuela were in dispute over the boundary between British Guiana and Venezuela, so while the vessel was under conversion she flew the flag of Argentina. But when she sailed from Grangemouth for La Guayra as *Zamora* on 5th November 1896 and raised the Venezuelan flag, she was stopped and detained in the Forth by HMS *Edinburgh*. Under pressure from the USA government, which applied their Monroe Doctrine of intervening when a European power interfered in affairs concerning the American continent, *Zamora* was subsequently released and allowed to proceed on her way. She called at St Michaels in the Azores to top up her bunkers and safely reached Venezuelan waters in early December.

Mishaps and incidents

Some years saw more mishaps and incidents than others. In February 1895 *Grange* (2) ran aground on the Hermitage Causeway in the Thames but, although for a time her position was serious, she was refloated and continued her voyage northwards. *Caroline* was involved in a collision off Great Yarmouth on 4th June 1897 which resulted in the sinking, five hours later, of the Newcastle-owned steamer, *Dilston Castle* (1,626/1871). *Caroline* suffered only minor damage and proceeded to Bo'ness where she arrived on 8th June. In December 1901 *Grange* (2) was involved in two incidents in quick succession. On 5th December she ran aground off Plaistow Marsh in the River Thames. She was refloated next day by two tugs and proceeded on her voyage to Grangemouth, but on her arrival there on 9th December she ran aground in the River Carron. While attempting to refloat herself, she finished up lying across the river, blocking the entrance to the Carron Dock, and had to be extricated by two local paddle tugs, *Forth* (144/1895) and *Grange* (125/1895). She damaged her rudder in the second incident, and had to go into dry dock for repairs.

The year 1904 saw a series of mishaps. On 22nd January the twin-funnelled *Avon* (2) ran ashore near Inchkeith Island in the Firth of Forth whilst on passage from London to Grangemouth. She refloated herself four hours later and continued on her way to Grangemouth, but two days later she made her way down river again to be repaired in the drydocks at Leith. Then, on 7th June, she was involved in a collision in the North Sea with the Leith steamer *Abbotsford* (1,035/1870). Luckily no serious damage was incurred and *Avon* (2) continued her voyage to London. However, ten days later, on 17th June, the passenger steamer *Grange* (2) was in collision with a barge, *Susie*, in the Thames. But, again the Carron vessel suffered relatively little damage. She was not so fortunate in November 1904, whilst on voyage from Grangemouth to London in poor visibility. In an unusual incident, she came under fire from HMS *Thrush* when seven miles east of Inchkeith Island. Fortunately none of the crew were injured, but *Grange* (2) was hit several times. Her port anchor, part of the forward deck and the woodwork of the forecabin all suffered damage when one shot went directly over the bridge and another ricochetted against the hull. The warship was manned by reservists undertaking gunnery practice and her captain was subsequently court-martialled for endangering a merchant ship.

Autumn 1906 saw two mishaps. On 18th October *Avon* (2) ran aground on Newcomb Sands, near Lowestoft but fortunately refloated herself some seven hours later without damage. A couple of weeks later *Forth* (4) was in a collision with the collier *Poplar* (834/1886) near the Mouse Light Vessel. Again no serious damage was suffered, and she was able to continue her voyage to Bo'ness.

Ship improvements

In November 1905 *Forth* (4) was sent to Hawthorn and Company, Leith to have a new midship section added and arrived back at Grangemouth on 24th February 1906. This modification increased her length to nearer that of *Grange* (2) and *Avon* (2), and that summer *Forth* (4) carried 6,858 passengers. *Thames* (4) went round to the Henderson yard on the Clyde on 29th September 1906 to be lengthened, and Carron took the opportunity to have her re-boilered and to move the passenger accommodation amidships at the same time. These alterations cost £22,000 and the work was delayed by six weeks because of a strike at the yard.

In 1903 the Carron Works introduced a whole new range of manufactured products, including heavy-duty catering equipment for hotels, ships and hospitals. As water was increasingly installed in homes after the 1890s, the demand for baths, sinks and basins continued to grow and, by 1908, the output of porcelain enamelled baths had risen to 15,000 per year.

In November 1908 *Carron* (5), book value £3,030, was sold for demolition for £1,600 to the Forth Shipbreaking Company of Bo'ness, together with four lighters at £150 each. The lighters were probably *Nos. 1, 2* and *3* and either *No. 5* or *No. 6*.

The company suffered its second steamer loss when *Grange* (2) foundered at 10.15 am on 31st December 1908. She had sailed from Grangemouth at 7.45 pm the night before and ran into heavy weather off the Bass Rock. Loaded with 578 tons of cargo, she had a crew of 32 including a stewardess and was carrying 16 passengers. As the night progressed conditions became worse, with seas breaking over the ship. At 5.00 am, when 35 miles north east of the River Tyne, several huge seas hit the ship and her forward hold was found to be filling with water. Although all her pumps were working, she began to go down by the head, and Captain Henry Ison gave the order to abandon ship. By 8.00 am all the 16 passengers and the crew had taken to the lifeboats. When the Hartlepool steam trawler *Eleazar* (111/1895) was sighted, Captain Ison reboarded his sinking ship to blow the whistle to attract her attention. Having done so, he left his ship for the last time as she went quickly down by the head at 10.15 am. His brave action succeeded and the trawler picked up the survivors and landed them safely at Shields. At the subsequent Court of Enquiry in Edinburgh, it was considered that the loss was probably caused by a sudden inrush of water from below the forehold and stokehold, and found that neither the master, the chief officer, nor the chief engineer were to blame. *Grange* (2) had a book value of £8,957, but was insured for £13,365.

Forth (4) at sea after lengthening in 1906. *[Glasgow University Archives DC101/1160]*

This loss was made good by placing an order for a new passenger steamer with Scotts' Shipbuilding and Engineering Co. Ltd. in May 1909. The alternative had been building another cargo-only vessel for the Bo'ness trade. The passenger steamer, named *Carron* (6), was delivered to the company on 6th December 1909, well in time for the 1910 season. *Carron* (6) cost £55,639 and on her trials reached a speed of 15.41 knots. She had accommodation for 122 first-class and 78 second-class passengers. One improvement that was much appreciated by her passengers was the fitting of hydraulic cranes to handle cargo. As cargo was usually discharged as soon as the ship docked, however early that might be, the noisy steam cranes tended to disturb the early morning sleep of the passengers.

In 1910 the sailings maintained by Carron Company were:

Avon (2) and *Carron* (6) from Grangemouth to London (passengers and cargo) on Wednesdays and Saturdays, returning from London on the same days

Forth (4) and *Thames* (4) from Bo'ness to London (cargo only) on Tuesdays and Thursdays, returning on Mondays and Fridays

Caroline (cargo only) from Grangemouth to Hull and King's Lynn weekly.

Disruptions of war

When war broke out in August 1914 the Carron fleet consisted of three relatively new passenger ships, *Forth* (4), *Thames* (4), and *Carron* (6), together with the recently-refurbished *Avon* (2), and one cargo vessel, *Caroline*. Immediately, all sailings were suspended for two weeks. On 4th August 1914 *Carron* (6) and *Caroline* were lying at Grangemouth, and were joined by *Avon* (2) on the 8th August, whilst *Thames* (4) and *Forth* (4) were in

Bo'ness. They stayed put until convoys were organised and arrangements made to have them covered under a recently-introduced Government War Risks scheme.

After this two-week suspension, *Forth* (4) and *Thames* (4) were allowed to resume sailings between London and Grangemouth, and *Caroline* continued to serve Hull and King's Lynn. *Carron* (6) was not brought into service again at the end of September because of delays caused while convoys were being organised, but then in November 1914 she was taken over by the Admiralty as an Armed Boarding Vessel. When this happened *Avon* (2) was brought back into service again. After the Admiralty closed Grangemouth and Bo'ness to all merchant shipping from the end of November 1914, Carron's London to Grangemouth sailings were transferred to Leith, whilst those between Bo'ness and London were discontinued, never to be resumed. Sailings to Hull and King's Lynn continued until January 1916 when *Thames* (4) was hired by the Admiralty for a period and *Caroline* transferred to the London sailings. The carriage of passengers was suspended on 15th December 1914 and never resumed after the war.

The First World War and the resultant transfer of operations from Grangemouth to Leith was not good for Carron. They suffered both in tonnage moved and from higher costs. In the second half of 1913 their sailings showed a profit of £12,718, but for the same period in 1914 there was a loss of £5,667. Although this could be partly attributed to the cost of lodging their staff from Grangemouth in Leith (£1,175 per month), Carron's revenue in the second half of 1914 fell dramatically compared with the same period in 1913 (see table 1).

The Grangemouth to London passenger traffic was reduced from 6,942 in 1913 to 2,197 in 1914; only 30 passengers travelled during November and December

Table 1: Comparison of half-year revenue, 1913 and 1914

Route	Half-year revenue, June to December 1913	Half-year revenue, June to December 1914
Grangemouth-London	£64,217	£35,440
Bo'ness-London	£38,077	£27,550
Grangemouth-Hull	£19,453	£8,820
Grangemouth-King's Lynn	£17,728	£9,851

1914; and the number of passengers on the Bo'ness to London sailings dropped from 2,603 in 1913 to 1,055 in 1914. It is also likely that many of the passengers travelling in 1914 were military and naval personnel joining their units. In 1915 Carron reported a loss of £5,911, despite receiving £10,412 from the Admiralty for the hire of *Carron* (6).

Three of Carron's vessels were lost as the result of enemy action. On 9th April 1916 *Avon* (2) struck a floating mine near the North Foreland whilst sailing from London to Leith with general cargo. Two of her crew of 31 perished: the second engineer and a fireman. Her book value at the time was £28,355 and under War Risk Insurance she was covered for £42,000. Later the same year, on 9th December, *Forth* (4) was mined off Suffolk, and on 26th May 1918 *Thames* (4) was torpedoed off Seaham. Earlier that year, on 28th March *Caroline* sank following a collision with the recently completed Newcastle steamer, *Merida* (5,951/1918) off Flamborough Head, Yorkshire. Only *Carron* (6) survived, but she was not to see her home port for five years. Her wartime experiences are the subject of an accompanying article.

Peace and replacements

A proposal that the company, together with the London and Edinburgh Shipping Company of Leith and the Dundee, Perth and London Shipping Company should amalgamate to operate joint sailings from East Scottish ports to London was made in November 1917, but rejected by Carron as not in its interests.

After the loss of *Thames* (4) in May 1918, Carron did not have a ship available to operate the London sailings so they chartered the Aberdeen Steam Navigation Company's *City of London* (2)(977/1871) for three months at a cost of £2,500 per month as a stop gap measure.

In November 1918, when Carron was re-registered under the Companies Acts of 1908 and 1917, it found itself with just one ship, *Carron* (6), but she was still under requisition. With the low volume of cargo traffic on offer, together with the high cost and uncertain delivery of new ships, Carron considered buying second-hand tonnage. But in the meantime they chartered the steamer *Highlander* (1,216/1916) from the Aberdeen, Newcastle and Hull Steam Company Ltd. and weekly sailings from Grangemouth recommenced on 14th October 1918.

During the half years between January 1918 and June 1919 the company continued to suffer financial losses as the tonnage they carried between Leith and London fell from 21,694 to 13,962 tons (compared with 55,396 tons in the second half of 1915), and this was despite receiving payments for the hire of certain of their vessels (see table 2).

Table 2: Breakdown of costs June 1918 to June 1919

	Half-year ending		
	June 1918	December 1918	June 1919
Loss: Leith-London sailings	£7,723	£8,009	£6,826
After allowing for hire of:			
Carron (6)	£6,504	£6,691	£5,817
Lighter *No. 10* (2)	£301	£49	£123
Other lighters	£1,198	£1,395	£872
Profit / Loss	**£280**	**£126**	**-£14**

Carron (6) was paid off by the Royal Navy on 6th January 1919 and then passed to Portsmouth Dockyard for reconditioning after her wartime service. As the records covering her surveys are no longer in existence, what happened next can only be surmised. It would appear that she was back at Grangemouth by 24th January and then laid-up. At sometime prior to September 1919 she arrived at Leith and her tail shaft, machinery and boiler was examined under a Special Survey. On 9th October 1919 she arrived back at Grangemouth, and made her first sailing to London on 21st October, returning to Grangemouth a week later. By now few passengers wished to travel by sea, rail or road transport was preferred and it was no longer viable to operate a large passenger ship like *Carron* (6). After only four trips she was laid up and put on the sale list in December 1919. For the half year to 31st December 1919 cargo carried was down to 2,128 tons, whilst losses reached £10,238. An offer of £111,000 was received for *Carron* (6) from Allan Adams and Company Ltd., Southampton but had to be rejected because the charter of *Highlander* was due to terminate on 31st January 1920 and no other vessel was available to maintain the sailings. Although consideration was given to chartering a variety of vessels, *Purfleet Belle* (1,401/1888) of London, *Ashton* (990/1884) of Grimsby, *Dresden* (807/1865) of Leith, all were too expensive, and *Arbroath* (1,014/1909) of Dundee was too large. Though she was expensive to run, there was no alternative to bringing *Carron* (6) back into service at the end of January 1920 on cargo-only sailings, until a suitable replacement was found. *Carron* (6) was finally laid up on 27th July 1920, and eventually sold on 8th September 1921 to Bland Line of Gibraltar for £60,000. She sailed for Gibraltar, still named *Carron*, on 6th October 1921 arriving on 12th October. Renamed *Gibel Zerjon* some days later, she took up passenger sailings to Tangier and was to operate under two owners in and about the western Mediterranean until broken up in 1934.

In the face to strong competition from the railways, it was essential that regular weekly sailings were maintained, but because of dock labour problems and shortages of coal, one steamer could not guarantee such a service. It became essential for Carron to have two steamers. To meet this commitment two second-hand cargo ships were purchased from Coast Lines Ltd., Liverpool in spring 1920. Following the amalgamation of several companies to form the Coast Lines Group in 1919, a number of steamers became surplus to requirements and two of these were bought by the Carron Company. On 6th March 1920 the 27-year-old *Princess Beatrice* was purchased for £62,500. She was handed over in London on 16th April 1920, but did not arrive at Grangemouth until 21st June after developing a crankshaft fault which had to be corrected before she could be brought into service. Built in 1893 for M. Langlands and Sons, Glasgow, essentially for their round Britain service, she was renamed *Avon* (3) and sailed for London on 26th June. At this stage Carron were still considering re-introducing passenger services so they acquired ships capable of carrying passengers if required. In fact, this facility was never re-instated. In May 1920 the 37-year-old iron steamer *Cloch* was purchased from Coast Lines, but this time there was a much quicker handover. She was taken over in London on 19th May still named *Cloch* and arrived in Grangemouth on 24th May, but did not sail as *Grange* (3) until 31st July. She had originally been built for the Clyde Shipping Company of Glasgow and employed as a spare on the various services the company operated to Ireland and the south of England, before passing to west of England owners. But following her purchase traffic was light, and *Grange* (3) was mostly laid up between 29th April and 4th November 1921, except when relieving *Avon* (3) for a short spell whilst the latter was in drydock. For the second half of 1922 the two second-hand steamers produced a profit of £1,863 for the company. Between them they carried 23,773 tons of cargo in the half-year ending on 31st December 1921, and 25,229 tons in the following six-months.

With trading conditions showing signs of

Avon (3) *ex-Princess Beatrice* in the River Thames. *[World Ship Photo Library.]*

improvement at the beginning of 1922, the tonnage carried rose from 25,229 tons in the first half year of 1922 to 32,579 tons in the second half. Carron considered whether it was better to replace the two steamers with faster vessels or to purchase a third steamer cheaply. They also kept watch on the prospects for re-opening the Hull sailings, and on the possibility of opening up a sailing to Ipswich because other traders were already operating irregularly on these routes. To improve the returns from the Carron Wharf on the Thames, agreement had been reached with the General Steam Navigation Company of London that their Rotterdam service steamers use this berth from 1st January 1920.

The decision taken in 1922 to increase sailings from three per fortnight to twice weekly required the purchase of a third steamer. After inspecting *Warlingham* (786/1891) at London, *Langland* (744/1906) at Rochester, *Portlaurie* (700/1921) at Hull, and *Glasgow* (1,068/1894) at Leith, it was decided in October 1922 to buy *Glasgow* for £6,750, and she was towed to Grangemouth for refurbishing. Registered in Glasgow, she was built in 1894

for James Rankine and Sons, Grangemouth, which operated sailings to the Low Countries before their merger with George Gibson and Co. Ltd. in 1920. In the past James Rankine and Sons had chartered ships (*Caroline* in 1889 and *Tay* in 1898) from Carron Company to operate sailings to Holland. *Glasgow* was surplus to requirements after the Rankine and Gibson companies merged, and was a very suitable vessel for Carron's trade. She had deck cranes for cargo handling, a form of equipment that had always been used on the company's steamers. She was taken over on 28th November 1922, having achieved a speed of 12 knots in trials conducted on 27th November. Such speed was necessary to ensure she could achieve a passage during a period of three tides. It was essential that a tide was not missed either at Grangemouth, where vessels had to be locked into the docks, or at the London berth, where ships had to lie on the mud at low water, because a loss of time would effect subsequent voyages. She made her first sailing to London on 5th December 1922, but it was not until 6th January 1923 that she carried the name *Carron* (7).

Carron (7) in the River Thames on 5th August 1933. *[John G. Callis]*

These three steamers remained in service until 1924, but with the volume of trade declining (a loss of £7,810 was suffered in the first half of 1925, dropping to £5,545 in the second half), two vessels were usually sufficient to meet demand and the 42-year-old *Grange* (3) was often taken out of service. Her final arrival at Grangemouth was on 8th May 1925, where she was laid-up pending a survey. Since the cost of bringing her up to standard was prohibitive, she was sold for £2,535 in June for breaking up at Bo'ness.

In 1926 sailings were disrupted by the General Strike. The miners came out on 30th April and the rest of the nation's work force came out in their support on 4th May. Sailings had to be cancelled for two weeks, and even when the strike ended on 12th May, coal shortages meant that only one weekly sailing could be maintained despite German imports. As a result, there were 40 rather than 51 sailings in the half-year, and a loss of £52 for the last six months of 1926.

With the sailings back to twice weekly by 1927, the company decided that *Avon* (3), the 34-year-old running partner of *Carron* (7), should be replaced, but not with a vessel that was fitted with accommodation to carry passengers. An order was placed with the Clyde Shipbuilding Co. Ltd. of Port Glasgow for a suitable steamer at a cost of £57,778. Named *Forth* (5), she carried out trials on 4th February 1928, and immediately went into service. However, on 22nd February she was withdrawn to be fitted with a new propeller as she could not maintain her specified speed. She made her second voyage from Grangemouth to London on 3rd April 1928. On 30th March *Avon* (3) arrived at Grangemouth for the last time, and then in July 1928 she was sold to breakers for £2,450. From a loss situation at the end of 1926, the Shipping Department of the company was back in the black again and showing a profit of £6,973, rising to £10,696 in the second half of that year. In 1928 profits for the year came to £15,553. But warning signs were appearing: this state of affairs could not continue because the amount of cargo carried northwards continued to remain low. In 1930 *Carron* (7) was re-boilered and refurbished to make her more compatible with her new partner.

Despite the grim conditions in the early 1930s, Carron maintained its reputation for a wide range of high quality products. As well as continuing with armaments it also produced castings for items ranging from steam engines to golf-club heads. The heyday for Carron Works was the inter-war years when they manufactured products such as mantles, firegrates, and fireplace suites, the latter based on original designs and in various styles from Jacobean through Tudor to Georgian and the famous Adam fireplace. Such products remained in great demand and their transportation to markets outside Scotland allowed a pattern of sailings to be maintained by *Forth* (5) and *Carron* (7), the former leaving Grangemouth on Saturdays and the latter undertaking the mid-week sailings.

But with the depression deepening the whole country was suffering, and by 1931 the annual profits of the Shipping Department dwindled to £3,258. Some of the downward trend was attributed to a strike of Thames dockers from 4th January to 16th February during which time no overside goods (those transferred to and from lighters) could be handled. Eventually, however, traffic started to increase and for the next eight years *Forth* (5) and *Carron* (7) gave reliable and virtually trouble-free service.

During the First World War Carron's steam and dumb lighters were employed by the Royal Navy for supply duties, with *No. 10* (2) carrying explosives from Rosyth Dockyard to the fleet lying in the Firth of Forth. In 1920 Carron had retained a number of these lighters for collecting and delivering coal and pig iron between Grangemouth and Glasgow and for transporting bunkers from Carronshore to the steamers at Grangemouth. But as rail services improved and road transport developed this use of lighters became uneconomic. One by one, as they became of no further use, the dumb lighters were laid up at Burnhouse Basin and put up for sale. In August 1920 *No. 10* (2) (1871) was sold for £2,750 to Tyne owners, whilst *No. 7* (1866) and *No. 8* (2) (1866) were sold in September 1922 and January 1923 respectively, the former for use by the Royal Gourock Yacht Club. Next to go, in August 1924, was *No. 9* (1871), followed by *Number Twelve* (1878) in July 1925. The last steam lighter, *No. 13* (1878),

Forth (5) [Glasgow University Archives DC101/1161]

was purchased by Tyne owners in 1927. With the provision of coal hoists on the other side of Carron Dock, bunkering by lighter finished at Grangemouth by the end of 1928, and the last bunkering lighters, *Nos. 11* and *17*, were sold for £100 each.

War causes further disruption

In August 1939, with war looming and just two ships in their fleet, the 11-year-old *Forth* (5) and 45-year-old *Carron* (7) valued at £40,000 and £6,000 respectively, the prospects for Carron's Shipping Department seemed bleak. Carron approached both the London and Edinburgh Shipping Company of Leith and the General Steam Navigation Company of London to see whether either or both of them would consider running a service in association, but Carron's proposal met with no success.

Later that year they considered replacing their two vessels with a single, more economical vessel, but nothing came of this idea. Due to Admiralty restrictions and the need to wait to join convoys, Carron's two vessels were able to provide one sailing each fortnight, and made a loss of £9,554. Part of this loss was attributed to increased wages to the crews to cover war risks. A master's weekly wage had increased from £8.17s.6d. (£8.85p) to £10.10s.0d. (£10.50p). The weekly wage bill for a vessel with a crew of master, mate, second mate, a lamplighter, five able seamen, a chief engineer, second and third engineers, six firemen, a steward and a cabin boy rose by 38% from £77.6s.6d. (about £77.32p) to £106.8s.6d. (about £106.42p).

Forth (5) and *Carron* (7) maintained the London sailings until 16th February 1940, when the Admiralty purchased *Carron* (7) for £16,000 against the wishes of the Carron Company. She was to be used as a block ship at Scapa Flow, Orkney, and was stripped of many of her fittings before transferring to Rosyth Dockyard to be modified and filled with stones and cement. On 3rd March 1940 she was towed north and sunk in Water Sound, between the islands of Burray and South Ronaldsay, where her remains can still be seen adjacent to the causeway that now connects the two islands.

When commercial movements on the upper reaches of the Forth were prohibited by the Admiralty from March 1940, *Forth* (5) used Leith as her home port, and her sailings were co-ordinated with those of the General Steam Navigation Company, which had operated Leith to London sailings for many years. During the last half year of 1940 Carron's Shipping Department incurred a loss of £10,968 despite receiving revenue generated from the use of Carron Wharf by the Dundee, Perth and London Shipping Co. Ltd. and the Aberdeen Steam Navigation Co. Ltd. which both used Carron Wharf from March 1940. Revenue increased further when the London and Edinburgh Shipping Co. Ltd. moved to Carron Wharf after their Hermitage Wharf berth was destroyed in an air raid on 27th December 1940.

Forth (5) was formally taken up by the Ministry of War Transport under the Coasting Liner Requisition Scheme in August 1940 and remained under their direction until March 1946, although she mostly continued to be employed in her original trade. She suffered minor war damage in two incidents:

on 19th May 1943 she was damaged by splinters whilst lying at Wapping, River Thames during an air raid; and then on 25th April 1944 she was in collision with a destroyer off May Island at the entrance to the Firth of Forth.

In September 1942 Carron were offered several vessels including four motor coasters in lieu of the requisitioned *Carron* (7), but they were all unsuitable. They were not fitted with deck cranes, essential equipment in the company's handling operations. In fact, Carron never owned or operated a motor vessel throughout its long history.

When George Pate retired as manager in 1944 at the age of 82 he had been with the company for 51 years and manager since 1913. He died the following year at Carron Grange, the manager's official residence. Only Joseph Stainton had served Carron as manager for a longer period.

Forth (5) remained under Ministry of War Transport direction until March 1946. From June to December 1944 she made only 15 voyages between Leith and London, but in the first half of 1945, with no convoys to wait for, she made 27 sailings. Her master, Captain R. S. Little since 1933, was awarded an MBE for his services during hostilities.

Sale of the last steamer

Immediately after the Second World War, as after the First, there was very little cargo requiring transportation. With the change of Government in 1945 came nationalisation, and the coal mines and coking furnaces, some of Carron's oldest and greatest assets, were taken over by the National Coal Board. In October 1944 there had been a movement amongst Scottish east coast companies to come together and dovetail their various sailings to their mutual advantage. In October 1945 London Scottish Lines Ltd. was formed to operate a joint service between Leith and London, and Carron were one of the main shareholders. The others were the London and Edinburgh Shipping Co. Ltd. of Leith, the General Steam Navigation Company, and the Clyde Shipping Co. Ltd. of Glasgow. Although the Dundee, Perth and London Shipping Co. Ltd. and the Aberdeen Steam Navigation Co. Ltd. both had the opportunity to join this organisation, they opted out because it would not have been in their best interests. By October 1945 Carron knew that London Scottish Lines would not be interested in purchasing *Forth* (5) when they took over.

The wartime pool working arrangements continued until 30th September 1945, after which *Forth* (5) was chartered to London Scottish Lines at £81.11s.3d. per day (or about £571 per week). As a result the company declared a record profit of £8,256 for the final half of 1945.

Carron (7) lying in Water Sound, Scapa Flow as a block ship. *[Graeme Somner collection]*

Forth (5) made 36 voyages during the period from January to the end of June 1946. Until March 1946, *Forth* (5) was on charter to London Scottish Lines, but thereafter revenue from all the ships on the service was pooled. The first division of the pooled revenue received from the London Scottish Lines for the period 3rd March to 30th June 1946 turned out to be a bitter disappointment to Carron's Shipping Department. Carron reported a half yearly loss of £5,645, a sorry state of affairs after the previous period.

When the London Scottish Lines acquired their third steamer, *Forth* (5) was withdrawn from service on 25th February 1947. She was sold at the lucrative price of £57,000 to Indian owners, who took her over at Leith on 4th April 1947. But prior to the sale her cannon ball main mast emblem was removed and handed to the Falkirk Museum for safe keeping. She sailed from Leith for Bombay on 17th June 1947, now named *Bharatbal*, and was to see service in Indian coastal waters for seven years before being wrecked.

Epilogue

There was an old saying that 'cargo follows the passenger'. Although carriage of goods could be more profitable, it was considered essential to develop a reputation as a passenger line as a way of securing large consignments of cargo and keeping ships fully employed. This theory was clearly espoused by the Carron Company which advertised their passenger services from early on. Initially their policy was to offer cheap fares to those who could defend their vessels from pirates (or worse!). Later they had faster and larger ships (even one with two funnels, no doubt to impress intending passengers). The withdrawal of passenger services in 1920 may have marked the beginning of the end for the Carron Company. Over the next 20 years their fleet slowly dwindled from three cargo steamers, to two, and then just one. After 165 years Carron's vessels, with their distinctive emblem of a cannon ball incorporated into the mainmasts, could no longer be seen in Grangemouth docks, although the Carron Company was still in production at Falkirk.

Traffic continued to decline after the ports of Bo'ness and Grangemouth were taken over in January 1948 by British Railways (Scottish Region), later the British Transport Commission. In 1956 Grangemouth handled just 11,000 tons of coal, compared with some 871,000 tons in 1923. At Bo'ness and at Grangemouth silting was a continual problem: the cost of dredging was high, and the dredgers themselves needed to be replaced. By 1960, with the coal mines closing down and the use of the docks continuing to decline, the British Transport Commission decided to close the port of Bo'ness, and left the dock to silt up. However, the increased movement of oil extracted from the North Sea fields and piped to Grangemouth for refining maintained the level of traffic out of Grangemouth. An oil loading jetty was developed at Hound Point, lower down the Firth near South Queensferry, to allow tankers which were too large to be accommodated at Grangemouth to load refined products pumped down to this point from the refinery.

Even the London Scottish Lines, which the Carron Company joined in October 1946, was only to survive until 1958. After these sailings were withdrawn, there was no direct cargo services to London from either Grangemouth or Leith. There remained just one slender link by sea between London and the Forth - that from the small Fife port of Kirkcaldy. But this too was severed in the summer of 1962 when the Aberdeen Steam Navigation Co. Ltd. withdrew its sailings. From that time, the Forth (and indeed the whole of the east coast of Scotland) ceased to have a regular sea connection with London and the south. The Carron Works at Falkirk, still standing adjacent to the Forth and Clyde Canal, which was closed to commercial traffic in 1963, continued to turn out many tried-and-

known products, together with the addition of new items such as plastic baths, stainless steel sinks, pillar boxes, and gas and electric cookers. Reproductions of the company's original carronade gun were now in great demand. Today replicas can be seen on the gun decks of HMS *Victory* at Portsmouth, and on Jersey in the Channel Isles where they replaced those removed by the Germans during the Second World War. But despite the company having a nationwide sales force, Carron's products could no longer be distributed by sea.

Carron Company's last profitable year was 1979, by which time there were dark clouds on the horizon. Despite the installation of new and more economical plant and a reduced work force to cut costs, Carron owed the banks some £12 million and the receivers were called in on 3rd August 1982. Various product departments were sold off, and all the original works' buildings that were not in use were demolished in 1983 and the land redeveloped with houses and a shopping centre. However, the stainless steel department, the most profitable, was retained and subsequently became Carron Phoenix Ltd. Today it produces modern sinks in a variety of materials and colours. When this new company was, in turn, sold in January 1990 to the Franke Group of Switzerland, control finally passed to foreign entrepreneurs after 231 years' control by local interests.

The quay in Carron Dock in Grangemouth, which the Carron Company used for so many years, is now quiet and deserted. Gone for ever are the golden days of rush and bustle as cargoes were loaded and unloaded.

Forth (5) showing the company crest on her stern. *[Falkirk Research Centre]*

HM Boarding Ship Carron

The only ship in the fleet to survive the war was *Carron* (6), despite the fact that she had sailed to distant parts and had to contend with many and varied weather conditions for which she had not been built. Having been requisitioned by the Admiralty in November 1914, on 9th December 1914 she was commissioned at Millwall Dock, London as HM Boarding Ship *Carron*, under the command of Lt. Commander James Park, RNR. She had by this time been fitted with two 4-inch guns. On the 20th she sailed for Plymouth, arriving there the next day and sailed on 2nd December on her first patrol. Her duties were to stop and search, if necessary, any foreign or neutral ships coming up the English Channel, her patrol covering between the Eddystone Light, the Lizard and the Longship Light. She returned to Devonport on the 28th having been relieved on patrol by the *Sarnia* (1,498/1910).

Carron went to sea again on 30th December and did not return to harbour until 3rd January 1915. Command of the vessel passed to Lt. Commander William H. Kelly, RNR on 8th February 1915. She maintained the pattern of patrols in the English Channel until March during which time she met with continuous gales and heavy seas, on one occasion resulting in the sea breaking the ladders and doors in the forecastle, and damaging the guns and crane on the foredeck. To make good this damage, she entered the Dockyard on 4th March for a week. During her next patrol she had an encounter with an unknown submarine. At 1.38 am on 14th March the engineer on duty reported that he had heard a heavy grating sound on the ship's bottom. At the same time the lookout on the bridge reported the sighting of a periscope a short distance away, but time was too short to fire a shot before it disappeared below the waves. Subsequently a patch of oil was sighted on the surface but nothing further was seen. Two days later at 2.52 am whilst steaming at 11 knots a light was suddenly sighted under her starboard bow and despite going full astern and altering course, she struck a trawler not showing proper lights. *Carron* commenced escorting the seriously damaged trawler to port but was called away to search for a submarine sighted in the area. This was one of her more eventful patrols.

Sunshine and sand

Carron was back in Dockyard hands between 8th and 12th May and sometime between 22nd May and 17th August 1915 (the Deck Log for the period is missing) she was transferred to support the Dardanelles campaign, where landings had been undertaken on 25th April 1915 from 200 vessels. *Carron* was based in the Mudros anchorage, an inlet on the island of Lemnos in the Aegean Sea, some 50 miles west of the entrance to the Dardanelles. She was employed patrolling the Bulgarian (today Greek territory) coastline to the north of the area of operations, or in the Gulf of Smyrna (now known as Izmir) to the south east, and with the constant threat of submarines attacking the fleet supporting the landings, had to maintain a zig-zag course at all times. When at the fleet anchorage at Mudros much time was taken up by having to replenish bunkers from colliers, and to assist the crew carrying out this operation in the hot conditions prevailing, a working party of about 30 Arabs was normally employed.

On 24th August 1915 she stopped the Greek vessel *Oxpana* and, when the Boarding Officer was not satisfied as to the correctness of the ship's voyage, a prize crew of one midshipman, one leading seaman, and two able-bodied seamen were placed on board with instructions to take her to Mudros for a full examination. Towards the end of 1915 *Carron* had a change from patrol duties as on 24th November she was despatched on a voyage to Piraeus on the Greek mainland - it seems probable that this voyage was undertaken to convey Rear Admiral Sir John de Robeck, Commander-in-Chief, Eastern Mediterranean Squadron, who had been forced to leave his command for a period of rest and also for consultations in London.

The Dardanelles campaign was faltering badly due to the strong resistance put up by the Turks, resulting in heavy casualties on both sides. The weather also had changed and the tremendous rain storms made conditions on land even worse, with troops being drowned as well as being shot at. Within six weeks of a new commander taking over, there was pressure on the British Government to withdraw the force of some 30,000 men from Gallipoli before winter began in earnest, but it was not until 8th December 1915 that withdrawal was authorised. Commencing on the night of 13th December *Carron* made four trips to the Anzac and Sulva Bay beaches to evacuate to Mudros some 3,000 troops, brought out on lighters to her, picking up the last of them on the night of 19th December. British and Allied forces at Cape Helles were also gradually reduced under cover of darkness and total evacuation of the area was complete by the morning of 9th January 1916.

From 27th December 1915 to 23rd January 1916 *Carron* maintained a submarine patrol off the island of Psara in the middle of the Aegean Sea, a point which all vessels had to pass on their voyages to and from the Dardanelles. This was an area in which submarines frequently patrolled in the hope of sinking one of the many hospital and troop ships retiring southwards. Serious losses in the past had occurred in the Aegean Sea, including the sinking of transport *Royal Edward* (11,117/1908) on 13th August 1915 with the loss 132 lives when she was on passage from Egypt to Mudros. On 10th February 1916 *Carron* commenced her last patrol to the Bulgarian coast and after her return to Mudros on the 14th, made ready for a return to home waters.

Having embarked at Mudros a number of British military prisoners for Malta, where they were to serve their sentences, *Carron* sailed on 15th February 1916. She arrived back at Devonport on 29th February 1916 and was in need of maintenance so was despatched to London for the necessary work to be undertaken at Millwall Dock. Her crew were granted 10 days' leave.

Cold and ice 1916

On 21st April 1916 *Carron* sailed for Lerwick in the Shetland Islands, arriving there on the 24th. After loading 106 tons of coal, she sailed the same day for Kola Sound in northern Russia. Kola Sound runs roughly north to south and is at the mouth of the River Tuloma, on the east bank of which is situated the town of Murmansk. The weather is grim, and from December to middle January each year the sun does not rise above the horizon, with the facilities in this place of wooden buildings being practically nil.

With Germany dominating the entrance to the Baltic, and Turkey dominating the entrance to the Black Sea, the only possible way to supply Russia with coal and munitions was through northern Russian ports. Archangel in the south east corner of the White Sea was the main port, but was closed by ice from November to May each year. The Russian Government was having to develop the facilities at Murmansk, which was ice free. To move the materials southwards to where they were needed, a railway was developed connecting Murmansk with Archangel and places further south. In two years the tonnage moving through the two ports was to rise 25 times above the normal peacetime trade of the White Sea.

During 1914, the Russians faced greater problems from the weather than from the Germans, but by early 1915 the Russia Government became concerned that minefields might be laid by German surface and underwater vessels on the approaches to the White Sea. The Admiralty recognised this danger and, despite the many demands on resources, allocated some old and obsolescent warships to keep the White Sea open. Six minesweeping trawlers were also sent out in June but by then the German minelayer *Meteor* - the

175

Carron (6) lying off Portsmouth in 1918, when commissioned as an Armed Boarding Ship. *[Public Record Office ADM176/890]*

ex-Leith, Hull and Hamburg Steam Packet Company's *Vienna* (1,912/1903) seized at Hamburg on the outbreak of war - had already laid 285 mines in the approaches to the White Sea. As a result ten Allied freighters were sunk between June and October 1915. Once the minesweepers started to sweep ahead of the convoys, losses dropped dramatically with only one further casualty being suffered. Regrettably, one of the six trawlers, *Lord Denman* (309/1914) of Hull, sent out to undertake this task, was lost after a collision on 22nd October in the White Sea.

Fearful that another surface minelayer - *Meteor* herself had been sunk in the North Sea on 9th August 1915 after laying mines in the Moray Firth - might attempt to lay mines in the area again in the Spring of 1916, the Admiralty despatched, amongst other ships, *Carron* and another Armed Boarding Ship, *Stephen Furness* (1,712/1910), the latter owned by the Tyne-Tees Steam Shipping Company. *Carron*, having arrived in Kola Sound on 30th April, commenced her first patrol on 4th May, covering an area of the Barents Sea to the north of Kola Sound right up to the edge of the ice field, but had to return to base on the 9th with engine trouble. On the 15th May, despite thick ice, *Carron* penetrated the White Sea, situated some 300 miles to the south-east of Kola Sound, but soon had to retire to Yukanski Bay, some 200 miles east of Kola Sound, at the entrance to the White Sea. Here she loaded 289 tons of coal on 20/21st May. Previously her worst enemy was heavy seas, now it was ice and fog. She remained iced in until 2nd June and finally returned to Kola Sound on 9th June. She sailed the next day back to the White Sea to continue to patrol and act as a guard ship to the anchorage at Yukanski Bay. Patrols continued and on one of them she anchored off the port of Kem, situated on the west coast of the White Sea, and on the railway line to Murmansk. During another patrol she stopped and boarded the Leith cargo ship *Petunia* (1,749/1889) on 18th September - no doubt news of home was welcome.

With the presence of British warships in the area, northern Russian waters were kept free from enemy action until September 1916, when German submarines commenced laying mines and attacking vessels. Between September and early December five U-boats operated in the area between North Cape and Kola Sound, resulting in 34 allied and neutral ships being sunk.

With winter approaching and the prospect of being unable to patrol because of ice, preparations were made by *Carron* to sail home. She sailed with a convoy from Yukanski Bay on 1st December 1916 bound for Lerwick. On the 5th she had to take HM Trawler *Bombardier* (305/1915) in tow because she was suffering from boiler trouble, but during the next three days the tow parted twice in rough conditions, with the trawler being adrift for periods of up to 12 hours. On the 9th the convoy arrived off Lerwick and *Bombardier* was able to steam the last few miles under her own power. On the 11th *Carron* sailed for Liverpool and entered Wellington Dock for maintenance, no doubt badly needed after eight months' service in northern Russian waters, with few shore facilities available.

More cold and ice 1917

On 3rd March 1917 Lt. Commander Louis A. Brooke-Smith, RNR took command of *Carron* and on the 13th the vessel was towed into Brunswick Dock to complete her refit. On 7th April she sailed for Busta Voe on the west coast of the Shetland Islands, and on 23rd sailed from there bound once again for Kola Sound in a convoy. *Carron* was detailed to tow two drifters, *London County* (80/1909) and *Oswy* (95/1916), which were to be employed in Russian waters as minesweepers. Again heavy weather was met with and the tows parted on several occasions, but eventually on 4th May *Carron* and her two drifters arrived at Kola Sound. On the 6th she sailed up to Murmansk and three days later started her patrols again.

Whilst the danger from mines laid by surface vessels had disappeared, the danger from attack by U-boats, or from the mines they scattered off various headlands, became greater. June 1917 saw five British ships sunk or attacked. *Carron* was Guard Ship at Yukanski Bay again from 18th June and remained there until 15th July. She was relieved of that duty by another Armed Boarding Ship, *Grive* (2,037/1905 - owned by the General Steam Navigation Company of London), before sailing on patrol again. She unfortunately ran aground during fog on 9th August near Cape Cherm on the Murman coast, between Yukanski Bay and Kola Sound, but refloated three hours later with the timely assistance of no other than HM Trawler *Bombardier*.

Carron then remained in port under repair until 3rd September when she sailed in convoy for Archangel, in the White Sea, with minesweepers working ahead because of the danger of mines. She arrived at Archangel on 5th September and sailed again for Kola Sound on the 7th, where she arrived on the 8th. Unfortunately, whilst *Carron* was in the White Sea, *U 28* again arrived in the area to the west of Kola Sound, resulting in loss of two more steamers. In September and October shipping was ordered to proceed independently via the Norwegian Inner Leads - neutral waters - in an attempt to reduce the losses being suffered further south, and off Kirkenes or Vardo armed trawlers met the inward vessels and then escorted them through to Archangel - the U-boats were, however, not long in finding the weak link in the chain further to the east.

With the Russian Revolution of the previous March now causing disruption even in the far north, British forces commenced reducing their numbers in the area, in the face of the impending takeover of the country by the Bolsheviks. By this time the British naval force had grown to include the old battleship HMS *Glory* for service as a depot ship at Murmansk, three old cruisers, four armed boarding steamers, two yachts, 23 trawlers, and four drifters. *Carron* sailed from Yukanski Bay for Scapa Flow in the Orkney Islands on 16th September 1917. She arrived at the naval anchorage of Longhope on the 23rd, and on the 25th proceeded to Liverpool where she was moored in Wellington Dock. After *Carron* had departed from the area, two further ships were torpedoed and sunk by *U 46*. Would the presence of *Carron* have prevented these losses one wonders?

In port and resting 1918

It must have been decided that repairs were of such a magnitude that they would be better undertaken in a Royal Dockyard, so on 4th October she sailed to Portsmouth. Now started a depressing period of her naval service, being moved from berth to berth, and never going to sea again.

Whilst still in Portsmouth harbour, a change of command took place on 25th July 1918 when Lt. Commander Charles H. Lightoller, DSC, RNR was appointed. Lightoller had had an adventurous career, having been wrecked and stranded on the desolate island of St Paul in the Indian Ocean in November 1889 (still an apprentice on his second voyage) when serving on the Liverpool four-masted barque *Holt Hill* (2,441/1884), survived the sinking of the *Titanic* (46,269/1912) in April 1912 (on which he was second officer), the stranding and loss off Foula, near the Shetland Islands, of the Armed Merchant Cruiser *Oceanic* (17,274/1899)(on which he was serving as a Lieutenant, RNR) in September 1914, the loss by collision of his second naval command, the destroyer HMS *Falcon*, in the North Sea in April 1917, and finally brought into port, his seriously-damaged next command, the destroyer HMS *Garry*, as the result of ramming *UB 110* in July 1918. His command of *Carron* was obviously to give him some rest from his arduous service. But the posting was not to his liking and he protested most strongly at being posted to such a backwater.

On 12th August *Carron* was towed to the Southampton shipyard of Camper and Nicholsons for a refit. The work was completed by 10th September and she was towed to Fountain Lake Jetty, Portsmouth to load ammunition. But, the war having ended, she discharged her ammunition on 4th November, almost finally being paid off on 3rd January 1919.

During the period of just over four years when *Carron* had been in naval service, she had been on patrol in the English Channel, the eastern Mediterranean, and in northern Russian waters, but in all that time she had only seen a submarine periscope once, and fired only one round from her guns, when a Russian icebreaker failed to stop when challenged. She had steamed many thousands of miles far away from the North Sea route she had been built for, and hopefully just her presence in Mediterranean and northern Russian waters had at least deterred submarines from attacking shipping.

Carron's last commanding officer, Lt. Commander Lightoller, as ever a man of action, had been promised the command of a new destroyer then being fitted out at Portsmouth. But he never took this ship to sea, the Armistice intervening. As one of the Carron Company's own masters was not appointed to *Carron* until 24th January 1919 at Grangemouth, one wonders if Lightoller himself was given the task of delivering the ship back to her owners.

Derivations of Carron Company names

Avon River rising east of Cumbernauld, west Stirlingshire, flowing about 18 miles east and north through Stirlingshire, entering the Firth of Forth about three miles west of Bo'ness.

Carron River rising in the Campsie Fells, west Stirlingshire, and flowing east for 20 miles, entering the Firth of Forth at Grangemouth.

Clutha The Latinised name for the River Clyde (which see below).

Clyde River rising near Elvanfoot, south-east Lanarkshire, flowing north west through Glasgow to Dumbarton, where it becomes the Firth of Clyde.

Derwent Not identified but probably the River Derwent in Yorkshire.

Forth River rising north of Ben Lomond, Argyllshire, flowing east towards Stirling where, after passing Alloa, it becomes the Firth of Forth, entering the North Sea some 40 miles to the east.

Grange Burn (stream) rising in south east Stirlingshire, flowing north east for eight miles, and entering the Firth of Forth to the east of Grangemouth.

Greata Derivation not traced.

Tay River, the longest in Scotland, rising on the north slopes of Ben Lui, Argyllshire, flowing through Loch Tay, and then on beyond Perth, becoming the Firth of Tay at Newburgh, entering the North Sea at Buddon Ness, some eight miles east of Dundee.

Thames River rising on the eastern slopes of the Cotswolds, flowing east through Oxfordshire, towards the City of London, entering the North Sea at The Nore.

Avon (2) at the company's London wharves. *[World Ship Society collection]*

Fleet lists

Details of some early vessels are fragmentary.

Sailing vessels managed on behalf of the Carron Company by Samuel Garbett and Co. (1763-1772) and by the Carron Shipping Company (1772-1805).

1. GLASGOW (1) 1763-1786 Sloop

1763: Built for Samuel Garbett and Co., Carron as GLASGOW.
1778: Sold to the Carron Shipping Co., Carron.
7.11.1786: Stranded near Lowestoft whilst on a voyage from Carron to London.

2. PAISLEY 1764-1781 Sloop

1764: Built for Samuel Garbett and Co., Carron as PAISLEY.
1778: Sold to the Carron Shipping Co., Carron.
25.11.1781: Wrecked at Whitby, Yorkshire whilst on a voyage to London with military stores.

3. STIRLING 1767-? Sloop

1767: Built for Samuel Garbett and Co., Carron as STIRLING.
1778: Sold to the Carron Shipping Co., Carron.
1797: Still in service.

4. FORTH (1) 1768-1782 Sloop

1768: Built at Carronshore, Stirlingshire for Samuel Garbett and Co., Carron as FORTH.
1778: Sold to the Carron Shipping Co., Carron.
1782: Wrecked off Great Yarmouth with heavy loss of life.

5. KINGSTON Sloop

1770s: In service with Samuel Garbett and Co., Carron.

Sea-going vessels owned by the Carron Company

1. CARRON (1) 1765-? Sloop

1765: Built for the Carron Company, Carron as CARRON.
1779: Still in service.

2. KING OF SPAIN/EARL OF DUNMORE 1777-? Frigate

1777: Acquired to deliver guns to the King of Spain.
1782: Renamed EARL OF DUNMORE.

3. LADY CHARLOTTE

1778: In service.

4. FALKIRK (1) ?-1782 Sloop

1770s: In service.
1782: Wrecked.

5. ROEBUCK Sloop

1770s: In service.

6. ROBERT AND MAY Sloop

1770s: In service.

7. EAGLE Sloop

1777: In service.

8. FURNACE Sloop

1777: In service.

9. EMPRESS OF THE RUSSIAS 1785-?

1785: Acquired to trade in the Baltic.

10. JAMIE AND JENNIE 1785-1875 Sloop

O.N. 22515   29 reg.   38 x 13 x 7 feet
1785: Completed at Airth for the Carron Company, Carron as JAMIE AND JENNIE.
3.1806: Registered at Bo'ness.
1.1817: Re-registered at Grangemouth after rebuilding by Lawrence Lawson, Carron.
10.1875: Sold to John Robertson, Aberdeen.
5.1878: Sold to M. P. Galloway, Leith.
2.1887: Existence of vessel in doubt.

11. CARRON (2) 1790-1838 Barge/sloop

33 reg.   54 x 16 x 8 feet
1790: Completed by William Steven, Carron for the Carron Company, Carron as a barge for service on the Forth and Clyde Canal.
8.1838: Sold to the Forth Steam Towing Co., Leith.
6.1846: Sold to Robert Innes, Leith and re-rigged as a sloop.
1.1849: Sold to Andrew Mercer junior, Leith.
10.1849: Sold to John Inkster, Leith.
1851: Broken up.

12. GLASGOW (2)

1792: In service on the Forth and Clyde Canal.

13. LEITH (1)

1792: In service on the Forth and Clyde Canal.

14. BANTON

1792: In service on the Forth and Clyde Canal.

15. FALKIRK (2)

1792: In service on the Forth and Clyde Canal.

16. PRINCE OF WALES

1792: In service on the Forth and Clyde Canal.

17. DESPATCH 1792-1828 Sloop

65 reg.   53 x 18 x 8 feet
1792: Completed at Port Glasgow for the Carron Company, Carron as DESPATCH.
5.1809: Registered at Bo'ness.
1.1817: Re-registered at Grangemouth after rebuilding by Lawrence Lawson, Carron.
1828: Lost.

18. THAMES (1)

186 reg
1793: Built at Southampton.

19. BELLONA 1794-1838 Sloop

68 reg.   52 x 18 x 9 feet
1794: Completed at Carronshore, Stirlingshire for the Carron Company, Carron as BELLONA.
1838: Broken up.

20. HAPPY RETURN Sloop

1794: In service, and still so in 1800.

21. PALLAS Sloop

1794: In service and still so in 1800.

22. APOLLO 1795-1882 Sloop

O.N. 1742   42 reg.   47 x 15 x 8 feet
11.1795: Completed at Carronshore, Stirlingshire for the Carron Company, Carron as APOLLO.
1840: Re-rigged as a smack.
8.1882: Sold to John Smith, Blyth.
18.10.1889: Stranded at entrance to Lossiemouth in fog and became a total loss, whilst on a voyage from Cullen, Moray Firth to Methil in ballast.

23. THETIS ?-1812

31.3.1812: Wrecked near Whitburn, County Durham, whilst on a voyage from London to Carron.

24. BANTON PACKET 1799-1894 Sloop

O.N. 22514   49 reg.   52 x 15 x 7 feet
1799: Completed at Carronshore, Stirlingshire for the

Carron Company, Carron as BANTON PACKET.
2.1894: Reduced to a coal hulk.

25. ARGO 1802-1877 Sloop
O.N. 22513 70 reg. 54 x 18 x 7 feet
1802: Completed at Carronshore, Stirlingshire for the Carron Company, Carron as ARGO.
5.1877: Sold and reduced to a crane barge on the Caledonian Canal.

26. PANOPE 1802-1838 Brig
122 reg. 72 x 18 x 12 feet
1802: Completed at Carronshore, Stirlingshire for the Carron Company, Carron as PANOPE.
29.11.1838: Wrecked on Gun Fleet Sands whilst on a voyage from London to Grangemouth.

27. ELIZA 1803-1838 Sloop
36 reg. 36 x 14 x 6 feet
1803: Completed at Bowling for the Carron Company, Carron as ELIZA.
1.1806: Registered at Bo'ness.
12.1838: Broken up.

28. REBECCA 1804-1844 Brigantine
153 reg. 76 x 22 x 14 feet
1804: Completed at Kincardine for the Carron Company, Carron as REBECCA.
1815: Registered at Grangemouth.
1844: Vessel not seaworthy and broken up.

29. DORIS
1805: In service.

30. MELAMPUS 1805-1865 Sloop
O.N. 24037 63 reg. 61 x 19 x 9 feet
1805: Completed at Carronshore, Stirlingshire for the Carron Company, Carron as MELAMPUS.
1816: Registered at Grangemouth.
8.1865: Sold to Robert McArthur, Greenock.
12.1866: Sold to A. Hamilton, Belfast and re-rigged as a smack.
4.1887: Sold to P. Mitchell, Rothesay and reduced to a hulk.

31. MINERVA 1805-1852 Snow
O.N. 5751 177 reg. 78 x 20 x 14 feet
1805: Completed at South Shields.
1813: Owners the Carron Company, Carron.
6.1852: Sold to John Finlay, Leith.
3.1853: Sold to William Mackenzie, Blyth.
10.1874: Sold to foreign owners.

32. GALATEA Sloop
9.1806: In service.

33. SAINT PATRICK 1807-1844 Sloop
56 reg. 58 x 15 x 6 feet
1795: Completed at Belfast.
1807: Owners the Carron Company, Carron.
1844: No longer seaworthy and broken up.

34. FAME Sloop
10.1810: Captured by French privateer off Northumberland coast, but recovered by Royal Navy.

35. PENELOPE 1810-1852 Schooner
115 reg. 70 x 20 x 11 feet
10.1810: Completed at Lyme Regis for the Carron Company, Carron as PENELOPE.
9.1852: Sold to George Hennet, Exeter.
16.12.1852: Whilst under tow, driven ashore on Herd Sand, Shields, whilst inbound from London, and became a total loss.

36. JUNO (1) 1812-1832 Brig
190 reg. 79 x 24 x 13 feet
6.1812: Completed at South Shields for the Carron Company, Carron as JUNO.
7.1832: Broken up.

37. LATONA 1812-1865 Sloop
O.N. 1338 67 reg. 61 x 19 x 9 feet
4.1812: Completed at Carronshore, Stirlingshire for the Carron Company, Carron as LATONA.
1833: Rebuilt by John Graham, Carronshore.
5.1865: Sold to William Airth, Arbroath.
30.9.1867: Lost at Peterhead.

38. PROSERPINE 1812-1852 Schooner
O.N. 24169 156 reg. 74 x 23 x 12 feet
11.1812: Completed at Lyme Regis for the Carron Company, Carron as PROSERPINE.
1836: Re-rigged as a smack.
11.1852: Sold to George Hennet, Exeter.
10.1853: Sold to Perrin Freestone and Co., Bristol.
1.1858: Sold to T.V. Venn, Bristol.
12.1859: Sold to Catherine Gyles, St Ives.
21.11.1860: Abandoned at Malta whilst on a voyage from Gergenti to Liverpool.

39. MILO 1815-1841 Sloop
83 reg. 57 x 18 x 10 feet
8.1815: Completed at Liverpool for the Carron Company, Carron as MILO.
5.1841: Sold to Henry Doran, Liverpool and re-rigged as a schooner.
11.1870: Existence of vessel in doubt and removed from register.

40. DYNAMENE 1818-1852 Smack
O.N. 20972 40 reg. 73 x 21 x 16 feet
12.1855: Lengthened, re-rigged as a brig, tonnage now 161.
7.1818: Completed by Richard Russell and Sons, Lyme Regis for the Carron Company, Carron as DYNAMENE.
1836: Re-rigged as a schooner.
11.1852: Sold to George Hennet, Exeter.
1.1854: Sold to John Crossman, Exeter.
1.1863: Sold to James Bradford, Belfast.
25.2.1863: Foundered off Carthagena whilst on a voyage from Port Talbot to Alexandria with a cargo of rails.

41. LUNA 1819-1852 Smack
O.N. 859 73 reg. 58 x 17 x 9 feet
1819: Completed by Humble and Hurry, Liverpool for the Carron Company, Carron as LUNA.
1847: Re-rigged as a schooner.
6.1852: Sold to Andrew Stenhouse, Limekilns, Bo'ness.
6.1862: Sold to G. Mathieson and Alexander Turnbull, Leith.
1877: Broken up.

42. NESTOR 1825-1865 Sloop
O.N. 15938 75 reg. 59 x 16 x 10 feet
1825: Completed by Humble and Hurry, Liverpool for the Carron Company, Carron as NESTOR.
9.1865: Sold to John Wemyss, Glasgow.
10.1866: Sold to John Christie, Liverpool.
1.1876: Sold to William McBurney, Bangor.
12.1889: Lying submerged in Old Channel, Belfast and abandoned.

43. ABEONA 1825-1853 Smack
O.N. 15719   173 reg.   77 x 23 x 13 feet
1825: Completed by Richard Russell and Sons, Lyme Regis for the Carron Company, Carron as ABEONA.
1836: Re-rigged as a schooner.
9.1853: Sold to John Robertson, Grangemouth.
7.1855: Sold to Parminter Cardell, Plymouth.
3.1863: Sold to John Rendle, Plymouth.
10.3.1873: Wrecked at Ormeshead, Milford, South Wales.

44. JUNO (2) 1832-1852 Brigantine
O.N. 8473   163 reg.   79 x 24 x 13 feet
7.1832: Completed at Carronshore, Stirlingshire for the Carron Company, Carron as JUNO.
11.1852: Sold to Thomas Gibson, Perth.
2.1857: Sold to Thomas Aitken, Leith.
3.1857: Sold to Alexander Davidson, Aberdeen.
20.6.1867: Lost in the White Sea.

45. LILY 1836-1837 Sloop
O.N. 5850   38 reg.   46 x 16 x 6 feet
1792: Completed at Greenock for unknown owners.
5.1827: Acquired by Alexander McKinley, Dumbarton.
6.1836: Acquired by the Carron Company, Carron.
1837: Sold to Stewart Graham, Greenock.
5.1854: Sold to John Hendry and Alexander Ferguson, Greenock.
25.11.1864: Foundered in Firth of Clyde.

46. VULCAN 1840-1853 Schooner
O.N. 19551   161 reg.   83 x 21 x 13 feet
3.1840: Completed by R. Menzies and Sons, Leith for the Carron Company, Carron as VULCAN.
2.1853: Sold to Fraserburgh Seal and Whale Fishing Co., Peterhead.
2.1862: Sold to George Thompson and others, Aberdeen.
3.1864: Sold to J. Elsmie, Aberdeen.
24.10.1868: Wrecked at Johnshaven, Kincardineshire whilst on a voyage from Sunderland to Aberdeen with a cargo of coal.

47. CARRON (3) 1851-1859 Iron steamer
O.N. 17667   349g 267n   167.4 x 22.0 x 14.5 feet
Engine, 80 HP.
12.1851: Completed by Smith and Rodgers, Glasgow for the Carron Company, Carron as CARRON.
14.7.1859: Sank following a collision with VISCOUNTESS CANNING (164/1842) of Guernsey five miles off Lowestoft whilst on a voyage from London to Grangemouth.

48. CLYDE 1851-1863 Iron steamer
O.N. 17625   345g 267n   167.4 x 22.0 x 14.5 feet
1860: 490g 345n   181.0 x 22.0 x 14.5 feet
Engine, 90 HP.
12.1851: Completed by Smith and Rodgers, Glasgow for the Carron Company, Carron as CLYDE.
10.1863: Sold to Frederick H. Powell, Liverpool.
1.1867: Sold to T. R. Oswald, Sunderland.
4.1.1870: Foundered off Hirtshals, Jutland.

49. THAMES (2) 1853-1860 Iron steamer
O.N. 17632   369g 213n   167.8 x 23.3 x 14.5 feet
Engine, 80 HP.
6.1853: Completed by Barclay, Curle and Co., Glasgow (Yard No. 5) for the Carron Company, Carron as THAMES.

8.1860: Sold to James Hamilton (partner in shipbuilder Barclay, Curle and Co.), Glasgow.
8.1860: Sold to Thomas S. Begbie, London.
10.1861: Sold to foreign owners, no further record.

50. FORTH (2) 1855-1862 Iron steamer
O.N. 17690   406g 253n   177.3 x 22.8 x 13.9 feet
Engine, 85 HP.
28.4.1855: Launched by J and G. Thomson, Glasgow (Yard No. 21).
4.1855: Completed for the Carron Company, Carron as FORTH.
7.1862: Sold to Barclay, Curle and Co., Glasgow.
5.1863: Sold to the General Steam Navigation Co., London.
8.11.1875: Stranded in thick weather in River Maas and became a total loss.

51. GRANGE (1) 1856-1867 Iron steamer
O.N. 13542   408g 263n   175.0 x 25.2 x 14.2 feet
2-cyl., 90 HP.
2.8.1856: Launched by J. and G. Thomson, Glasgow (Yard No. 29) for the Carron Company, Carron as GRANGE.
8.1856: Completed.
12.1867: Sold to John Edmund Swan (of Barclay, Curle and Co.), Glasgow.
1.1868: Sold to Burrell and Co., Glasgow.
10.2.1873: Stranded near St Nazaire and became a total loss.

52. CARRON (4) 1860-1884 Iron steamer
O.N. 28676   447g 286n   181.0 x 25.7 x 14.5 feet
2-cyl.; 120 HP.
1887: C. 2-cyl. by Kincaid and Co., Greenock, 85 HP.
4.1860: Built by Barclay, Curle and Co., Glasgow (Yard No. 80) for the Carron Company, Carron as CARRON.
17.2.1883: Stranded at Amble, Northumberland whilst on a voyage from Grangemouth to London but later refloated, and repaired at Grangemouth.
1884: Sold to P. Barr, Stranraer.
5.1889: Sold to McLachlan and Co., Glasgow and renamed MIDLOTHIAN.
2.1896: Sold to Chaber et Castanie, Oran, Algeria and renamed VILLE DE MELLILA.
1900: Sold to J. Muro Saenz, Almeria, Spain and renamed EL FOMENTO.
1903: Sold to Sociedad Anonima 'La Mediterranea', Barcelona, Spain and renamed LA MEDITERRANEA.
1907: Sold to A. Lamourelle, Cette, France and renamed MARIE LOUISE.
1918: Broken up.

53. THAMES (3) 1860-1878 Iron steamer
O.N. 28677   454g 340n   180.5 x 26.1 x 14.5 feet
2-cyl. by Barclay, Curle and Co., Glasgow; 106 HP.
1880: C. 2-cyl. by Hawthorns and Co., Leith; 60 HP.
11.1860: Built by Barclay, Curle and Co., Glasgow (Yard No. 84) for the Carron Company, Carron as THAMES.
2.1878: Sold to Lamb and Clasper, Sunderland.
1.1880: Sold to James Cormack and Co., Leith.
6.1883: Sold to Brodie Cochrane, County Durham (James Cormack and Co., Leith, managers).
10.1885: Sold to John Young and Co., Newcastle-on-Tyne.
9.1889: Sold to the Thames Steam Ship Co. Ltd. (F. le Boulanger, manager), Swansea.
5.3.1893: Wrecked at Killala Bay, County Mayo, whilst on a voyage from London and Sligo to Ballina with a cargo of guano.

54. FORTH (3) 1862-1881 Iron steamer

O.N. 28679   499g 368n   188.1 x 27.1 x 15.8 feet
2-cyl. by Barclay, Curle and Co., Glasgow; 130 HP.
1890: T. 3-cyl. by Blair and Co. Ltd., Stockton; 85 HP.
28.9.1862: Launched by Barclay, Curle and Co., Glasgow (Yard No. 99).
9.1862: Completed for the Carron Company, Carron as FORTH.
9.1881: Sold to Robertson and Co. (James Miller, manager), Grangemouth.
7.1888: Sold to T. Simmons, Middlesbrough.
1897: Sold to J. M. Lennard and Sons Ltd. (William Lennard, manager), Middlesbrough.
8.1905: Sold to the Leven Steamship Co. Ltd. (Benjamin O. Davies, manager), Middlesbrough.
6.8.1906: Wrecked on Long Pierre Rock off Herm, Channel Islands, whilst on a voyage from Middlesbrough to St Malo.

55. CLUTHA 1864-1881 Iron steamer

O.N. 45545   534g 394n   191.5 x 27.3 x 15.0 feet
2-cyl. by Barclay, Curle and Co., Glasgow; 140 HP.
1888: C. 2-cyl. by the Cardiff Junction Dry Dock and Engineering Co. Ltd., Cardiff; 120 HP.
7.7.1864: Launched by Barclay, Curle and Co., Glasgow (Yard No.120).
7.1864: Completed for the Carron Company, Carron as CLUTHA.
17.12.1873: Stranded at Broadness Point, Gravesend, but later refloated.
10.1881: Sold to Robertson and Co. (James Miller, manager), Grangemouth.
8.1888: Sold to W. Harkess (J. M. Lennard and Sons Ltd., managers), Middlesbrough.
22.12.1894: Sailed from Middlesbrough for Aarhus with a cargo of iron and disappeared.

56. AVON (1) 1865-1888 Iron steamer

O.N. 45529   552g 360n   192.3 x 28.0 x 14.9 feet
2-cyl. by Barclay, Curle and Co., Glasgow; 120 HP.
1872: C. 2-cyl. by Barclay, Curle and Co., Glasgow; 120 HP.
6.10.1865: Launched by Barclay, Curle and Co., Glasgow (Yard No. 139).
21.11.1865: Completed for the Carron Company, Carron as AVON.
16.7.1874: Struck Bass Rock whilst on a voyage from London to Grangemouth but was able to proceed on voyage.
5.1888: Sold to the Avon Steamship Co. (Thomas Jack junior, manager), Larne.
13.10.1891: Sold to Henry Williams, Liverpool.
30.4.1894: Sold to Richard Hughes and Co., Liverpool.
16.5.1894: Owners became the Avon Steamship Co. Ltd. (Richard Hughes and Co., managers), Liverpool.
27.4.1897: Owners became Richard Hughes and Co., Liverpool.
4.2.1905: Owners became Richard Hughes and Alexander Hutson, Liverpool.
21.7.1909: Owners became Richard Hughes and Co., Liverpool.
19.9.1909: Sank after a collision with the steamer PACUARE (3,891/1905) in the Crosby Channel, River Mersey, whilst on a voyage from Fowey to Liverpool. with a cargo of china clay.

57. GREATA 1867-1888 Iron steamer

O.N. 56930   580g 395n   192.3 x 28.0 x 15.1 feet
2-cyl. by Barclay, Curle and Co., Glasgow; 120 HP.
1871: C. 2-cyl. by Barclay, Curle and Co., Glasgow; 120 HP.
13.6.1867: Launched by Barclay, Curle and Co., Glasgow (Yard No. 164).
11.1867: Completed for the Carron Company, Carron as GREATA.
24.1.1887: While on a voyage from Grangemouth to London, ran on to Beamer Rock, near North Queensferry, Firth of Forth, and stoved in bottom.
15.2.1887: After cargo discharged, refloated, towed to Leith, and placed in dry dock for repair.
1.1888: Sold to Napier Shipping Co. Ltd., Glasgow.
1.1891: Sold to Macas and La Roda, Valencia, Spain and renamed VICENTE SANZ.
1906: Owners became La Roda Hermanos.
27.2.1914: Burnt out whilst at anchor at Melilla, North Africa.

58. DERWENT 1874-1896 Iron steamer

O.N. 68177   598g 307n   193.7 x 28.0 x 15.9 feet
C. 2-cyl. by Barclay, Curle and Co., Glasgow; 127 HP.
4.1874: Built by Barclay, Curle and Co., Glasgow (Yard No. 241) for the Carron Company, Carron as DERWENT.
9.1896: Sold to Venezuelan Government and renamed ZAMORA (being classed as a first class cruiser with a crew of 40 and 50 marines).
1909: Broken up.

59. TAY 1875-1899 Iron steamer

O.N. 68183   597g 295n   194.3 x 28.1 x 16.1 feet
C. 2-cyl. by Barclay, Curle and Co., Glasgow; 130 HP.
1.9.1875: Launched by Barclay, Curle and Co., Glasgow (Yard No. 256).
9.1875: Completed for the Carron Company, Carron as TAY.
11.1899: Sold to Thomas Ronaldson and Co., London.
8.1900: Sold to Antwerp Steam Ship Co. Ltd., London.
21.3.1901: Sank after being struck by German steamer CHEMNITZ (2,758/1889) whilst lying in Flushing Roads sheltering from heavy weather, having sailed from Antwerp for London with a general cargo on 19.3.1901. There were only two survivors.

60. MARGARET 1878-1889 Iron steamer

O.N. 76870   393g 230n   160.0 x 24.2 x 14.0 feet
C. 2-cyl. by the Barrow Shipbuilding Co. Ltd., Barrow; 90 HP.
16.5.1878: Launched by the Barrow Shipbuilding Co. Ltd., Barrow (Yard No. 56).
5.1878: Completed for the Carron Company, Carron as MARGARET.
3.1889: Sold to Ayr Steam Shipping Co. (David Rowan, manager), Ayr and renamed MONA for service as a fish carrier.
17.8.1908: Wrecked on Chubaidth Rock, south west of Colonsay, western Scotland, whilst on a voyage from Bunessan, Mull to Stranraer with livestock and nine passengers. The passengers landed on Oronsay and the crew were picked up by the steamer FERN (503/1900).

61. CAROLINE 1878-1918 Steamer

O.N. 76872   618g 308n   192.8 x 28.1 x 16.1 feet
C. 2-cyl. by Laird Brothers, Birkenhead; 168 HP.
6.1878: Launched by Thomas Royden and Sons, Liverpool (Yard No. 192) for the Carron Company, Carron as CAROLINE.
17.7.1880: Stranded during fog on Fidra Island, Firth of Forth and submerged at high water.
24.7.1880: Raised by pontoons, floated off and taken to Leith for repair.
9.2.1891: In collision with steamer LAMBETH (923/1879) in the River Thames and sunk.
16.2.1891: Raised, patched up and taken to Grangemouth for repair.
23.5.1898: In collision with the steamer GLASGOW (1,068/1894) off the River Tees but suffered only minor damage.
28.3.1918: Sank after collision with the steamer MERIDA (5,951/1918) off Flamborough Head, whilst on a voyage from Grangemouth to London with a general cargo.

Forth (4) turning in the River Thames, sometime after 1906. *[Graeme Somner collection]*

62. CARRON (5) 1883-1908 Steamer
O.N. 81136   636g   300n   195.0 x 29.0 x 15.7 feet
C. 2-cyl. by J. Jack and Co., Liverpool; 180 HP.
12.1883: Launched by Thomas Royden and Sons, Liverpool (Yard No. 225) for the Carron Company, Carron as CARRON.
24.7.1893: In collision with Norwegian steamer TRONDA (634/1875) under the Forth Bridge, the latter vessel sinking, though subsequently refloated.
11.1908: Broken up at Bo'ness by Forth Shipbreaking Co.

63. FORTH (4) 1886-1916 Steamer
O.N. 90902   930g   353n   230.0 x 34.2 x 13.7 feet
1906: 1,159g   535n   268.9 x 34.2 x 13.7 feet
T. 3-cyl. by A. and J. Inglis, Glasgow; 292 HP.
11.1886: Launched by A and J. Inglis, Glasgow (Yard No. 196) for the Carron Company, Carron as FORTH.
1906: New midship section added by A and J. Inglis, Glasgow.
3.11.1906: In collision in the River Thames near Gravesend with the steamer POPLAR (834/1886), but able to proceed on voyage to Bo'ness, and then on to Leith for repairs.
9.12.1916: Mined and sunk four miles south west of Shipwash Light Vessel, whilst on a voyage from London to Leith with a general cargo. No lives were lost.

64. THAMES (4) 1887-1918 Steamer
O.N. 90903   930g   353n   230.0 x 34.2 x 14.3 feet
1907: 1,327g   672n   279.5 x 34.2 x 14.3 feet
T. 3-cyl. by A. and J. Inglis, Glasgow; 292 HP.
1.1887: Launched by A. and J. Inglis, Glasgow (Yard No. 197) for the Carron Company, Carron as THAMES.
1907: New midship section added by builders.
15.2.1918: Attacked by German submarine in the North Sea but torpedo missed.
26.5.1918: Torpedoed and sunk by the German submarine UC 17 when six miles south east by east from Seaham Harbour, whilst on a voyage from London to Leith with a general cargo. Four lives were lost including the master.

Thames (4) in the River Thames. *[Graeme Somner collection]*

Grange (2) proceeding down the River Thames. *[Graeme Somner collection]*

65. GRANGE (2) 1892-1908 Steamer

O.N. 90908   1,519g   541n   280.0 x 36.2 x 17.7 feet
T. 3-cyl. by Wigham, Richardson and Co., Newcastle-on-Tyne; 622 HP, 17 knots.
12.5.1892: Launched by Wigham, Richardson and Co., Newcastle-on-Tyne (Yard No. 274).
8.1892: Completed for the Carron Company, Carron as GRANGE.
27.2.1894: Ran down the schooner ANNIE CROSSFIELD (83/1890) in Limehouse Reach, River Thames.
26.5.1895: Ran down the schooner TOPAZ of London off Flamborough Head, Yorkshire. The crew were picked up and landed at London.
5.12.1901: Ran ashore on Plaistow Marshes, River Thames, but refloated and proceeded on voyage to Grangemouth.
9.12.1901: Ran aground in River Carron and whilst trying to refloat herself, finished up lying across the river blocking the channel to the dock. Later refloated and taken into dock.
31.12.1908: Foundered in bad weather 35 miles north east of the River Tyne, whilst on a voyage from Grangemouth to London. All passengers and crew were saved.

66. AVON (2) 1897-1916 Twin-screw steamer

O.N. 90917   1,722g   472n   290.0 x 37.6 x 17.7 feet
Two T. 4-cyl. by Wigham, Richardson and Co., Newcastle-on-Tyne; 553 HP.
5.3.1897: Launched by Wigham, Richardson and Co., Newcastle-on-Tyne (Yard No. 330).

5.1897: Completed for the Carron Company, Carron as AVON.
22.1.1904: Ran ashore on Inchkeith Island in the Firth of Forth but refloated on the next high water.
7.6.1904: Collided with the steamer ABBOTSFORD (1,035/1870) of Leith in the North Sea whilst on a voyage from Grangemouth to London but continued to London.
4.1913: Refurbished by Scotts' Shipbuilding and Engineering Co. Ltd., Greenock, tonnages now 1,574g, 670n.
9.4.1916: Mined and sunk south east by south from the Tongue Light Vessel, whilst on a voyage from London to Leith with general cargo. The mine had been laid by the German submarine UC 7. Two of her crew were lost.

67. CARRON (6) 1909-1921 Steamer

O.N. 124460   2,351g   1,076n   294.5 x 40.7 x 18.8 feet
T. 3-cyl. by Scotts' Shipbuilding and Engineering Co. Ltd., Greenock; 600 HP, 15 knots.
14.10.1909: Launched by Scotts' Shipbuilding and Engineering Co. Ltd., Greenock (Yard No. 429).
6.12.1909: Completed for the Carron Company, Carron as CARRON.
11.1914: Requisitioned by the Admiralty as an Armed Boarding Vessel, and fitted with two 4.7 inch guns.
10.1919: Returned to owners.
8.9.1921: Sold to M. H. Bland and Co. Ltd., Gibraltar and renamed GIBEL ZERJON.
9.1928: Sold to Compagnie de Navigation Mixte, Marseilles, France and renamed DJEMILA.
9.1934: Sold to Merallia Ricuperi, Turin, Italy for breaking up.

Avon (2) sailing down the River Thames. *[Graeme Somner collection]*

Carron (6) on her trials in the Firth of Clyde. [Glasgow University Archives DC101/0114]

68. AVON (3) 1920-1928 Steamer

O.N. 99898   974g 387n   236.0 x 34.1 x 14.8 feet
T. 3-cyl. by D. and W. Henderson and Co. Ltd., Glasgow; 174 HP.
8.3.1893: Launched by D. and W. Henderson and Co. Ltd., Glasgow (Yard No. 365) for M. Langlands and Sons, Glasgow as PRINCESS BEATRICE.
6.1919: Owners taken over by Coast Lines Ltd., Liverpool.
3.1920: Acquired by the Carron Company, Carron and renamed AVON.
5.4.1928: Withdrawn from service and laid-up at Grangemouth.
9.7.1928: Arrived at Bo'ness for breaking up by P. and W. McLellan.

69. GRANGE (3) 1920-1925 Steamer

O.N. 87721   745g 373n   216.0 x 28.7 x 15.0 feet
T. 3-cyl. by J. and J. Thompson, Glasgow; 190 HP.
9.1883: Launched by Dobie and Co., Govan (Yard No.133) for George J. Kidston and James Cuthbert, Glasgow as CLOCH.
17.2.1893: Owners became the Clyde Shipping Co. Ltd., Glasgow.
11.5.1894: Sold to George P. Bazeley, Penzance.
15.5.1894: Registered in Penzance.
15.12.1905: Owners became George Bazeley and Sons Ltd.
3.3.1920: Owners became Coast Lines Ltd., Liverpool.
28.5.1920: Acquired by the Carron Company, Carron.
7.1920: Renamed GRANGE.
12.6.1925: Arrived at Bo'ness for breaking up by P. and W. McLellan.
7.1925: Breaking up began.

70. CARRON (7) 1922-1940 Steamer

O.N. 102662   1,068g 492n   240.0 x 32.0 x 16.1 feet
T. 3-cyl. by W. B. Thompson and Co. Ltd., Dundee; 228 HP.
6.1.1894: Launched by W. B. Thompson and Co. Ltd., Dundee (Yard No. 122) for James Rankine and Sons, Glasgow for the Carron Company, Carron as STIRLING but renamed GLASGOW before completion.
10.1903: Owners became the Rankine Line Ltd.
7.1917: Requisitioned by the Admiralty as a supply vessel.
12.1918: Returned to owners.
1.1920: Owners became George Gibson and Co. Ltd., Leith.
11.1922: Acquired by the Carron Company, Carron and renamed CARRON.
2.1940: Sold to the Admiralty as a potential block ship and stripped of her fittings at Grangemouth.
3.3.1940: Sunk as a block ship in Water Sound, Scapa Flow, Orkney Islands.

71. FORTH (5) 1928-1947 Steamer

O.N. 149391   1,058g 410n   240.0 x 36.2 x 16.0 feet
T. 3-cyl. by the Clyde Shipbuilding and Engineering Co. Ltd., Port Glasgow; 226 HP.
1.1928: Completed by the Clyde Shipbuilding and Engineering Co. Ltd., Port Glasgow (Yard No. 351) for the Carron Company, Carron as FORTH.
8.1940: Requisitioned by the Ministry of Shipping, London; later Ministry of War Transport.
3.1946: Returned to owners.
3.1947: Sold to Dinshaw Brothers, Bombay, India and renamed BHARATBALA.
7.1948: Sold to Bharat Line Ltd., Bombay.
31.3.1954: Stranded on Savai Bet Reef, Shayal Bet, near Port Albert Victor, Gulf of Cambay (north of Bombay), and became a total loss.

Forth (5) on the Thames *[National Maritime Museum P10359]*

Tugs and lighters

1. ROB ROY 1854-1871 Wooden paddle tug

O.N. 22511   40g 19n   63.5 x 13.1 x 6.8 feet
Engine, 22 HP.
1847: Completed by James Jackson, Middlesbrough for James Robertson and William Adam, Grangemouth as ROB ROY.
2.1850: Owners now Andrew Cowie and James Robertson, Grangemouth.
1.1854: Acquired by the Carron Company, Carron.
12.1871: Broken up.

2. JAMES 1854-1877 Wooden lighter

O.N. 11517   50 reg.   59 x 13 x 4 feet
1.1854: Built by J. and R. Swan, Larkhill, Lanark for John

Yule and John Wilkie, Glasgow as JAMES.
7.1854: Acquired by the Carron Company, Carron for £400.
1877: Broken up.

3. No. 1 1857-? Iron lighter

1857: Built by J. and G. Thomson, Govan, Glasgow (Yard No. 34) for the Carron Company, Carron as No. 1.

4. No. 2 1857-? Iron lighter

1857: Built by J. and G. Thomson, Govan, Glasgow (Yard No. 35) for the Carron Company, Carron as No. 2.

5. No. 3 1860-? Iron lighter

1860: Built by J. and G. Thomson, Govan, Glasgow (Yard No. 48) for the Carron Company, Carron as No. 3.

6. No. 4 1860-1881 Iron lighter

1860: Built by J. and G. Thomson, Govan, Glasgow (Yard No. 49) for the Carron Company, Carron as No. 4.
1881: Run down and sunk by the steamer GLENCOE (310/1867) of Middlesbrough between Grangemouth and Bo'ness.
11.1882: Claim of £1,324 for vessel and cargo finally settled.

7. LEITH (2) 1861-1894 Wooden barge

O.N. 28680 26 reg, 56 x 11 x 4 feet
1861: Built at Carronshore, Stirlingshire for the Carron Company, Carron as LEITH.
2.1894: Reduced to harbour work only.

8. NUMBER ONE 1861-1887 Wooden barge

O.N. 45541 20 reg, 52 x 15 x 4 feet
1861: Built at Carronshore, Stirlingshire for the Carron Company, Carron as NUMBER ONE.
6.1887: Reduced to harbour work only.

9. No. 5 1865-? Iron lighter

Probably similar to No. 4 above and used on inland waters only.

10. No. 6 1866-? Iron lighter

Probably similar to No. 4 above and used on inland waters only.

11. No. 7 1866-1923 Iron steam lighter

O.N. 130123 60g 46n 65.7 x 16.6 x 7.1 feet
2-cyl.; 45 HP.
1866: Built by Thomas Adams and Co., Grangemouth for the Carron Company, Carron as No. 7.
10.1914: Registered.
8.1923: Sold to James Stewart, Glasgow and used at the Royal Gourock Yacht Club.
4.1925: Sold to C. L. Stewart, Glasgow.
5.1931: Broken up.

12. No. 8 (1) 1866-1923 Iron lighter

1866: Built.
Not registered so probably used in Forth and Clyde Canal coal trade.
1923: Sold to Andrew Hutton and Sons Ltd., Middlesbrough.
Disposal unknown.

13. No. 9 1871-1924 Iron steam lighter

O.N. 62888 47g 37n 65.6 x 16.7 x 6.3 feet
2-cyl. by Barclay, Curle and Co., Glasgow; 14 HP.
5.1871: Built by Barclay, Curle and Co., Glasgow (Yard No. 217) for the Carron Company, Carron as No. 9.
1922: Laid up in Burnhouse Basin, Carron.
8.1924: Sold to H. D. Pochin and Co. Ltd., Manchester.
6.1935: Sold to John Baxter and Co., Newcastle-on-Tyne.
1.1938: Broken up at Dunston-on-Tyne.

14. No. 10 (1) 1871-1895 Iron steam lighter

O.N. 62887 37g 25n 64.8 x 14.2 x 6.2 feet
2-cyl. by Barclay, Curle and Co., Glasgow; 20 HP.
9.1871: Built by Barclay, Curle and Co., Glasgow (Yard No. 218) for the Carron Company, Carron as No. 10.
5.1895: Sold to J. Grieve, Blairmore.
2.1903: Sold to E. R. Lester, Plymouth.
7.1907: Sold to William Sim, Arran.
5.1916: Sold to James Hamilton, Ayr.
7.1916: Transferred to the No. 10 Steam Ship Co. Ltd. (James Hamilton, manager), Ayr.
12.1934: Broken up.

15. No .11 1874-1925 Coal lighter

43g
1874: Built.
Not registered and used in Forth and Clyde Canal in the coal trade.
1920: In service as a coal barge at Grangemouth.
1928: Sold.

No. 10 (1) discharging coal on a beach, probably some time after 1907 when she was Clyde owned. *[Glasgow University Archives ALB179]*

Number Twelve on the Forth and Clyde Canal. *[Ballast Trust]*

16. NUMBER TWELVE 1878-1925 Iron steam lighter
O.N. 76869   64g 44n   66.1 x 17.0 x 7.5 feet
2-cyl. by Kincaid, Donald and Co., Glasgow; 16 HP.
7.1878: Built by H. Murray and Co., Port Glasgow for the
Carron Company, Carron as NUMBER TWELVE.
1922: Laid up in Burnhouse Basin, Carron.
7.1925: Sold to John Day, Hull.
4.1940: Broken up.

17. No. 13 1878-1927 Iron steam lighter
O.N. 76871   64g 44n   65.9 x 17.0 x 7.5 feet
2-cyl. by Kincaid, Donald and Co., Glasgow; 16 HP.
1878: Built by H. Murray and Co., Port Glasgow for the
Carron Company, Carron as No. 13.
12.1926: Laid up in Burnhouse Basin, Carron.
1927: Sold to Gray's Wherries and Stevedoring Co. Ltd.,
Newcastle-on-Tyne.
4.1957: Existence of vessel in doubt: no trace of owners for
10 years.

18. No. 14   ?-1928 Coal lighter
Not registered and used on Forth and Clyde Canal.
1927: In service but probably disposed of the following
year.

19. No. 15 ?-?
Not registered, and out of service by 1920.

20. No. 16   ?-1923 Pig iron lighter
Not registered
1920: On hire at Grangemouth.
1923: Sold to Andrew Hutton and Sons Ltd.,
Middlesbrough.
Disposal unknown.

21. No. 17 ?-1928 Coal lighter
Not registered and used on Forth and Clyde Canal.
1920: In service in Grangemouth.
7.1928: Sold.

22. No. 18   ?-1923   Pig iron lighter
78 dwt.
Not registered and probably used on Forth and Clyde
Canal.
1920: On hire.
1922: Sold to John White, North Queensferry, Fife.
Disposal unknown.

23. No. 19   ?-1923   Pig iron lighter
75 dwt.
Not registered and probably used on Forth and Clyde Canal.
1923: Sold to Andrew Hutton and Sons Ltd.,
Middlesbrough.
Disposal unknown.

24. No. 20   ? -1928 Lighter
No further details.
1922: Laid up at Grangemouth.
1928: Probably disposed of by this time.

25. No. 10 (2) 1905-1920 Steam barge
O.N. 90924   81g 46n   65.9 x 17.6 x 8.0 feet
C. 2-cyl. by the Carron Company, Carron.
11.1905: Built by J. Cran and Co., Leith (Yard No. 54) for
the Carron Company, Carron as No. 10.
8.1920: Sold to the Consett Iron Co. Ltd., Newcastle-on-
Tyne and renamed CONSETT LIGHTER.
1957: Deleted from register, existence in doubt.

26. No. 8 (2) 1906-1923 Iron steam lighter
O.N. 45663   63g 34n   64.6 x 17.9 x 7.6 feet
2-cyl. Lawrence Hill and Co., Port Glasgow; 14 HP.
12.1866: Built by Lawrence Hill and Co., Port Glasgow for
their own account as ST. ROLLOX.
2.1869: Sold to Parlane McFarlane, Arrochar.
2.1906: Acquired by the Carron Company, Carron and
renamed No. 8.
1.1923: Sold to Andrew Hutton and Sons Ltd.,
Middlesbrough.
12.1950: Broken up.

INDEX OF SHIPS

All ships mentioned in histories and fleet lists are indexed. Names in CAPITALS are those of ships which have a main entry in one of the fleet lists, the page for which is shown in **bold type.** Pages shown in *italics* carry a photograph of the ship.

190

Manchester Explorer (see page 51). *[Fotoflite incorporating Skyfotos]*

Manchester Liners Ltd.

Joseph Fisher and Sons
Joseph Fisher and Sons Ltd.

Steamship Knutsford Ltd.
Manager Robert B. Stoker
Two flags are recorded: 'KS' in 1910 and 'S' in 1912.

 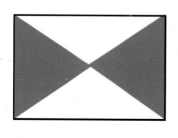

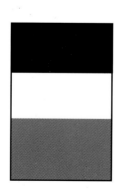 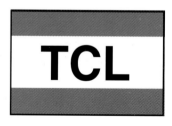

Pachesham Steamship Co. Ltd.
Barberry's Steamship Co. Ltd.
Managers: Runciman (London) Ltd.

Transatlantic Carriers Ltd.
Managers: Walter Runciman and Co. Ltd.